WITHDRAWN

Spenser's Narrative Figuration of Women
in *The Faerie Queene*

RESEARCH IN MEDIEVAL AND EARLY MODERN CULTURE

Medieval Institute Publications is a program of
The Medieval Institute, College of Arts and Sciences

# WESTERN MICHIGAN UNIVERSITY

RCC
CB
351
.S831
v. 55

Spenser's Narrative Figuration of Women in *The Faerie Queene*

Judith H. Anderson

Research in Medieval and Early Modern Culture

MEDIEVAL INSTITUTE PUBLICATIONS
Western Michigan University
Kalamazoo

APR 2 3 2018

Copyright © 2018 by the Board of Trustees of Western Michigan University

Library of Congress Cataloging-in-Publication Data

Names: Anderson, Judith H., author.
Title: Spenser's narrative figuration of women in the Faerie Queene / Judith H. Anderson.
Description: Kalamazoo : Medieval Institute Publications, 2018. | Series: Research in medieval and early modern culture | Includes bibliographical references and index.
Identifiers: LCCN 2017046483 | ISBN 9781580443173 (hardback : alk. paper)
Subjects: LCSH: Spenser, Edmund, 1552?–1599. Faerie queene. | Women in literature.
Classification: LCC PR2358 .A924 2018 | DDC 821/.3--dc23
LC record available at https://lccn.loc.gov/2017046483

ISBN: 9781580443173
eISBN: 9781580443180

All rights reserved. Without limiting the rights under copyright reserved above, no part of this book may be reproduced, stored in, or introduced into a retrieval system, or transmitted, in any form, or by any means (electronic, mechanical, photocopying, recording or otherwise) without the written permission of both the copyright owner and the author of the book.
    Every effort has been made to obtain permission to use all copyrighted illustrations reproduced in this book. Nonetheless, whosoever believes to have rights to this material is advised to contact the publisher.

Printed and bound by CPI Group (UK) Ltd, Croydon, CR0 4YY

in memory of A. C. Hamilton

Contents

Acknowledgments ix

Introduction: Spenser's Narrative Figuration of Women 1

1 Parody and Perfection: Spenser's Una 13

2 Belphoebe's "mirrours more then one": History's Interlude 49

3 Britomart: Inside and Outside the Armor 75

4 Phantasies, Pains, and Punishments: A Still-Moving Coda 121

Notes 149

Index 189

Acknowledgments

THIS BOOK HAS GROWN out of my teaching, writing, and talking about Spenser over many years. Its debts are numerous, among them to the scholar and friend to whom it is dedicated, A. C. Hamilton. I regret that he did not live to see this effort, since he once challenged me to write it. Every student of Spenser has benefitted from Bert Hamilton's many scholarly achievements, including his pioneering book *The Structure of Allegory in "The Faerie Queene,"* his collection of *Essential Articles for the Study of Edmund Spenser*, his editorship of *The Spenser Encyclopedia*, and his indispensable, annotated edition of *The Faerie Queene*. His encouragement, out of the blue, meant a great deal to me. It came early, the time when encouragement is most needed.

With respect to the project at hand, I want to thank Tamara Goeglein for reading and thoughtfully responding to the evolving project in manuscript form, and William Oram for his invaluable comments first on the initial chapter and later on the whole manuscript once it was finished, or, as it turned out, nearly so. Earlier, I also had the benefit of a convivial and provocative conversation with my colleague Kathy Smith about chapter 1. A grant from the Office of the Vice-Provost of Research at Indiana University funded the final stage of my project.

With the permission of the original presses, three essays published earlier have been revised and recontextualized for inclusion in this book: "'In liuing colours and right hew': The Queen of Spenser's Central Books," in *Poetic Traditions of the English Renaissance*, edited by Maynard Mack and George deforest Lord (New Haven, CT: Yale University Press, 1982), 47–66; "Busirane's Place: The House of Rhetoric," *Spenser Studies* 17 (2003): 133–50; and "Britomart's Armor in Spenser's *Faerie Queene*: Reopening Cultural Matters of Gender and Figuration," *English Literary Renaissance* 39 (2009): 74–96. These essays have been repurposed, expanded, and greatly revised to become parts of chapters 2 and 3.

Introduction: Spenser's Narrative Figuration of Women

THE FOCUS OF THIS book is the figuration of women within Spenser's narratives in *The Faerie Queene*. Its introduction addresses my reason for using "figuration" in the title and begins to show why "narrative" is also featured—begins, because the proof of this pudding is in the showing, the demonstrable effect of the moving, temporal dimension of narrative on meaning as each chapter explores it. My use of "women" in the title is lexical, the designation of an initial, recognizable grouping. Within Elizabethan society and culture, including poetry and drama, *women* was a functioning term, however much diversity it masked, enabled, or suppressed. I use the term in this historical, yet still open, still moving, sense.[1] In *Rethinking Feminism in Early Modern Studies*, Ania Loomba and Melissa E. Sanchez observe that a key issue in early feminist criticism and theory—and one currently "far from settled"—was "how to define 'woman,'" to which I would add, "and especially how to respect and account for a multitude of differences between *women*."[2] Each chapter that follows contributes to the significance of these terms in Spenser's culturally encyclopedic text, refining and modifying what they encompass. In this way, each illuminates women's plights and possibilities in the age of Elizabeth.

In emphasizing an unsettled use of language in its plural form, however—*women*, not *woman*—I am implicitly privileging history, analytics, and difference over universalization, psychosociology, and theory, although I am not excluding the latter trio, and in fact will bring it into discussion when productive, clarifying, or in some other way helpful for my purpose to do so.[3] Simply, if not too simply, put, my allegiance is more Aristotelian than Platonic in this study. One entailment of such prioritizing is my commitment to textual detail and specifics, and this means close reading.

* * *

Spenser's figuration of women in *The Faerie Queene* is widely various, with figures ranging from static to mobile, from mono- to multidimensional, from monstrous to idealized, from purely fictive to strongly historicized, with many a variant in between. Like the figures of men, they develop with respect to the thematic focus of each book, some crossing from book to book. Metaphorically and analogously, that is rhetorically, they also relate to one another in interwoven, textual ways that resemble a network or web and resonate with social and cultural structures, past and present. Political and religious connections of this sort, together with gendered ones, have been in evidence for decades, as have legal ones more recently. Spenser's richly figured text is a cross section of all these, and all further resonate with my own longstanding interests in rhetoric and figuration, which, accompanied by a heightened attention to narrative, this book engages. The ancient roots of rhetoric and law, for example, are thoroughly intertwined, as a number of studies have emphasized with respect to intention, probability, inference, equity, and character.[4] To these, I would add the suggestive relation to the Spenserian text of the accumulative, comparative role of precedents in English common law and of the case-based reasoning of casuistry in ethics and religion.[5] My central concern, however, is with the interwoven, resonating, paralleling, developing Spenserian text itself—a text that is variously parodic, analogous, allegorical, and intertextual. This concern accords with other broad structural phenomena, even as it connects the figures of women in Spenser's more epic narratives in *The Faerie Queene* with those in his more romantic ones—Una with Florimell, for instance.

Renewed interest in character in the past two decades and the controversies it has spawned and continues to spawn, especially in Shakespeare criticism, have also generated additional angles from which to view Spenserian figuration, and vice versa, and I have incorporated them. Perhaps above all, these developments, together with others mentioned, have further highlighted the critical function played by the lenses we choose through which to examine early modern writings. This critical function will be salient throughout my argument, as will the multiple lenses I openly use—a different lens, sometimes more than a single lens, in each chapter.

Relevant terminology, itself a basic lens, has been prominent in recent studies of Shakespearean character, involving word-concepts such as *personification, person* or *persona, figure,* and *character* itself. *Personification* and *character* in their modern senses, it turns out, are not properly Renaissance terms, although this fact in itself does not disqualify their informed use with respect to Renaissance texts.[6] André G. Bourassa offers a thorough discussion of the history in French of the word-concepts *personnage* and *caractère* from ancient Greece to the Renaissance, which is virtually the same as that of the cognate terms in English (83–85). *Person* goes back to Latin *persona*, or "mask," and George Puttenham's term in his English rhetoric for the counterfactual in "personation," namely *prosopopoeia*, similarly goes back to Greek *prosôpon*, "something covering the face."[7] Both terms involve fiction and identity, or questions of identity, and both imply rhetoric, poetry, and, still more broadly, culture, society, and civilization itself. Once freed from Proteus's cave in Spenser's fourth book, for example, Florimell "mask[s]" her affection "with modestie" as she prepares to return to society.[8]

The term I prefer with reference to *The Faerie Queene* is nonetheless *figure*, with an occasional exception, notably in chapter 3, which treats Britomart, the figure of a woman in Spenser for whom the term *character* also makes considerable sense, as it does in the criticism of Shakespeare's plays. For the same reason, notably in chapter 3, I also bring the modern theories of figuration of Paul Ricoeur and Jean-François Lyotard into the discussion, as well as theories of psychoanalysis and important discussions of gender. These theoretical excursions, and several others, are relatively brief, not focal, however. Their purpose is specific, meaningful connection, rather than overarching explanation for the entirety of the present book. *The Faerie Queene* packs the sort of variety found in the panoply of Shakespeare's plays into the 35,000 lines (rounded) of an evolving narrative written over many years. The word-concept *figure* is particularly useful with respect to Spenser's massive poem and greatly various figures of women because it encompasses a continuum from an emblem such as Speranza, to an emotive image such as Acrasia, to a character such as Britomart in dialogue with her motherly nurse about love-sickness. It further encompasses the vital connection between rhetoric and personation. Characters in Shakespeare's plays can also be, and variously have been, called figures too.

Like *persona* and *prosopopoeia*, the English word-concept *figure* has an ancient and expansive, revealing genealogy.[9] It derives via Latin *figura* from *fingere*, "to form or fashion by art," and, like its Latin parent, was the customary rendering for Greek *schema*, "perceived shape." The range of historical significations the *Oxford English Dictionary* (*OED*) affords for *figure*, notably cross-referenced with the verb *feign*, which is also derived from Latin *fingere*, serves my present purpose well. These significations start most generally with "form, shape," then proceed to "the proper shape or distinctive shape or appearance (of a person or thing)," specifically including "an embodied (human) form"; a "represented form" or " image, likeness," including an imaginary one; "a phantasm"; a "statue, image, or effigy," or even a part enacted; "an emblem, type"; "a written character," whether alphabetical, musical, or mathematical; or "any of various forms of expression, deviating from the normal arrangement or use of words ... a figure of speech."[10] The list might be said to suggest a movement from top to bottom, from finished creation to basic materials, from objective, embodied person or thing to signs and their uses—notational or poetic, purely referential or creative. The developing process of figuration within the narrative, specifically as it affects Spenser's major figures of women, the ones about whom lesser figures constellate, is at the heart of this book. My term for it is *narrative figuration*.

The role of the narrator in *The Faerie Queene* also bears on terminology and, as I inescapably found in writing this book, it recurrently bears on the interpretation of Spenser's figures of women. It does so all the more because the function of Spenser's narrative in the portrayal of these figures is crucial—more than perhaps we have thought. Long since, writing a book on Spenser and the medieval poet William Langland, I encountered the importance of the narrator's role and at first attempted to keep the term "poet," that is, the poet's voice in the poem, apart from the term "narrator," but I found this distinction increasingly difficult to maintain as Spenser's poem developed. I finally abandoned it, explaining this fact in my discussion of the 1596 installment.[11] These Spenserian voices recurrently interact with and blend into each other, as do voices in Chaucer's General Prologue, another of Spenser's models. More recently, in a chapter on "Chaucer's and Spenser's Reflexive Narrators," I compared the narrative personae of Chaucer and Spenser, making use of poststructural theory; in another chapter, "What Comes after Spenser's *But* in *The Faerie Queene*," I considered both these narrators from the perspective of linguistic minutiae, in Spenser's instance the diction, rhetoric, and grammar of his sixth proem.[12] In the present book, I have referred in specific contexts of *The Faerie Queene* to the "perceptual unreliability of the narrator" or to the "sometimes unreliable narrator," to the narrator as "a persona, himself a mask, now to be trusted, now not, now within the fiction, now apart from it," and to a Spenserian narrator who is inconsistent "even in his masking." Like the other figures of Spenser's poem, "its narrator also evolves and shifts. His own figure is contextualized." These views reflect those in my earlier publications, but I have found them newly pertinent in considering Spenser's figures of women, as will be evident in the chapters to follow. In these, I have used the terms "poet," or "Spenserian poet," and "narrator," or "Spenserian narrator," as the context has invited them. In passing, I'll mention that I encountered similar issues regarding poetic and narrative voices in discussing Milton's *Paradise Lost*, whose poet considered Spenser his "Original."[13]

Another issue this project raises is that of separating out Spenser's figures of women for discussion. This separation risks decontextualization, as to varying extents do any other kinds of selection, for that matter. I hope to have lessened this danger by being keenly aware of it and by having considerable familiarity with the poem, enough (I hope) to recognize when more context is needed. Spenser's massive poem is verbally intricate, and its interwoven plots and multiple characters are challenging to remember, not unlike those in Shakespeare's *King Lear* or his earliest *Henry* plays. Overlooking Spenserian specifics blurs or distorts Spenser's poem, which responds most fully to careful, reflective reading. The relation of reading to rereading is another issue bearing on interpretation as well as on teaching, which analysis should consider, and I do.

A compensating advantage of choosing to focus on Spenser's narrative figuration of women has been the surprising perceptions and connections that have not been seen before or have not been seen the same way, something that I found happening both with new chapters and with those that incorporate revised segments of earlier publications. Despite my interest in the narratives of *The Faerie Queene* over the years, focusing on its figured women has highlighted the importance of these narratives still further. Taken together, their stories themselves have a distinct tale to tell about the function of narrative in *The Faerie Queene*. Storytelling is a basic, perhaps the most basic, age-old way of organizing and understanding experience, and the multiple, multiplying narratives of Spenser's poem are not an exception. That the stories of the figures I treat in detail are moving narratives—at points or in instances sadly stilled ones—is vitally important in itself. As the figure that Spenser names *Mutability* realizes, only what moves lives and, while living, changes. In addition to illuminating the work of Spenser's storytelling, his narrative figurations of women also differ to such an extent that they resist easy generalizing, or indeed, isomorphic theorizing, in this respect reflecting his still moving, metamorphic poem as a whole. *The Faerie Queene* is fundamentally committed to process and exploration, and a reading of it should be as well.

* * *

In the first three of the chapters that follow, I have concentrated on the three major figures of women in *The Faerie Queene*, namely, Una, Belphoebe, and Britomart, including the interlinked relations of their stories with those of Florimell, Amoret, or both. Other women-figures enter the discussion as well, certainly Duessa, Una's wicked double.[14] Each of these chapters, as their titles signal, makes the figure of a woman the focal subject. The fourth chapter groups other figures of women on the basis of stillness and movement, constancy and change—figures found in a single location or situation and those that move into different places and contexts. It then concentrates on several figures in the mobile grouping, namely, Aemylia, Serena, Mirabella, and Pastorella—particularly Serena. Although these figures lack the prominence of the titular figures of my first three chapters, they are much more than features of an allegorical landscape and prove particularly challenging with respect to reading it.

Some years ago, I passed up an invitation to write an article on "Spenser's Women" for *The Spenser Encyclopedia* because I did not see how to treat them together compactly for that format without producing something that looked like essential femininity or "Woman." As already noted, they are much too various. Accordingly, each of the following chapters takes an approach that fits the narrative figures in it, using a different lens and sometimes more than a single lens. Chapter 1 approaches Una through the history of parody and specifically through Spenserian parody. In the early cantos of every book of *The Faerie Queene*, parody plays a significant role, which includes parodic self-citation. It also includes both parodic content and parodic expression and both criticism and sympathy. Its subject is often sacred, as in the instance of Una and as it frequently is in the Middle Ages and, much later, in the poetry of John Donne. Broadly conceived as "comic quotation, imitation, or transformation," parody enables a shift of perspective that makes Una at once less simple and more accessible.[15] Parody is committed to *play*, not simply in its ludic sense but also in its open, or loosening, complicating, moving, one.

A telling instance of Spenserian parody that I examine in chapter 1 links the sexual assaults on Una, Florimell, and Duessa (faked in her case). The memorably onomatopoeic word "blubbered," which applies in the 1590 poem only to these three figures, occurs in all three assaults. The contextualized precedent of Una's blubbering, defined by similarity to and difference from that of the other two figures and vice versa, opens up larger issues that pertain to her figuration more generally and to the widely contrasting critical responses that it has evoked in recent publications. A number of these responses make Una either wicked or otherworldly, mere flesh or mere spirit. They miss the integrity of her *figural being*.

Other salient instances of parody in the first chapter that pertain to Una include the opening cantos of Book I and the satyrs' forest, a place of Ovidian myth and *kindness* in every punning sense of this word and one that only Una in Book I and Hellenore in Book III get to visit. A major portion of this chapter concerns the culminating return of Una to Eden, together with Redcrosse, her chosen dragon-slayer. This is a return that extensively parodies both the biblical garden that is lost forever and its restoration. Many readers of *The Faerie Queene*, including me, have again and again used the words "parodic" or "parody" with reference to specific parts of it. My argument in this chapter is that a shift of perspective to recognize parody more fully and openly enables the recovery of Una's figural being, which is distinctly that of a woman. That it should do so with respect to Una, a human figure of Truth, affords a particularly stringent test and meaningful confirmation. That this shift should occur in the opening book of the poem, moreover, makes it especially notable in what follows, as appropriate—that is, not as a totalizing template but as a single, recurrent possibility.

Taking a different approach, chapter two focuses on Belphoebe, who enters the poem in Book II. Belphoebe is named after a classical moon goddess, a mythologized aspect of nature, and not, like Una, named after a metaphysical conception. Further unlike Una, who is betrothed to her human lover at the end of her story, Belphoebe is relentlessly virginal and never reconciled with her twin sister, Amoret—"Love." In further contrast to Una, Belphoebe appears in three successive books, each a different thematic context. Increasingly, these books seek some form of balanced relationship that progressively involves others. Depiction of Belphoebe begins with a long, all-inclusive, idealizing portrait of her early in Book II, a momentary pause narratively framed by the parodic, low-life figure of Braggadocchio, her lustful contrary. Nothing comes of this meeting of opposites, which abruptly ends with Braggodocchio's lecherous lunge and Belphoebe's raised javelin, then her flight. The opening portrait of Belphoebe is full of suspended tensions between mythic and mortal realities that the narratives of Books III and IV must further confront, and as early as the third proem, these tensions involve Queen Elizabeth's sometime-favorite, Sir Walter Ralegh. At the same time, they conspicuously affect the poet-narrator's role as recurrently he turns to lyric and myth. In Book III, a narrative impasse in the eroticized relation of

Timias and Belphoebe issues in the strange glorification of Belphoebe's rose, which is a virtual apotheosis, and then, in Book IV, in the entanglement of Amoret in the relation of Timias and Belphoebe. Amoret's plight becomes a thinly disguised reference to the secret marriage of Ralegh to Elizabeth Throckmorton and the disgrace of them both in the eyes of the queen. The poem becomes openly subject to history, as does my approach to it and as the subtitle of chapter 2, "History's Interlude," signals.

Although Timias and Belphoebe are reconciled, Amoret, first captured by Lust and later abandoned in the forest by Belphoebe and Timias, is subsequently found by Prince Arthur. Seeking shelter, Arthur unwittingly takes Amoret and her female companion to the House of Slander, an old hag whose figure is a hideous cartoon alluding unmistakably to the queen. Although parody is not my focus throughout the present book, here I would nonetheless stress that allusion itself is ludic (< *ludere*, "play," *alludere*, "play with"). *Serio ludere* is a Renaissance commonplace that embraces parody, from its more benign expressions to the more biting expressions into which it can blend. Again, parody persists as a possibility in *The Faerie Queene*, although it never encompasses the whole as it does in contemporary works by Rabelais and Cervantes. All or nothing is not the Faerie way.

Belphoebe never leaves the woods in the course of the poem, and her portrayal gives us no sense of her developing interiorly or consistently from one of her appearances to another. Her virginity is the only other consistency about her, and it begins to look like fixation. Whereas Una, another allegorical figure, learns from experience, Belphoebe evidently does not. In another figural contrast to Belphoebe, her twin, Amoret, is nearly always found in Houses or more broadly in cultural topoi in the poem—in situations set apart from the moving narrative of quest, if also in some sense part of it as a sort of way station. But even as *The Faerie Queene* invites categories and distinctions, it seems always to breach the one and trouble the other when read closely. The woods—in extreme intertextualized form the Wandering Wood—can be considered a topos as well, yet, in its wilder forms, the woods can still be distinguished from the more cultivated places. If, unlike her twin sister, Amoret herself ever really changes, she does so in the company of the questing Britomart, a subject treated in the third chapter, which focuses on this cross-dressed knight. Both Amoret and Florimell are part of Britomart's story. As earlier noted, I make Florimell a comparative part of Una's as well.

Britomart is the most complex of Spenser's figures of women. Instead of looking at her through a single lens, I use several sequentially in chapter 3, which not surprisingly is the longest in this book. The first lens derives from recent discussions of Shakespearean character, particularly Alan Sinfield's, and then shifts to a primarily rhetorical focus, as does Book III itself in its culminating episode of the House of Busirane.[16] My focus next becomes primarily mythic, iconological, and thereby gendered, tracing Britomart's arming and her armor itself from early episodes in Book III, through Book IV, to her final battle in Book V. Although the lenses I use are, like those of others, still selective, together they seem relatively more adequate to the nuances and development of her figuration than a single lens could ever be. Even so, they do not exhaust the possibilities.

From the opening episode of Spenser's Book III, Britomart's agency, her mind, and her inside, which differs from her armored outside, are emphasized. She has a father rather than a myth of origin, a kindly old nurse, and both a history and a projected future set firmly on earth. From the outset, moreover, she and her adventures are defined by their relationships to and differences from those of numerous others. She has a social existence more pronounced and complex than that of other figures of women in the poem. A number of additional "character effects" Sinfield finds in Shakespeare's women are also found in Britomart, for example self-reference and self-questioning, which include soliloquy and lying (58–59). Also included are indecision, decision-making, and informative conversations overheard by the audience (or readers), which raise questions about intentionality (59). Although I do not want to make Britomart into a cross-dressed Shakespearean heroine, I am not alone in having seen similarities between her and Shakespeare's Rosalind, Viola, or his other, ostensibly female cross-dressers.

Britomart's experiences prior to the House of Busirane lead into it and, like this place, they specifically increase her awareness—Sinfield's "developing interiority" or "consciousness" (62, 65). For Britomart, this perverted rhetorical House of Ovidian myths and Petrarchan conceits that spread over two cantos is a further education and initiation into the erotic culture in which she, too, has functioned to this point. The abusive Busirane, a poet-magician, has captured Amoret, *transfiguring* her from what she was in the Garden of Adonis to the Ovidian-Petrarchan love object, and Britomart's task is to free her from Busirane's spell and thus to enable arrested love. Busirane represents a fantasy and a culture of rape, but his ultimate wish remains only that. Britomart frees Amoret, and Busirane's artworks vanish, in 1590 leaving behind only a trace, an ambivalent hermaphroditic image.

When a continuation of the 1590 installment comes in 1596, this image and the actual reunion of Amoret with her knightly lover, which was imaged in the hermaphrodite, are gone. Instead, the action of Book IV opens with Amoret and armed Britomart on a single horse, thus in silhouette another hermaphroditic image. Britomart masks her identity as a woman from the apprehensive Amoret, who thinks that her fully armed rescuer is a man. Thus abusing Amoret by playing with and on her responses, Britomart performs and thereby explores her own manhood, as contemporary readers of myth could have imagined it. Thus feigning, abusing, and likely faining, she inherits something of Busirane's role, along with Amoret, whose role as victim Britomart had earlier entered empathetically while rescuing her. Psychologically oriented readers might recognize here a doubled traversal of fantasies.

The combined silhouette of Britomart and Amoret on the horse further anticipates the hermaphroditic statue of Venus within her eponymous Temple later in Book IV. Britomart by herself is an armed Venus—traditionally, a *Venus armata*—however, and for my purpose she is most significantly a combination of Venus and Mars, not simply a Venus-Virgo or even a Minerva/Athena. The principle of erotic coupling in *The Faerie Queene*, embodied in its principal couple, Britomart and her lover Artegall, requires four terms, not just two opposites. Each member of the couple variously includes the male or female other, and this is why the grotesque, immobile, hermaphroditic image of binary opposites at the end of Book III in 1590 proves inadequate. This is also why the true Britomart is not simply within the armor and why she is crucially wearing her armor when she finally fights Artegall in hand-to-hand combat and is reconciled to him. Her armor and her agency have become effectually the same in the course and process of Books III and IV. In Britomart's close combat with Artegall (disguised as the Salvage Knight), he is wounded, but she is not, although her horse is, and her ventail, or mask, is sheared off to show her face, framed by wisps of hair. As in the House of Busirane, she remains in control, and Artegall yields to her before she accepts him.

Britomart is an evolving figure in Books III to V, and, in their course, her armor figures the development of her integrity and its loss. Though armed in Book V, she is no longer armed distinctively in her own armor. Recurrently, her identity is mistaken or misinterpreted—first by Dolon, ironically named for a Trojan who betrayed his own side, and then by the ascetic priest of Isis, who ignores the personal and suppresses the passionate in Britomart's experience, overwriting them with dynastic concerns. What makes a crucial difference, however, is the extent to which the poem goes out of the way to *expose* the fact that Britomart herself does not realize what is happening in this process of transference and substitution—misappropriation, in another lexicon, still rhetorical but now also economic, or structural. It is openly done to, not by, her figure, bearing in this respect some similarity to Busirane's transfiguration of Amoret, with the significant difference that Britomart has not spent her whole preceding life in the sheltered Garden of Adonis (then in the similarly enclosed, protective Temple of Venus, if we factor in the 1596 installment). Accordingly, the description of Britomart's final battle with Radigund, Artegall's jailor, is specifically wasteful in sexual and generative terms. It witnesses the abuse of Britomart's figural integrity. Britomart pays a high cost for rescuing Artegall. Killing Radigund, she loses too much of herself, and, with this loss, the many inconsistent, problematical figures of women in Shakespeare that Sinfield and others address—characters with a "continuous consciousness" until it fails or falls silent—also come back into view, returning to memory like so many cultural ghosts.

As the main title of my fourth and final chapter, "Phantasies, Pains, and Punishments," signals, in it I shift from the single focal subject of the earlier chapters to take stock of the rest of Spenser's narrative figures of women. I have subtitled it "A Still-Moving Coda" for the relative brevity and generality of its first third, while signaling that this coda escapes its own generalizing soon after.[17] As earlier indicated, my approach to the rest of these fictive women has a basis in the paradoxical combination of stillness and movement—still moving. This basis derives from discussions in chapters 1 to 3, with respect to which it is a recurrent drumbeat. They lay the groundwork for it, as also happens in the developing context, book by book, of the poem itself. Both terms, *stillness* and *movement*, have positive and negative extensions: for example, *stillness* suggests stability, constancy, conceptualization, and lyric sublation or, conversely, fixation and death; *movement* suggests life, time, change, and narrative or, conversely, instability and inconstancy. On this inclusive thematic basis, one grouping of Spenser's fictive women consists of those found in a single location and condition—thus situated or placed. As presiding genius, any of these good or evil figures might move within her site, as do Lucifera and Alma, but not beyond it. The chapter offers Acrasia as a contained example of this group, insofar as her figure is central to questions about sex and gender in the poem. Explicitly mythological figures and statues of them I mention but do not pursue, because my concern is primarily with figures more distinctly human. Many of the former I have also discussed extensively elsewhere (and endnote as appropriate).[18]

My chief concern in the fourth chapter is with the relatively lesser figures of women who move into different places and contexts. While Duessa and Hellenore get attention, as Duessa already did in chapter 1, the mobile figures mainly treated in chapter 4—Aemylia, Serena, Mirabella, and Pastorella—are all in the 1596 installment, Aemylia in Book IV, and the other three in Book VI. With their inclusion in this project, all six books of the 1596 *Faerie Queene* are represented. Although relatively minor compared with Una, Belphoebe, and Britomart, each of the main figures of chapter 4 has narrative life—a story. Aemylia's is a story of transgression, suffering, and reform whose conclusion stands in marked contrast to that of Amoret. The interlinked stories of Serena and Mirabella are profoundly psychological studies of female misery, and they further extend and transfigure Amoret's and Belphoebe's twinned stories as well. The story of Serena in particular is simultaneously and significantly the story of her figuration. There is less to the story of Pastorella, but she is the last fictive woman of note in *The Faerie Queene* of 1596, and her story brings my discussion back to that of Una and Redcrosse at the end of chapter 1.[19] Like their story, Pastorella's ends with restoration. This ending is at once fit and parodic, the same yet also quite different—still moving.

Chapter 1

Parody and Perfection: Spenser's Una

THIS CHAPTER BEGINS WITH background that enables and introduces my focus on Una's figuration, while deferring her thematic dominance for a time. It moves from the general to the more specific, from a discussion of parody as a historical form to parody in the 1590 *Faerie Queene*, especially with respect to Una, Duessa, and Florimell, all three of whom resonantly "blubber" in the charged context of near-rape. Building on their parodic relation, the chapter then examines the problematizing of Una in stark terms of good or evil in recent criticism, which I interweave with my own readings of her experiences throughout Book I. It concludes with a substantial treatment of parody in Eden, where Una's story achieves a divinely comic ending.

* * *

My opening question is whether we have fully appreciated the extent and degree to which *The Faerie Queene*, like contemporary masterpieces by Rabelais, Shakespeare, and Cervantes, makes a defining use of parody, albeit not an exclusive or overwhelming use. Without denying the serious moral and religious force of the poem, might we do so? Would a greater, more specific recognition of the presence and function of parody in Spenser's epic, as apart from irony, satire, or simple contrast, shift our sense of it? In asking such questions, I am deliberately seeking a shift in perspective that will make Una both more accessible and less simple as a figure.

Each book of the epic uses comic parody early enough for it to be a formative influence and thereby signals a fundamental commitment to *play* in both the ludic and open senses of the word. This is also a commitment to process and exploration, which a reading of each book should reflect as well: just for example, in Book I, Archimago's parodic impersonation of Redcrosse initiates and intermittently propels a comic subplot;

in Book II, the figure of Braggadocchio reflects back parodically on both Guyon and his Palmer; the parodic Malecasta in Book III, together with Florimell, frames its first canto, and Florimell quickly accords with the thematic "mirrors more then one," her figure later to be parodied specifically by her double, the False Florimell.[1] Additional examples abound in the 1596 installment: in the opening cantos of Book IV, the outrageous parody of friendship by the false foursome; the parody that relentlessly dogs the execution of Artegall's justice in the early cantos of Book V; the parody in Calidore's quest throughout Book VI, evident in the ironic juxtaposition of pastoral and violence from the earliest cantos to Melibee's idyll. In the first of the *Mutabilitie Cantos*, Mutability's rebellion, itself already parodic, is then further parodied by Faunus. Such familiar examples are only a start, but, coming early in each book, they are, like other first impressions, important and lasting. Of course, as each narrative progresses, it is subject to modification and, in the instances of each book, to significant, even radical modification. The paired protagonists of Book I, Redcrosse and Una—perhaps Una most of all—afford an especially telling test of the parodic potential of Spenser's epic romance, and they will appear recurrently in subsequent discussion.

Whatever early preview of *The Faerie Queene* Spenser's friend Gabriel Harvey saw, parody aligns suggestively with his familiar response to it as "*Hobgoblin* runne away with the Garland from *Apollo*." Harvey's critical jest contrasts with the enthusiastic praise of Spenser's lost comedies that it follows.[2] In context, Harvey further compares what he has seen of *The Faerie Queene* unfavorably with Ariosto's model romance and instead recommends that Spenser return to the generic model of ancient and contemporary writers of dramatic comedy, including Aristophanes. Perhaps the academic Harvey was more of a generic purist than Spenser or, perhaps, less of a one. Anciently, Aristophanes also affords a familiar model—perhaps *the* model—of parody.

Parody might well be the major term from ancient Greece that describes "comic quotation, imitation, or transformation," although parody is also a practice that readily overlaps, merges with, or even blends into satire and irony, two other ancient terms.[3] Additional terms of relevance, such as *burlesque, travesty, pastiche, double-coding*, and *meta-fiction* are all more recent. Although these terms have variously been identified with parody, by themselves they are generally narrower or even other with respect to it. Both great parodies—the usual historical examples being by Aristophanes, Rabelais, Cervantes, and Sterne—and the ancient roots of parody are more complex and inclusive; they are capable of criticism, sympathy, or both at once—that is, of balance, ambivalence, or simple ambiguity. They include both parodic content *and* parodic expression, either of which can also constitute parody by itself. These, too—complexity and ambivalence, criticism and sympathy, and content, expression, or both—are further points of emphasis.[4]

John Florio's Italian–English dictionary of 1598 refers to parody, as does Henri Estienne's Greek dictionary in 1572. The widely read J. C. Scaliger discusses parody in his *Poetices libri septem* of 1561 (Rose 9–10). Strictly English sources, namely the clergyman Thomas Walkington (*The Optick Glasse of Humors*, 1607) and Ben Jonson in *Every Man in His Humor* (performed 1598, published 1616), employ the term. Anciently, the term *parody* occurs in Aristotle's *Poetics*, referring to the comic writings of Hegemon and Nicochares, parodists of epic style and matter.[5] Ancient commentators on the writings of Aristophanes extend the term to "all sorts of comic literary quotation and allusion" (Rose, 15). Quintilian also refers to parody as imitation and as an abuse of language, a sort of extended catachresis.[6] (Catachrestic form is a thought to ponder: in miniature, consider, analogously, the paradoxical phrases "coy submission" and "modest pride" to describe Milton's Eve, for whom either word alone is insufficient and a single, proper word is lacking.)[7] In the Middle Ages, comic wit and structural doubleness are notable in biblical parody, in musical and visual parody, in such an elaborate comic subplot as that of *The Second Shepherd's Play*, and in Chaucer's self-reflective *Tale of Sir Thopas* and *Tale of Melibee*, both tales important to Spenser. In medieval England and Germany, parodies of the Mass were endemic in "the underworld of clerical writing," as well as in the margins of religious and legal books; according to Miri Rubin, readers, hearers, and viewers were continually reconstructing the "eucharistic symbolic," using "old materials to signify new perceptions and to express altered points of view."[8] By the later Renaissance, Petrarchan parody is so widespread as to have become a subject in itself. Under Queen Elizabeth and King James, John Donne parodies sacred subjects in erotic poems and erotic poetry in holy sonnets. The historical, complementary co-existence of such parody signals its play, its double-sidedness, its loosening of boundaries, its potential for inclusion and connection.

Etymologically, *parody* derives from the Greek word for song or ode, *oidē*, and *para*, a prefix indicating "beside" or "against"—that is, either nearness or opposition—and by extension implying either sympathy, on the one hand, or contention, on the other. Use of the same prefix, *para*, in words such as paradox and parallel are analogously suggestive, particularly since they also convey notions of doubleness—with paradox, doubleness of thought; with parallel, doubleness of representation. Margaret A. Rose, to whose work I owe much, allows that humor was not always or necessarily present in ancient parody, but her own definition, sensitive to sourer and narrower modern theories, requires it: "*the comic refunctioning of preformed linguistic or artistic material*" (52). By *refunctioning*, she wants to signal creativity and, by *preformed material*, to get beyond the misleading reduction of parody only to style. Again, she stresses the comic nature of parody, while nonetheless acknowledging exceptions. The word *comic* itself, I would add, also has a range of meaning, applicable both broadly to humor and to a tale with a happy ending, for example.

For my present Spenserian purposes, parody has a specific connection with imitation and citation, including *self-citation* and *self-reflection*, and, in short, with *mirroring*, including refraction, or bending. It also involves incongruity and revisionary recreation, typically comic in some sense. *Irony*, probably the term most often used for a number of relevant passages in Spenser's epic, is at once broader and less specific. Although irony can describe a recurrent or continuing attitude, such as that of an eiron like Socrates or Chaucer, irony is traditionally classed as a figure—Puttenham's "Drie mock."[9] Although parody, like irony, can apply to a single sentence, it typically has more formal substance; we might announce an intention to write—to compose—a parody, less likely one to compose an irony. If extensively applicable, *irony* becomes an adjective; *parodic* becomes a noun—*parody*. Granted this last distinction, I note that it appeals to our experience of literature, which evokes responses. Again, however, I would stress both the tenuousness of provisional distinctions such as that between irony and parody *and* their usefulness for thinking.

Parody, as my description of it has indicated, is a flexible term. Maddening to anyone rigorously logical as this lack might be, *parody* has fuzzy edges, as do most other literary terms, such as those of rhetoric. Ideally, these terms outgrow the taxonomic fixation useful for beginning students, and the same applies to the distinctions of genre, whose most striking characteristic is that its forms are ever developing and changing.[10] Parody overlaps with other techniques, forms, and categories, and vice versa. Among these, in addition to irony, are allusion, comparison, and, in their loose senses, analogy and intertextuality, all of which are broader and less specifically—that is, neither exclusively nor absolutely—committed to the *comic*, in all the breadth of this happy term itself, than parody is.

Literary terminology is most valuable as a platform for the exploration of thoughtful, affective, exploratory response, not as a means of pigeonholing. Platforms are important, but they are only a start.

Parody and the 1590 *Faerie Queene*

Before returning to Archimago's impersonation of Redcrosse early in the second canto of Book I, which I briefly mentioned in the section above, I want to go back to the beginning of the first canto of this same book. In its initial stanzas, St. George's armor on a knight seeking a dragon, accompanied by a lady with a lamb on a leash, lends parodic potential to this overdetermined figure of the popular, as well as of the more elevated, imagination.[11] The knight and the lady, both nameless and set against a blank landscape at the outset, also trigger memories, further parodic, of many an iconic illustration in a book of hours or other devotional volume.[12] Of course, this is not all the initial descriptions suggest, but only what is to the immediate point: at the outset, these figures, which take shape progressively, remain silhouettes and outlines, still to be filled in—and filled out. The many verbal ambiguities inhering in them, especially in the figure of Redcrosse, only increase their potential. The narrator speculates that the figure of Una, whose whiteness is obscured by her black stole, "inly" mourns, a heavy care in her heart.

Skimming, for the present, over multivalent parodies in the first book, such as the Wandering Wood, its abiogenetic reptilian resident, the helpful heavenly maiden's advising Redcrosse to spend the night with Archimago, this tempter's mumbo-jumbo, his sprite's comic katabasis to the Cave of Morpheus, and more, I now return to Archimago's impersonation of Redcrosse. It is of particular interest because it involves the narrator's parodic self-citation. It begins when Archimago, having separated Una from Redcrosse and set her "wandring" once again through the woods, decides to disguise himself, trying out his extensive repertoire of "formes and shapes" (I.ii.9–10). These, especially his dragon number, unsettle him, "That of himselfe he ofte for feare would quake, / And oft would flie away." His fright anticipates the target of this proleptic parody, namely Redcrosse, who, fourteen lines later, is said to be fearfully running away from himself ("still flying from his thoughts and gealous feare": 12). Properly, the prolepsis belongs to the narrator, who sets up the parodic echo. Between prolepsis and subsequent echo, Archimago dons armor and accoutrements matching those of Redcrosse, and the narrator lingers over a detailed description of this impersonation, as if to savor its ourageous wickedness: "the mighty armes," the "siluer shield," a "bloudy crosse," a "bounch of heares" upon the helmet (11). Then comes the narrator's parodic self-citation of the opening stanza of the poem, in which we got our earliest glimpse of Redcrosse:

> Full iolly knight he seemde, and wel addrest,
> And when he sate vppon his courser free,
> *Saint George* himselfe ye would haue deemed him to be.
> (I.ii.11)

For the first time in the poem, the saint is named, if only as a seeming falsehood. As we know, the words, syntax, and stanzaic location of these breezy lines parody the first stanza of canto i: "Full iolly knight he seemd, and faire did sit, / As one for knightly giusts and fierce encounters fitt." Doing so, they simultaneously unsettle the identity of the figure within the armor we first met and the perceptual reliability of the narrator. Uncertain reliability becomes a heightened possibility upon which the poem will play—and play *variously*—thereafter. No figure, including the narrator, will be wholly exempt from it. Whether considered locally as parody or under an overarching umbrella of parody, such play takes on a role that need not be abrasive, corrosive, or, indeed, destructive, although in theory it could be. In striking examples from later books, the parody even of Artegall or Calidore in their first cantos does not cancel the fact that they are, as we say, more on the side of the angels than their vicious opponents are. Their virtues may be modified and redefined, critically scrutinized and profoundly questioned, but not wholly undermined or simply invalidated.

At the outset of Book II, there is again parody aplenty even before Braggadocchio's debut. Guyon's response to Redcrosse, then to Duessa, is itself parodic, and the Castle of Medina is surely a parody of true temperance. But my favorite instance is Duessa's so overplaying the part of violated virgin that the disguised Archimago has to tell her to dial it down (i.16). By parodic contrast, details of Duessa's botched audition recall Una's earlier response to the actual assault of Sans Loy in Book I. Duessa's "fowly blubbered" face and "garments rent," for example, disfigure Una's "ruffled rayments, and fayre blubbred face."[13] In response to this parody, what is called for, finally, is judgment—sensitive, critical judgment, which by its very nature is subject to demonstration, dispute, and, when justified, revision. Embracing the possibility of revision, such judgment is provisional, working within an ongoing process that includes play rather than excluding or shutting it down. Tonally, the difference between torn garments and ruffled raiments is both subtle and considerable, not to mention that between *fair* and *fowl*. *Raiments*, a word deriving from an Old French verb meaning *to array*, suggests finery, and "ruffled rayments" suggests merely disordered ones, whereas Duessa's ripped clothes and disheveled hair suggest something more brutally physical—cruder and rawer.

The memorably onomatopoeic word "blubbered" applies in the 1590 *Faerie Queene* only to Una, Duessa, and Florimell, linking their assaults, while further description radically differentiates them.[14] "Blubbered," is a word that originates in connection with bodies of water. It could well have been used to initiate an Ovidian metamorphosis into a brook or a spring, part of the landscape on the order of the nigh-raped nymph's "bubling fountaine" in Book II.[15] Applied to a human being, it is, at least potentially, an undignifying, even ugly and degrading, word, in all the weight of the notion of *dignity*, or human worth, in this period. This weight is religious, not simply social, insofar as it enters discussions of merit, justification, and punishment.[16] In short, "blubbered" is a carefully chosen word that befits a context of rape, whether actual or feigned.

I'll turn next to the events that open Book III and begin to define its context. They start with Britomart's unseating Guyon, proceed to the vision of the fleeing Florimell, and finally turn to the episode of Malecasta, an obvious parody of chastity. Recalling the figure of Verdant in the Bower of Bliss, at the outset of Book III the "fiery feete" of Guyon's horse "burne / The verdant gras" and doing so, parodically reinforce the comic justice, not to say the condignity, of this knight's come-down at the end of Britomart's spear (i.5). Biblically, "all flesh is grass," and, with Florimell on the narrator's horizon—proleptic but also close by—"all the goodliness thereof is as the flower of the field": Isaiah 40:6.[17] The castle of Malecasta displays a tapestry that is further mindful of the mythic potency of Acrasia's Bower, now transposed to a social landscape—a court, not an isolated island-coupling. This tapestry features eros and death in the story of Venus and Adonis, ending with a fictive woman bending over a dying man, another parodic recollection of the Bower.

Near the outset of Book III, Florimell bursts onto the scene as a sudden, striking impression that is gone almost as soon as it comes, although it also lingers memorably.[18] The forest setting is deeply shaded, and her appearance "out of the thickest brush" is white, gold, and sparkling against it:

> Vpon a milkwhite Palfrey all alone,
>   A goodly Lady did foreby them rush,
>   Whose face did seeme as cleare as Christall stone,
>   And eke through feare as white as whales bone:
>   Her garments all were wrought of beaten gold,
>   And all her steed with tinsell trappings shone,
>   Which fledd so fast, that nothing mote him hold,
> And scarse them leasure gaue, her passing to behold.
>
> Still as she fledd, her eye she backward threw,
>   As fearing euill, that poursewd her fast;
>   And her faire yellow locks behind her flew,
>   Loosely disperst with puff of euery blast:
>   All as a blazing starre doth farre outcast
>   His hearie beames, and flaming lockes dispredd,
>   At sight whereof the people stand aghast:
>   But the sage wizard tells, as he has redd,
> That it importunes death and doefull dreryhedd.
>   (III.i.15–16)

The impression Florimell's figure creates is beautiful, fearful, ethereal, portentous, ominous, and, paradoxically, both fleeting and lasting. At first, the view of the lady is frontal, starting with her face. In the second stanza, the view is from behind her as she passes from sight. The phrase "Still as she fledd" suggests movement and its opposite, stillness; she is at once fleeing and frozen in fear—like the nymph of the fountain in Book II. Comparison of her hair to the tail of a comet with "flaming lockes dispredd" enlarges her significance, associating her with anticipated sorrow and death, of which there is much in Book III. Notably, she is not named in the text until canto v, where her dwarf finally recounts the cause of her leaving the court to find Marinell, her wounded love. The fact that this cause is withheld until then resists identification of her in canto i too simply with "flower honey," a translation of the name Florimell. As ever in Spenser, we read the image as we go, not rushing to the typically reductive label that the narrator deliberately (parodically?) withholds until later.

In years past, this image of Florimell was identified primarily with Neoplatonic beauty. More recently, it has been read as desire or, specifically, male desire. In all instances, *eros* would be a better, broader, historically more accurate term. The fleeing beauty, after all, is followed by an image specifically of male lust in the figure of the forester with his punny, phallic "bore speare." The two male knights who join the chase are motivated by eros to pursue a beautiful and wondrous object of desire, rather than by lust in itself. Comic as may be the sight of two knights on a single horse in pursuit of their fleeing vision, Guyon, however given to outbursts of wrath, is still the patron of temperance, if now without the exclusion or denial of eros.[19] Bestial lust flees in another direction, and Timias, who, Harry Berger observes, is here first named in the text, goes after the would-be violator. Timias's proper name, deriving from "honor" in Greek, deflects readings of his motivation as merely its opposite.[20] By the same reading, honor may not be motivating the eros of Guyon and Arthur, but neither is animal lust.

The cross-dressed Britomart, now also named for the first time in the text, is constant to her own quest, indeed, explicitly to her own "mind," declining pursuit of either forester or Florimell. She cares not to "follow beauties chace" or "Ladies Loue" (i.19). Although these phrases are ambiguous (the chase of beauties, beauties' or beauty's chasing; the love of ladies, ladies' or lady's loving), Britomart's rejection of them simply comes down to the facts that she is not interested in chasing a fleeing woman or in flight as a means of escape. Florimell's fear of the slobbering boor who chases her is entirely justified, as later is her continued flight from a helmeted knight with unfamiliar insignia, not to mention the reader's awareness that the sight of her has erotically motivated this knight. Projection of Florimell's fear onto Britomart, however, is textually unjustified.[21] On the one hand, a flighty female is just not Britomart's type, and, on the other, Britomart, far from rejecting eros, actively and aggressively seeks Artegall. In the Castle of Malecasta, she also feels misplaced empathy for its impassioned seductress. Although Book III makes the theme of "mirrours more then one" focal, every figure is not interchangeable with every other one. Spenser's figures of women all have some relevance to one another, but they are not simple projections or doubles of Britomart. Their differences and contrasts are as defining as are their similarities and likenesses. Parody is well suited to enable the complexity of this mirroring.

Since I have made an issue of the word *blubbered*, I propose to follow it to its reappearance in Florimell's would-be rape by the fisherman, and then back to Una's by Sans Loy. The parodic relationship between these scenes is further defining. Ultimately, it will introduce consideration of what might be termed "the problem of Una." Recurrently analogized by the narrator to small, frightened, fleeing animals—a "light-foot hare," "a fearefull Doue"—and later to Ovidian figures fleeing in fear—"fearfull *Daphne*" and, more puzzlingly, "wicked *Myrrha*"—Florimell progresses from the natural fear of a predator to a fear that is culturally and mythically defined. This defining fails to distinguish Daphne's choice of virginity from Myrrha's incestuous guilt.[22] In short, Florimell's travel takes her from the erotic context on the near side of the Garden of Adonis into the seamier context on the far side, a context that at moments infects the narrator's perspective, too, as in the conspicuous instance of Myrrha. A similar development will bear on the depiction of Serena in Book VI, who might be seen to have stepped carelessly into the allegorical landscape that the Blatant Beast inhabits (iii.23–24).[23]

On the far side of the Garden, an impressive assortment of parodic perversions of eros emerges: the witch, her son, and her other misbegettings, namely the hyena-like beast and False Florimell; Argante and Ollyphant, twins in lust, incest, and predation; the Squire of Dames, a promiscuous figure who belongs in a fabliau; the dirty old fisherman and shape-shifting Proteus, exemplar of instability; Malbecco, Hellenore, and Paridell, who parodically figure the destructive force of eros in history; and finally Busirane and his aestheticized house of erotic horrors. Florimell's continual flight through the woods to the sea seems to descend through a scale of being: her flight into and through the woods, then the monstrous destruction of her signature white horse and the loss of her identifying girdle, the mixing of her garments with fish scales, and her abduction by the flux of the ocean. She suffers a near-metamorphosis into what her blubbered face portends—the foam or airy bubbles of the sea: faced by Proteus, she is "Ruffled and fowly raid with filthy soyle, / And blubbred face with teares of her faire eyes" (III.viii.32). The words "Ruffled" and "raid" (arrayed) echo the description of Una's raiments when the satyrs frighten Sans Loy away; "fowly" and "faire," respectively, recall Duessa's faking and Una's distress in comparable situations, as well. "Soyle" could indicate genital fluid, presumably spilled by the fisherman.[24] More obviously here, the victim is soiled by the victimizer.

I can't say that I find anything funny about Florimell's shame and fear when Proteus claims her. Now she is compared to "a fearful partridge, that is fledd / From the sharpe hauke,"

> And fals to ground, to seeke for succor theare,
> Whereas the hungry Spaniells she does spye
> With greedy iawes her ready for to teare.
>
> (III.viii.33)

Florimell comes closer to the physical brutality of rape than any other figure of a woman in the poem, with the partial, elusive exception of Serena and, still more symbolically and psychologically, of Amoret. Yet the run-up to Florimell's terror is a shameless parody of *double entendres*, such as her prayer to the old lecher "to guide the cock-bote well," since "the great waters gin apace to swell" (24). Whether this doubleness is perversely shameless or innocently so, as well as for whom it is either, are open questions, although at least we know that the old lecher—hardly offered as a role model—responds to Florimell's hapless words by "fondly grin[ning]" (24).

Nevertheless, Florimell's rescue from the fisherman parodies Una's from Sans Loy in Book I. Like Florimell's, the extremity of Una's fear, evident in her "fayre blubbred face," also finds expression in an image of natural instinct:

> She more amazd, in double dread doth dwell;
> And euery tender part for feare does shake:
> As when a greedy Wolfe through honger fell
> A seely Lamb far from the flock does take,
> Of whom he meanes his bloody feast to make,
> A Lyon spyes fast running towards him,
> The innocent pray in hast he does forsake,
> Which quitt from death yet quakes in euery lim
> With chaunge of feare, to see the Lyon looke so grim.
> (I.vi.10)

Although wolf, lamb, and lion carry biblical associations not found in Florimell's hawk, partridge, and spaniels, the affective content is similar.

Florimell's rescue, again like Una's, is preceded by an evocation of providential care that attests to her chastity and innocence, making the narrator's earlier comparison of her to Myrrha even more dubious, indeed, hasty and foolish:

> See how the heauens of voluntary grace,
> And soueraine fauor towards chastity,
> Doe succor send to her distressed cace:
> So much high God doth innocence embrace.
> (III.viii.29)

Proteus, hearing the shrieks of Florimell, hastens to her aid, much as do the satyrs to Una's. Less benign than the "wyld woodgods," as the satyrs are called in Book I (vi.9), however, the shape-shifting Proteus and the restless sea in which he lives realize Florimell's movement in some sense, even as he imprisons her because of her constancy—once again her *stillness* ("Still as she fledd": III.i.16)—in the rocky cave from which she then can fly no more. Movement and stillness, like eros and death, continue to inform her figure and parodically to recall the nymph of the fountain in Book II.

The evocation, or rather the invocation, of providence in anticipation of Una's rescue is more elaborate and emotional than in Florimell's, although the extremity of their peril is similar. Yet the "heauenly virgin" Una, who teaches truth among the satyrs, is a different figure in the narrative context of a different book, and her plight asks for discrimination.[25] Having snatched Una's veil from her face, Sans Loy tries flattery first, then force. At this point, the narrator exclaims, "Ah heauens, that doe this hideous act behold, / And heauenly virgin thus outraged see, / How can ye vengeance iust so long withhold" (vi.5)? The "shiekes" and "cryes" of the "pitteous mayden" follow, together with her "plaintes" to the heavens,

> That molten starres doe drop like weeping eyes;
> And *Phoebus* flying so most shamefull sight,
> His blushing face in foggy cloud implyes,
> And hydes for shame.
>
> (I.vi.6)

Whereas Florimell, like Serena later on, feels shame before her rescuer and hides her face in fear, here it is Phoebus who both flies from the shameful sight of violent assault and, hiding his own face, exhibits, as if by contagion, its shaming effect on him. The extravagant figure of stars that melt into tear drops could be considered either hyperbole or catachresis by Renaissance standards, in either case a figure associated with an excess befitting the situation.[26]

What happens next in stanza 6, however, is more controversial, and my own relationship to it has wavered over the years. Ending this stanza, the Spenserian narrator asks a question that might first be taken at face value: "What witt of mortall wight / Can now deuise to quitt a thrall from such a plight" as Una's? The answer comes instantly, at the outset of the next stanza, "Eternall prouidence exceeding thought, / Where none appeares can make her selfe a way: / A wondrous way it for this Lady wrought" (7). In retrospect, the question that ends stanza 6 might be considered rhetorical, but only if we overlook the difference between the wit of a human being and eternal providence, obviously God here. Yet Berger's observation that the sequence is comic, comparable to "operatic parody" and calculated to remind us that "in spite of all the fuss, everything is well under control," has traction. When Berger adds that the question and its answer "serve mainly to alert the reader to Spenser's own inventiveness," however, his reading offers to replace parodic multivalence with deflating skepticism and to exclude "Eternall prouidence" from the Spenserian equation.[27] The special virtue of parody is to enable a balance of empathy and comedy, seriousness and play. Una's plight engages, not only operatic excess, but also the violence of rape and the doctrine of grace—God's concern for truth and for human beings. If "the heauenly virgin" Una is never as physically imperiled as Florimell, her figural being modulates all these possibilities, and, in the immediate instance, it does so through the inclusive, nuanced potential of parody.

Parody and the Problem of Una

Una's blubbering, even more than that of the other figures of women, has opened up larger issues pertaining to her figuration, to critical response, and to parody. Una is conspicuous in the first book of the epic, and this book, as opening, is ground and backdrop for the working of the books that follow. Since the subject of Book I is religious—by its nature bearing on the most serious, ultimate of concerns—it also offers a particularly stringent test of the extent to which the poem might be considered parodic and its very allusiveness ludic (cf. allusive, < *ludere*, "play"). *Serio ludere* is a Renaissance commonplace that embraces parody. The conception of allusive parody, including the self-citational sort, begins to grasp the complex tonality of Book I, as the preceding section has suggested.

To judge from recent criticism, Una's *figural being*, the kind of figure she presents, has become more problematical than it was in days gone by. Without the extremities of recent criticism, in fact, Una might not be a problem or have one. We live in extreme times. Truth being the daughter of time, to cite the old adage, recent enlightenment might well be progress, although it is difficult to see how the extreme diversity of current views can all be equally enlightened. A number of readings find that Una is deficient, overbearing, emasculating, or simply evil, especially in the early cantos of Book I, whereas others have continued to find her benign or heavenly in updated or reinvigorated ways. My point is that the current problem of Una inheres in the reception of her in recent criticism and is made accessible by it. Accordingly, my plan is to interweave diverse, recent, broadly representative views of her figure—historicist, comparative, psychoanalytical, and theological—with my own readings and especially with the parodic potential of her figuration, thereby to recognize and include, if not to reconcile, them. Already in this chapter, I have found her figure touched by allusive parody, at once in retrospective rereading and immediately. In the end, discussion of parody in the twelfth canto, which treats Spenser's Eden, will offer a possible resolution of issues that bear on Una's figural being there and elsewhere.

One driver of the negative readings of Una is the fact that we never get inside her in the way or to the extent we do with Redcrosse. Her lamblike innocence—is it instead her simplicity, her oneness?—is hard to bear. Briefly, at least, Una, seeming to mourn "inly" from our first sight of her, comes to experience emotions such as grief, fear, anger, compassion, doubt, and joy, which connect her to the realm of human passion and indeed to humanity as we mortals know it, but she remains upright, despite her brief, despairing swoon when she encounters the dwarf with the armor that Redcrosse abandoned before Orgoglio seized him. If she falls, she does so ritualistically "Thrise" (I.vii.24), and we know she will get up: not operatic parody this time but an experience—yes, ritualized experience—that touches her and does so without causing a sustained and damaging descent.[28] Notably, she gets up before Arthur comes to the rescue, her renewed resolve and strenuous effort seeming to coincide with his arrival in the narrative (vii.27–29). Experience is not by definition corrupting (except in the mouth of Milton's Satan). Moreover, Una is a figure who, from start to finish in Book I, occupies substantial portions of text and even whole episodes, making her a major player in this book. Her experience, not only Redcrosse's, plays a defining role.

Claire McEachern calls Spenser's epic "This least inward of poems," and Una might well be the major figure to whom McEachern's remark most nearly applies.[29] More recently, Kathryn Walls has described Una as primarily an emblematic character, to an extent a designation comparable to McEachern's, although for Walls Una figures the Invisible Church, whereas for McEachern she figures the contemporary, national church of the Tudors: if there is similarity in these two views, there is more substantial difference.[30] Yet Una is not only an autonomous figure in the narrative of the poem, but sometimes crucially she also represents an aspect—an interior dimension, if you will—of Redcrosse, as, for example, when she intervenes both physically and psychically to stop his suicide. After she and Redcrosse are divided into "double parts" early in canto ii, neither is complete without the other, and both are potentially—not necessarily or always already—inside and outside one another.[31] Their relationship thereafter depends on demonstrable context; often, it is ironic, parodic, or both and therefore a sign of difference and distance—of divisive doubleness. Their reunion signifies wholeness, first incipient and in the end, if not perfected, at least assured.

From the beginning, when Una and Redcrosse wander through the Wood and stumble upon Error, Una is clearly characterized in the narrative as *contingent* truth, or truth in this fallen, human world. She does not possess infallibility or even the intuition of an angel. Complaints about her evil, deceptions, or failures arise from a reductive conception of her either as only a woman or else from too simple an assumption of her ideality, one so exaggerated as to replace the unfolding narrative by an a priori idea of her as purely an abstraction or a mystical sign. This is a false division of concept and signifying figure from narrative. Either extreme, Una merely as woman or merely as ideal, effectually replaces the working of narrativized figuration in Book I and bifurcates or denies her integrity as a figure.

When Una is abandoned by Redcrosse, she or, rather, her unfolding experiences organize the evolving forces of nature, history, and grace that will rescue Redcrosse—the lion, the satyrs, Satyrane, and eventually Arthur, in sum an ascending scale, as well as one that implies a historical progression. As Coelia puts it in canto x, Una "Hast wandred through the world," leading her "weary soles" (an obvious pun) and guided by grace, while the benighted Redcrosse has sunk into the darkness of himself (I.x.9). When Una mistakes the disguised Archimago for Redcrosse in canto iii and later, in canto vi, for a pilgrim, her error, which parodies, by similarity *and* difference, the initial response of Redcrosse to Duessa, again bears witness to the inescapable human fallibility of her figure. In a relevant, religious commonplace of the period, only God sees into the mind and heart and alone unerringly penetrates hypocrisy, which is Archimago's moral aspect (I.i.arg.). Not to be divinely unerring is not simply, in a sinful sense, to err; it might instead be an honest mistake and, if culpable at all, not willfully so: to err, the saying goes, is human, and, in Una's characterization, it is at once inevitable and further humanizing.

When Una's "pet lion" (as Richard Halpern comically dubs him) also fails to respond to Archimago's evil in canto iii, it is first and foremost because he is a lion, not because Archimago has morphed into Judas, as Walls suggests, nor because the lion has become Una's projection, as

Halpern indicates.[32] At the same time, Judas, as hypocrite, like any other egregious, historical expression of hypocrisy, could be considered a specific aspect of what Archimago conceptually represents, if this reading is invited by the context. Satan himself, the guileful father of lies, is surely another candidate, should we want one, since Archimago is said to hate Una "as the hissing snake" in the Garden of Eden, that is, as the shape-shifting Satan (I.ii.9).[33] In short, in the episodes involving Una, the figure of Archimago, when present, is a larger term for hypocritical guile even than the historical Satan, although Archimago's figure alludes more than once to Satan and will do so again in Spenser's Eden.[34]

In the developing narrative of *The Faerie Queene*, figures often represent many historical singularities, whether once or recurrently, rather than just a single one. Una's lion does not recognize Archimago because this guiler does not use force, as do Sans Loy and earlier Kirkrapine. In this failing, the lion is analogous—again, *analogous*, not an identical projection—as variously elsewhere, to Redcrosse, who can recognize and deal with the direct, martial threat of Sans Foy but fails to recognize anything wrong with the disguised, deceitful Duessa. The lion, after all, whatever else he might be, is an animal. He is evidently also truth-loving by nature, or kind, as are all God's human creatures and instinctively his nonhuman ones, too, especially when contextually animated—*anima*, or ensouled to an extent, as the word *animal* signals.[35]

McEachern's argument about Una concerns history, politics, and ideological representation—more exactly, the coding of ideological distinctions onto the female body. McEachern recognizes that Una is associated with the invisible Church but focuses instead on the challenges of representing this church, or Christian truth, in the world by the figure of a woman whose binary opposite, Duessa, is another such figure. McEachern observes that the very clothing of Una renders her vulnerable to imitation, and as supporting evidence she offers contemporary, overlapping illustrations of Queen Elizabeth and the Romish whore of Babylon (53–58). She suggests that Una's visibility as a clothed, attractive figure of a woman necessarily compromises her absolute purity by embodiment and her self-sameness, or identity, by susceptibility to duplication (45–46). Notably, however, Una only appears unveiled in her "self-resemblance" when restored to Eden, as distinct from her unveiled distortion by "blubbred" terror before Sans Loy (I.xii.8, vi.4, 9–10).[36] Although McEachern's generalization about the absence of inwardness in Spenser's epic is mistaken in my view, her problematizing of Truth's gendered expression in clothing and as beauty is valuable.[37] Berger seems to agree when he finds that, "Una is no less visible than Duessa and no less an idol," but then he explains this overlap as the product of androgenesis, because Una, no less than Archimago's specter of her, Duessa, is under male instruction—simply the same from this perspective.[38] Such views as McEachern's and Berger's seem extreme. Put most simply, Una and Duessa, one and two, are not equal—period; yet, as numbers or numerical concepts, in addition to whatever else they are, they are both comparable *and* differential.

In contrast to McEachern's historicism, Syrithe Pugh's emphases are primarily comparative and generic. Her perceptive discussions of Una include the Ovidian features of the Wandering Wood, Ovid's literary compassion for his heroines, and the Ovidian forest of Spenser's satyrs.[39] Deserted by Redcrosse, Una, in Pugh's reading, resembles Vergil's Dido and Ovid's Ariadne in the *Heroides*, the opening of whose epistle Una's meeting with the lion and subsequent complaint recall (66). Ariadne is also rescued by Bacchus and his satyrs in "one of Ovid's favourite myths" (67), and Pugh notes that Redcrosse and Una's retreat from a rainstorm into the Wood of canto i alludes to that of Aeneas and Dido from a rainstorm into a cave. All these episodes qualify as sympathetically comic parody. Pugh further observes that the "innocent wandering" in the Wood by Spenser's couple turns into confusion, however—an implicit criticism of the Vergilian antecedent—as, unwittingly, they draw closer to Error's cave (50). A sharp difference exists between Pugh's allusive reading of Redcrosse and of what she terms Una's "innocent wandering" and that of Walls, who speaks of "complicity" in the couple's mutual desire to enter the Wood and of their guilty fear before God, from whom they "run away" into it (26, 29). But the rain-making deity of canto i is significantly Jove, not simply the Christian God, and his violent emission into his leman's—that is, his mistress's—lap is more suggestive of an Olympian rape than of the biblical flood found in Walls's reading (28). Redcrosse and Una don't run into the Wood; they just enter it, being "Enforst" by nature (rain) to do so (I.i.7). They seek shelter in the Wood because, in a relevant pun, they have enough sense to get out of the rain. The pagan culture of the ancient world and nature, especially human nature, which includes common sense and the fleshly senses, are thematic throughout Book I. The pagan is also the (merely) natural until nearly the end of this book. Yet nature has been divinely created and, if in time fallen, in time also redeemed, as it will be decisively first in the eighth canto by Arthur and then progressively by Una and Redcrosse in the rest of Book I.

Pugh's description of the forest in canto vi—another woody, or natural, and mythological place (*topos*)—to which the satyrs take Una after her narrow escape from "the paradigmatic Ovidian danger, that of rape," is especially attractive:

> [This forest] is the world of Ovidian myth, metamorphosis, and natural magic as a benign and sheltering place, characterized by pity for the unprotected female and by a natural instinct of religious awe, though ill-expressed as idolatry. By making Sylvanus's crew the agents of divine providence, Spenser begins to suggest a certain compatibility between Ovid and Christianity, especially in his pity for the weak and vulnerable, and in his interest in the miraculous [67].

The satyrs' forest, benign if idolatrous, fits well the parodic ambivalence, or doubleness, that repeatedly touches the figures of Book I and affects our response to them. At its sharpest point, it includes the notoriously benighted but comic efforts of the satyrs to worship Una's "Asse" when she discourages their idolatrous worship of her own person (vi.19). Naturally, in a resonant word, the satyrs do not quite desist.

For Halpern, Una represents "the invisible Church or Christian Truth," a distinction that has always seemed a bit fuzzy to me, too (1). He carefully asserts that Una's "lion becomes to some degree a psychic projection of Una" and therefore intuits Una's wishes in clawing open the door to Corceca's cottage (2). But soon, Halpern's Corceca likewise signifies Una's "blindness of heart" for two reasons: first, Una does not interrupt "her lion's murderous rage," and second, "When a Spenserian hero arrives at a particular locale, we generally understand the place to embody his or her spiritual condition at that moment" (2). This generalization, although plausible, is an oversimplification. The simultaneous presence of *two* (or more) visitors in the Houses of Book I, not to mention evidence from the Houses of subsequent books, instead suggests that every House has some special pertinence to each visitor, not an identity with each: Redcrosse is not Coelia, and Britomart is not Amoret, the latter a distinction that I pursue in chapter 3. If, in some ways and to some extent, Una represents the Church, in addition to Truth, she has a distinctly social, cultural, and historical dimension, to which the role of an abbess (Abessa) and Corceca's incessant use of prayer beads perversely pertain. Details, particulars, and distinctions, not only similarities and generalizations, are ever important to the working of Spenserian allegory. Those who are deficient, or lacking, and blind of heart—Abessa and Corceca—pertinently contrast with Una's presence and needs as an abandoned woman, as Truth, or as Church, rather than simply exposing her interiorized hang-ups. The other problem, Una's not restraining the lion, vanishes if we do not just assume that he is her projection. Lions respond instinctively to violence, as does Una's lion to the violent intrusion of Kirkrapine.

Insofar as Una figures Truth, she certainly has some degree of intuition, as philosophers assert we all do, and she also has some knowledge of the ur-dragon, that dragon of dragons, that is besieging Eden. To ask why Una, who eventually recognizes the Wandering Wood as the site of Error's den, should be "familiar at all" with such a place overlooks this background (Halpern, 2). No more than experience need knowledge be corrupting: "Evil into the mind of God or Man / May come and go, so unapprov'd, and leave / No spot or blame behind," to recall *Paradise Lost*, for whose poet Spenser was the "Original."[40] Una is noticeably quicker than Redcrosse to read the signs of danger in the Wood and then to recognize Error. She cannot do so sooner precisely because, as this episode signals, she is *contingent* truth here. She is no longer in Eden or even in the court of Gloriana, having entered the world of quest in order to end the siege of Eden by evil. Now she participates in a quest narrative that is committed to experience, to encountering its perils and learning from them. That she does learn from them is one reason she can see through Archimago's disguise in canto xii, as she cannot earlier, in cantos iii and vi. Of course, in canto xii, she is also back in Eden, and the dragon is dead, at least for now.

Halpern takes Una to task for advising Redcrosse to stay the night with Archimago, and his doing so invites a closer look at her advice, which, on the face of it, does seem odd. There is something parodic about it, since her role recalls the damsels who people romances and either help the hero or, alternatively, entrap him. The stated reasons for Una's advice are that night is approaching and the battle-weary Redcrosse needs some sleep. True: these reasons respond sensibly to natural needs, of which Una evidently and appropriately has knowledge, and, as elsewhere until canto xii, she is unable to penetrate the hypocritical Archimago's disguise. Again, the truth she embodies is contingent, not divinely omniscient, and she is about to learn a hard lesson concerning the natural condition of her chosen knight.

Halpern's reading merges Una and Archimago at this moment, however, and tellingly, he cites as evidence a sequence of two stanzas in which, he suggests, we might suppose at the outset of the second, that Archimago, not Una, is speaking (3). In the first of these stanzas, Una addresses Redcrosse:

> Now (saide the Ladie) [it] draweth toward night,
> And well I wote, that of your later fight
> Ye all forwearied be: for what so strong,
> But wanting rest will also want of might?
> The Sunne that measures heauen all day long,
> At night doth baite his steeds the *Ocean* waues emong.

The next stanza continues,

> Then with the Sunne take Sir, your timely rest,
> And with new day new worke at once begin:
> Vntroubled night they say giues counsell best.
> Right well Sir knight ye haue aduised bin,
> Quoth then that aged man [Archimago].
>
> (I.i.32–33)

In the middle of the second stanza, Archimago reinforces, indeed cleverly exploits, Una's advice, but the reasonable and grammatical supposition at its start is that Una is still speaking. If the identity of the speaker wobbles for a line in the middle, unless we *already* suspect Una of evil, there is no more reason to pin the wobble on her than to give the guileful Archimago due credit for it. Without a reason to blame Una here, Halpern's *already* having identified her with Corceca and the murderous lion in canto iii, thereby having violated the narrative sequence of the poem in order to imply a reason in canto iii to suspect Una's motive here in canto i, is suspect but strategic. Simultaneously, this strategy welcomes, even provokes, reexamination of the text, as well as of the method of reading it, which is hardly separable from Halpern's critical argument. Ironically, it is useful to my purposes in highlighting the importance of narrative sequence to the development, the unfolding process, of the poem. From the Wandering Wood to the battle with Error, to Archimago, Redcrosse and Una travel through an increasingly perilous landscape that requires greater discrimination from all who encounter it, not only from the immediate travelers in the poem. The challenge to reading, whether figures and landscape or verbal text, is tricky.

Another of Halpern's arguments is provocative, since it aligns with his shift from a defining lack in Una to Freud's notion that castration defines the psychological condition of woman and doing so aligns with other engagements of psychoanalytical readings in this chapter and the third one. Halpern reads Una (woman) as a lack that becomes a "promiscuous unity . . . drift[ing] into" Archimago or other unsavory figures, because her very basis is an absence of substantive being. This argument is comically seductive, and, indeed, there is a certain tongue-in-cheek quality throughout Halpern's essay, initially delivered as a luncheon address—more *serio ludere*, perhaps? The argument starts by claiming that the Latin word *una* is exclusively a modifier, an adjective or adverb, and not a grammatical entity, or noun (5).[41] According to Latin or English lexicons, this claim is mistaken. English o*ne* or Latin *unus/-a/-um* as a noun variously signifies a numeral equally represented by the figure 1 or the word *one*; it can also signify the concept of singleness, or unity, and someone, a singularity. The relation of the noun to the adjective is often ambiguous—a dynamic, portentous pun that simultaneously looks two ways, to heaven and earth, for example, and in short, to a unity. In an unfolding temporal narrative, such unity becomes at most continuity in this world, which is, to my mind, what Una comes actually to embody.[42]

A maxim in Spenser's Book V comes to mind: "truth is one in all"—that is, one always and everywhere one, an inspiring thought that the immediate context challenges in the later, more secular book (xi.56).[43] But how does this familiar maxim apply to Una in Book I? The argument to its second canto specifically refers to Una as "Truth," which is the only singular, specific name besides Una she gets. *Truth*, understood as medieval *trouthe*, which is an understanding readily available in the sixteenth century, has ontological, epistemological, and personal dimensions—as the godhead, objective reality, and subjective, affective loyalty (cf. modern, plighted *troth*)—all of which pertain to Una. If I had to choose between Una as invisible Church or as Truth, the options Halpern specifies, I would choose Truth hands down as the broader, more conceptual term and regard the invisible Church as one important expression of it—more exactly, as one expression of the poetic figure of Una when justified by the text, and never as an exclusive expression.

Aside from the awkward fact that Una is quite visible, the presence in Augustine of the Protestant doctrine of the invisible Church is itself debatable. This doctrine, which, for Walls, Una represents, is certainly present in Calvin, who probably thought he found it in Augustine, and it is earlier present in Luther. The Protestant reformers had somehow to account for what the Spirit was doing during all those centuries of blindered Catholicism, whereas, in quite a different historical context,

Augustine had had to fend off the Donatists by defending the institutional church, something he did vigorously. Many are the versions of Augustine's ecclesiology to be found, whether in the Renaissance or the present. Such a learned bishop in the English Protestant Church as Lancelot Andrewes, a contemporary of Spenser, speaks not of the invisible Church, but more traditionally of the "mystical body of Christ," referring this to Saints Paul and Augustine.[44] But I am *not* choosing between Una's conceptual identities, merely prioritizing one, namely Truth.

Between 1998 and 2004, Berger published three related articles, all of which treat the figure of Una to some extent.[45] In them, his approach is theorized and frankly psychoanalytical, for example, including the castration principle, narcissism, scapegoating displacements, redistributed complicities, and what he calls the discourses of victims and sinners, both of which are forms of false consciousness. He interprets Spenser's Book I in modern terms of gender and sexuality, thereby to show that Christianity scapegoats woman (1998:177–80). He also intends to demonstrate that Spenser exposes this scapegoating and its associated expressions of bad or diseased conscience, rather than participating in them (1998:180).

The proof of the critical pudding is how well it works with Spenser's text. Berger reads by the light of a laser beam, and his localized insight is always illuminating, but I am not so sure that his larger argument holds up. His discussion of the end of Despair's canto in Book I affords a striking example, as well as an opportunity to consider the relevant text: here, Una, who has entered the cave of Despair with Redcrosse (ix.35), intervenes suddenly to snatch the dagger from her knight's suicidal hand, sharply to reproach him (52), and urgently to remind him of divine mercy and of his own election (53). At the very end of the canto, Redcrosse does what Una advises, "Arise . . . and leave this cursed place," namely, the landscape of Despair (I.ix.53). His doing so recalls his cooperation with Una early in the book to defeat Error, however temporarily, and it is a small, imperfect sign of their reunion as they leave Despair for the House of Holiness. In Berger's reading of this episode, however, Una's intervention effectually infantilizes, emasculates, and castrates Redcrosse.[46] Yet Una has just interrupted a suicide, the temptation to which Despair's *coup de grâce*—oops, forget *grâce*—has been to excite the deranged knight's imagination of damnation. Suicide is imminent, the dagger poised in the knight's uplifted hand, and immediate intervention is needed. The terror of damnation is what the knight flinches from—not from divine forgiveness, as Berger suggests, but from its erasure by the insidious working of Despair, now at its critical moment (1998:176). Nothing is heard from Una of "heauenly mercies" until the critical moment requiring her immediate action has passed (I.ix.53).[47] Insofar as Una's figure points to heavenly intervention in this episode, she is grace—saving grace—but she is also love, and she is truth, *trouthe*. Her acting directly to save her knight also expresses an assurance and a strength of conviction not evident in *her figure* before. These will be evident again before the book is finished.

In another of the articles, Berger treats the "transmigration" of meaning from one character in Book I to another in ways that intersect with my own and others' arguments about Una in the present essay. The term "transmigration" is evidently more than a translation of the term "metaphor," or continued metaphor ("allegory"), however.[48] "Transmigration" substitutes here for psychoanalytical displacement, and it displaces metaphor's maintenance of difference, or, indeed, of narrative distance. Thus the meanings of the names Abessa and Corceca "transmigrate to Redcross," as instanced in "his blindheartedness" and in his fleeing from Una, thereby absenting himself (Berger, 2004:225). Yes, but also no. What's in a name when each of these two figures of women is disembodied and returned to the status of a common word? Transmigratory reading subsequently turns Abessa and Corceca into additional displacements of the failings of Redcrosse, as cultural representative and protagonist, onto woman. But other kinds of relationship between Abessa/Corceca and the fleeing knight are surely possible, a leading candidate being parody or, more blandly and locally, ironic commentary. Rather than being sucked into the vortex of Redcrosse's psyche, through ironized parody this episode distances it, comments on it critically, and puts it into a much broader historical perspective.

We witness Redcrosse's blindness to Una's loyalty and his flight both from her (and figuratively from himself) considerably before Abessa and Corceca appear in the narrative, and so Abessa/Corceca's commenting on Redcrosse's failures can only be retrospective—simultaneously a backwards connection of their meaning to his *and* an outward migration of his meaning to theirs. Yet transmigrating, or simply blending, their meaning (and subsequently Kirkrapine's) backwards into Redcrosse's without their ever laying eyes on him reprioritizes and compromises their own figuration and function in the narrative, as it does Una's. Abessa's name, for example, has many meanings—notably, absence of being, abbess, and a meaning that usually gets forgotten, absenteeism, which applies both to former Catholic and current Protestant abusers of benefices.[49] If the spelling and etymology of Abessa's name also relate her to Duessa and thence to the larger plot of Book I, the connection appears to be more strongly thetic and historical than psychic and internal in this instance (cf. Berger, 2004:225). Allegory, as a continued form of metaphor, is, once again, about differences, as well as similarities: Abessa is a withdrawal from being, Duessa a doubling and, implicitly, a fragmentation of it and therefore a more positive threat. Relatively simple, relatively outward, and relatively emblematic as are figures such as Abessa and Corceca, their figuration in the narrative resists reduction to Redcrosse's psyche, as, indeed, does Una's. Again, yes, but also no: relationship is not identity: metaphor, including allegory, always combines similarity with difference.

Allegorical projections and momentary or partial identifications occur in Spenser's Book I, as well as in other Renaissance writers, but they also respect figural differences and narrative distances and ask for specific, immediate textual support. These expectations apply even to the personified, hence tropic, figure of Despair, who looks like Redcrosse emerging from Orgoglio's dungeon and knows all about the knight's betrayals, but fails of full identity with Redcrosse, with whom he dialogues, interacts, and in speaking momentarily even merges, and whom he desperately wants simply to become. Yet Despair cannot *become* Redcrosse without the knight's actual, bodily death as the fulfillment and finality of his desperation. Precisely labeled, this haunting tropic figure is the *temptation* to despair. Another representative instance of the textual support expected occurs in Archimago's retrospective-proleptic parody of Redcrosse already discussed, by which this magician frightens himself with his own disguises and then dons the armor of the fleeing knight, thus impersonating him.[50]

Whereas Halpern and Berger prioritize Freud and Lacan, Walls's book on Una reprioritizes Saint Augustine, the Bible, and religion more generally. It too features perceptive, localized readings,[51] but I part fundamentally with her central thesis that Una, from the time that she is abandoned by Redcrosse, is consistently and primarily the invisible Church, also understood as Augustine's City of God or the human community joined with Christ and thereby representing him. Consistency and primacy are the major sticking points. In an episode such as Una's sojourn with the satyrs, Walls's thesis is plausible, but not exclusively so, in view of Pugh's reading of the same episode, which to me is more compelling. It is thus not that Walls's argument is simply wrong, but that it is too absolute. Her argument requires that, prior to Redcrosse's abandonment, Una is, as she puts it, "chronically fallible" (20). Reading Una's role in entering the Wandering Wood, in recognizing Error's den, in her encouragement to Redcrosse when he fights Error, and in advising Redcrosse to lodge with Archimago, Walls outdoes Halpern's criticism of Una, which she cites for support. For instance, although neither Redcrosse nor Una enters the cave of Error, Una is nonetheless "in error" (32). This view denies Spenser's narrative: both may approach Error, but Una recognizes it, warns Redcrosse, and stops short of it. Subsequently, the knight peeks boldly into Error's cave, his "glistring armor" exhibiting the parodic light of a votive candle—"a litle glooming light, much like a shade" (I.i.14). Then, once Error has effectually paralyzed him by coiling her tail, python-like, around him, Una calls out to him, "Add faith vnto your force, and be not faint" (I.i.19). Walls criticizes Una at this moment for conceiving of faith as merely "a supplement to 'force,'" and Redcrosse for responding, "not because his faith in God has been awakened but because his pride has been stung" (21–22). If she is right about Redcrosse's response, this is his failing, not Una's, and, as Walls notes, Una's encouragement at least works to strengthen her knight.[52] (A parallel but near-farcically parodic incident comes later, in Lucifera's House, when Duessa encourages Sans Joy, and Redcrosse responds instead by mustering his strength.) Even aside from what Una intends in her cry of encouragement, its result is that Redcrosse responds "with *more then manly* force" and beheads the reptilian monster (i.24: my emphasis). In short, her encouragement works.

But is it fair to conclude that Una conceives of faith as merely a supplement? First, remember the narrative situation: Redcrosse is in dire physical straits, the serpent enveloping him; what role should his force play? And is Una's outcry to add faith to force—belief to effort—really compromising in this moment? Consulting the *OED*, Walls finds that "'to add faith to [something]' was once an idiomatic expression for 'to give credence to [it], to believe in [it].'" But she adds that, "Faith in the context of this definition is quite distinct from religious faith, faith (that is) in God" and bases her assertion on the historically relevant supporting citations in the *OED* that are secular—specifically prudential or erotic (23). There are two problems here: the first hardly counts against Walls's scholarship, which precludes the endless rechecking of mutating electronic sources; nonetheless, the third edition of the OED (2010), contravening her claim, includes the following religious citation, dated 1560, for the expression "to add faith to": "Iudas repented & confessed his sinne, . . but . . because he added not faith vnto his repentaunce, confession and satisfaction, all was in vaine."[53] The second problem is larger and more significant insofar as it bears on the use of negative evidence, that is, on an absence. Although

Spenser's use of the phrase was apparently not instanced in the edition of the *OED* Walls consulted, negative evidence is weak in the face of textual use. For good reason, the *OED* invites readers to furnish any overlooked example of variant usage, which, in the instance of Redcrosse's battle with Error, further shows that the expression in question occurs in the context of religious faith.

Walls also suggests that "force," as Una uses it in her outcry, is "probably . . . no more than 'strength,'" which is "tantamount to believing in 'himself'" or in an "intensified egotism" and quite in contrast to Una's admonishing him nine cantos later, when he faces Despair, to believe in God's mercy (23–24). Yet consider that we are at the beginning of an evolving narrative and that one of the things we initially read about the nature of Redcrosse's quest is how much his heart yearns to test his puissance "Vpon his foe, and his new force to learne" (I.i.3). Untried, overeager, and overconfident, the young knight has much to learn, but he is nonetheless on a righteous quest, not only to confront his dragon (or dragons) and by experience to learn the force of his foe, but also to learn the nature and source of his own force, which includes his having been chosen to wear the armor of Ephesians 6:11: the crucial phrase from Spenser's alexandrine, "his new force to learne," reads both these ways. Una's urging, only sixteen stanzas later, "Add faith vnto your force," taken whole as an independent clause, with its major stress on the immediate predicate "faith" rather than on "force," the later object of a preposition, for all these reasons refers not exclusively to physical strength or to faith as merely a supplement but functions instead as the salvific intervention that Una's words intend. Redcrosse's true self, the one he is questing to realize, is, if as yet immature, not just egotistical, as both Una and Gloriana presumably believed when they chose him and he took upon himself the full armor of God. In short, Una's encouragement to Redcrosse is appropriate to the context of his first battle and to his present condition, rather than simplistically flawed or disconcertingly secular (Walls, 24).

Aside from the episodes prior to Una's abandonment, Walls's opposite, idealizing assertion that Una is somehow transformed, or elected, into her role as the invisible Church during the night at Archimago's hermitage is for me a hard saying. This transformation of Una is, in Walls's words, "most important" yet also "secret" and "unspecified" (4; cf. 38, 178). It is as invisible, or hidden, as the true Church itself—that is, it happens outside our sight and, indeed, beyond Spenser's text. Thereafter, Una's adventures mirror those of the Church in Augustine's *City of God*: the satyrs, for example, represent the Church's mission to the Gentiles, which is not invisible, although Una, in reality, is.[54]

Arthur, like Redcrosse, once he reforms, and like everyone else who helps Una, barring the lion (read as a Christ figure), is a constituent part or replica, indeed, an aspect, of Una's unique singularity for Walls (178–79). From start to finish, Book I is really about Una, not Arthur or even Redcrosse, seemingly its equal or more focal protagonist; she, always already communal, is its only subject. In short, although Walls's book is valuable in ways and at moments, not least in seeing something at once communal and larger than life in the figure of Una, its commitment to an all-consuming argument challenges credibility, a word some might hear with irony. Spenser's epic is a narrative committed to temporal sequence and development. It resists totalizing, systemic impositions, be they psychoanalytical or religious, modern or late antique.

Parody in Eden

Parody persists in the final third of Book I, for example, in the figure of Despair as guide and counselor, quoting and skewing classical and Christian commonplaces, or in the initial behavior of the ungainly, overweight dragon, "Halfe flying, and halfe footing in his haste" and, in a pun, shadowing the land "vnder his huge waste" (I.xi.8). Initially, Una's figure might seem free of parody at the end, but her homeland, Eden, and the events occurring there certainly are not, and the more closely we look, her figure is vitally touched by parody as well. It is so because she is a major player in these events, one finally, if momentarily, again crucial.

But what in the world might Eden be in the twelfth canto of Book I? What sort of place (*topos*)? Many readers, perhaps thinking of Milton's "paradise within," have assumed Eden's innerness, a reasonable assumption that I share and one that correlates with the inner dimension of other houses (*topoi*) in this book. Notably, however, these other houses, even the minor residences of Archimago or Aesculapius, the one a hermitage, the other a cave in the pit of hell, are not *exclusively* inner.[55] The name *Eden* openly evokes, indeed insists on reference to, the Edenic garden of Genesis, gone forever as an unfallen, earthly paradise, and so it evokes exile, together with return, loss along with triumph. This name further strengthens the necessity of Eden's innerness, even while accentuating its lost outerness and consequent fictitiousness.

If Spenser's Eden were only inner, the lengthy, folksy scene-setting early in the canto would be odd and seem out of place: mirthful children, women with timbrels, a rabble gaping, gazing, and frightened by the idea of lingering life in the dragon. Memorably and typically realistic, a mother warns her child away from the dead dragon's claws, while others boldly measure the beast, as if it were a beached whale. In this context, a reader might well recall the parodic tie of Saint George to the popular imagination when the first canto opened. Now, in canto xii, such domestic scene-setting—also suggestive of genre painting—signals an outer, social dimension, as well. The realm of Eden is the conclusive counterbalance to that of Lucifera. Both places have inner and outer being in the poem, and their relationship is effectually parodic.

A. C. Hamilton notes in his edition that the line describing Redcrosse's joy at his betrothal to Una—"His heart did seeme to melt in pleasures manifold"—"recalls the parody of his present state" during his erotic dream of her at Archimago's hermitage in the first canto.[56] A different parodic reminiscence, also noticed by Hamilton, ties Spenser's Eden to Lucifera's House of Pride. During the betrothal ceremony in Eden,

> sweete Musicke did apply
> Her curious skill, the warbling notes to play,
> To driue away the dull Melancholy;
> The whiles one sung a song of loue and iollity.
> (I.xii.38)

The *OED* offers the penultimate line of this inset as an example of *melancholy* meaning "sadness, dejection . . . gloominess; pensiveness or introspection; an inclination or tendency to this."[57] The same line recalls the time that Redcrosse entered Lucifera's hall to battle Sans Joy and found there that "many Minstrales maken melody, / To driue away the dull melancholy" (I.v.3). That dull melancholy needs to be driven away in the House of Pride, where Sans Joy is about to be battled, is not surprising, but that this need exists in the palace of Eden's king is so, unless we remember that an earthly Eden is a memory of failure, exile, and loss, not just a triumphant return. This is a doubleness with which readers of Milton's Eden, envisioned from a fallen world, will be familiar. In this world, the attainment of a Miltonic paradise within will also co-exist with another awareness, if only, in such ideal attainment, a memory of what has been lost. Duessa might be foiled but not eliminated—that is, not killed or destroyed.

Another revealing instance of parody that occurs when Arthur first enters the picture in Book I resonates with the present one. The phrase "exceeding shone" in Arthur's introductory description recalls that of Lucifera, in which it occurs twice, and these two figures parodically share an additional, iconic affinity with a dragon, the one on his helmet, the other beneath her feet (iv.8–9, vii.34). The description of Arthur has other verbal memories of unsavory figures who appear earlier, including Orgoglio and Archimago. The broader bearing of parody on the figure of Arthur, whose elf queen originates in Chaucer's comic *Tale of Sir Thopas*, which is itself a parody, is one I have told elsewhere.[58] Again and again in Book I, the idealized figure of Arthur, best of knights and magnanimous epitome of all the virtues, is touched and humanized by parody, as are all its major figures, Una included. The ambivalence of parody, whose roots spread over Book I, might be seen to penetrate the entire epic, not to undermine or destroy its ideals, but at once to recognize and to ensure their ties to the human conditions of language, of storytelling, and of life.[59] Again, parody can be gentle and forgiving.

It is with this broadly parodic perspective that I want to return to the problem of Una, insofar as it is also the problem of the whole twelfth canto, which has fully satisfied few modern readers, perhaps because we have had other expectations or desires. Noticeably, the twelfth is also a relatively short canto, in fact the shortest in Book I. Space and time are not features that Spenser, the poet who puts the Garden of Adonis in the middle of Book III and its fertile mount "in the middest of that Paradise," easily ignores (vi.43).[60] A tongue-in-cheek, highly rhetorical, and, frankly, coy question about Archimago's arrest near the end of the twelfth canto openly signals that this arrest will be temporary and brief, as readers discover early in Book II: "Who then would thinke, that by his subtile trains / He could escape fowle death or deadly pains?" (I.xii.36). The tone of this parodic question by the narrator—a question generically reminiscent of one in a book for children—comes when the threat to the betrothal is over and right before its consummation proceeds.

For the purpose of discussion, canto xii can be broken into two halves: first, triumphant return and, second, betrothal, and so, in effect, past present and future present. At the beginning of the second half comes the spoiler, the guileful messenger of fragmentation and disunity, that is, of Duessa: double being, duplicity, dualism. This messenger, Archimago, destined for near farce recurrently in Book II, is akin to Ate, the messenger with the apple of discord at another, earlier wedding in ancient myth, destined to play a part in later books of the poem.[61] Duessa's emissary, Archimago, the old man of Ephesians 4:22–24, as well as an evil image-maker and himself the arch (chief) image, presents her claim to the person of Redcrosse.[62] The claim, "that writt," is not just something written (xii.25). A writ is more exactly "a written command, order, or authority," "a legal document or instrument," "a written command precept, or formal order issued by a court in the name of the sovereign, state, or other competent legal authority, directing or enjoining the person or persons to whom it is addressed to do or refrain from doing some act specified therein."[63] The legalese would have been familiar to Spenser, himself a litigant and the deputy clerk of the Council of Munster.[64]

The writ itself includes Duessa's claim to Redcrosse "or liuing or else dead," phrasing that strangely recalls a memorable, biblical ambiguity in the initial description of Redcrosse at the opening of Book I, where this knight is said ever to wear a bloody cross in "remembrance of his dying Lord . . . And dead as liuing euer him" adore (i.2). Despite a possible echo of Revelation 1:18, "I am he who liveth that was dead," exactly what "dead as liuing" means is ambiguous and elusive at the outset of the opening canto. The emphasis on death that the phrase "dying Lord" contributes to this context two lines earlier only heightens its ambiguity. "Dead as liuing" could mean "dead as if living" or "dead as when living" or "dead and living." There is more than one touch of ambiguity in Redcrosse's figure at the beginning of the first canto, but this particular ambiguity is special, insofar as it concerns the young knight's faith, the extent and degree to which he grasps—fully understands or fully embodies—the burden, at once the weight and the meaning, of the redemptive armor he wears. In each of the possible readings of the ambiguous phrase, death seems to vie with or even to preempt life, as it does in the tale Duessa tells Redcrosse after his defeat of Sans Foy. She portrays herself as the betrothed widow of a prince slain by foes, who travels far and wide to seek his "blessed body," further emphasized and parodically degraded five lines later to a "woefull corse" (I.ii.24). Since Duessa's father is the Emperor of the West with a throne by the Tiber, she is clearly a representative of the Roman Catholic Church here, and her single-minded search for the body of her slain prince glances at the enormous emphasis on the *Corpus Christi* in the late medieval history of Catholic ceremony and sacrament, which carried over to the sixteenth century, and it intimates that this emphasis might be considered a death cult.[65] In the writ of canto xii, her claim to Redcrosse holds a threatening memory of these earlier necrotic passages. Little wonder that "dull melancholy" has to be driven away after the intrusion of Archimago-Duessa and their reassertion of failure and loss at the end of Book I.

Archimago's intrusion to deliver Duessa's legal writ also evokes and parodies a scene common in both dramatic and nondramatic writing from the Middle Ages to the sixteenth century, namely the devil's legalistic assertion of his right to Adam and all his descendants. Together, the charge and the argument against it were a theological commonplace. Langland's *Piers Plowman*, known to Spenser, affords a representative example of its poetic treatment.[66] When Christ comes to harrow hell and free the pious pagans, Lucifer explains to his fellow demons that if Christ

> "reue [bereave] me my riȝt he robbeth me by maistrie.
> For by right and by reson the renkes [race ("men")] that ben here
> Body and soule beth myne, bothe goode and ille.
> For himself seide, that Sire is of heuene,
> If Adam ete the Appul alle sholde deye
> And dwelle with vs deueles."
> (XVIII.277–82)

He then adds, "'I leeue that lawe nul noȝt lete [allow] hym the leeste [the least of them]'" to escape (285).[67] Lucifer's argument belongs to the Old Law, which casts further light on the words and images in Archimago-Duessa's claim: "the burning Altars," "bold periury," and "polluted" pledges, for example (xii.27).

With further relevance to what happens next in Spenser's twelfth canto, Langland's Satan picks up the thread after Lucifer:

> "but I me soore drede,
> For thow gete hem with gile and his Gardyn breke,
> And in semblaunce of a serpent sete vpon the Appultree
> And eggest hem to ete, Eue by hirselue,
> And toldest hire a tale, of treson were the wordes;
> And so thou haddest hem out and hider at the laste."
> (XVIII.286–91)

Then Goblin, another devil, chimes in: "'For [because] god wol noȝt be bigiled ... ne byiaped [tricked], / We haue no trewe title to hem, for thoruȝ treson were thei dampned'" (293–94). In Spenser's Cave of Mammon in

Book II, Mammon will receive a common epithet for the devil, "Guyler," variously repeated throughout the debate among Langland's devils and then in Christ's answer to them. Its application to Mammon in Book II will only confirm what Archimago and Duessa share proleptically with him (vii.64). When, in *Piers Plowman*, Christ confronts the devils' legalism, he, too, first answers in terms of the Old Law, observing that beguilers deserve beguilement, that guile had deceived Adam and Eve, and that his own life has paid on the cross for theirs and redeemed their debt: in short, an eye for an eye and a fulfillment of the Law (XVIII.330–60). The further point that pertains to the writ of Archimago-Duessa, however, is that their legalism has been superseded by a new covenant of grace, redemption, and mercy, which Langland's Christ next asserts at length. In all these passages—the exchanges between the devils and then Christ's declaration to them—lies the backgrounding gloss on Redcrosse's response to the charges of Archimago-Duessa and Una's intervention to support the truth of his claims. She is "trouthe," after all, Truth, no longer veiled, and she is also love, the love of and for Redcrosse. It is fitting at this point that, as unveiled truth, she should penetrate Archimago's disguise for the first time.

Redcrosse responds explicitly to the writ against him, which urges Duessa's rights, not Una's. This distinction should not be misleading, however: Duessa's rights cannot exist without the cancelation of Una's, nor can Duessa (re)appear without Redcrosse's separation from Una, as happened in canto ii. Notably, Duessa does not come herself to Eden's court. Likewise, now in reverse, Duessa's rights must first be disabled before Una's are fully restored. Redcrosse's response blames Duessa for leading him astray "vnwares" (twice: xii.31–32), and it thus recalls earlier characterizations of him, such as "since no'vntruth he knew" (about his response to the dream of a false Una: I.i.53) and "too simple and too trew," the narrator's ironic and ambiguous observation when Redcrosse embraces the guileful deception of Duessa-Fidessa by the tree of Fradubio; there the narrator's observation referred at once to the swooning Duessa's overdone deception and to the naïveté and vulnerability of the young knight, thus merging them at least syntactically and verbally (I.ii.45).

In the present canto, Redcrosse's response to the writ and then Una's support of his words now accord with what Langland's devils fearfully anticipate and what Christ actually says to Satan: "'For the dede that thei [Adam and Eve] dide, thi [thy] deceite it made; / With gile thow hem gete ageyn alle reson" (XVIII.333–34). Based on deceit and guile, Duessa's claim is without legal standing; it lacks truth. Christ's argument in Langland next makes redemptive grace and the love of the creator for his creature still more crucial as its positive culmination. This ending too will be recalled in the conclusion to Spenser's first book.

In light of *Piers Plowman*, Una, together with Redcrosse, is vitally touched by parody at the end of canto xii—explicitly by sacred parody, a cultural staple in medieval and Renaissance times. Importantly, it is together that they act to invalidate the writ, sharing the exposure of its origin in deceit. But Una's role goes beyond this exposure. She embodies not only personal loyalty ("trouthe," or troth) and Truth ("trouthe") but also love, at once human love in the narrative and godly love more broadly and symbolically. It is she who, at the crucial moment, acts to support Redcrosse and indeed to save him from the guile and dualism that Archimago and Duessa represent. Britomart will play a similar role simultaneously as Artegall's love and the vehicle of redemptive love in Book V, where the fallen Artegall is imprisoned "Vntill his owne true loue his freedome gained" (v.57): Artegall's "true loue" is at once Britomart, who loves him, and his true love (trouthe, troth) for her.[68] Book V is a different context, and Britomart's figure is different from, not simply related to, Una's, however, a matter to which my third chapter will in time return.

After Redcrosse's acknowledgment of his "mishaps" with Duessa (31–32), it is Una's support for his story (33–34) by which her father, the King, is "greatly moued," resulting in Archimago's arrest and the consummation of her betrothal to Redcrosse (35). Una is not Christ, still less is Britomart much later, but both figures intimate an analogy between his redeeming love and the love of a woman for a man and a man for a woman—in canto xii of Book I, especially a woman's for a man.[69] Earlier in this canto, the narrator has described the "glorious light" of Una's "sunshiny face," which Hamilton glosses suggestively with Revelation 12:1, the woman clothed with the sun (23). In Spenser's *Epithalamion*, not to be published or written until 1594–95, the poet will refer to the beauty of his own bride's "sunshiny face," a memory (at least for his readers) of Una's human, as well as of her distinctively heavenly, aspect.[70]

Hamilton's notes also gloss the last half dozen stanzas of canto xii of Book I with references to numerous marital contexts: the marriage supper of the Lamb, the numerological symbolism of marriage in the Old Testament, pagan Roman rites, and Spenser's *Epithalamion*.

Hamilton specifies the sweating of the walls and posts with sprinkled wine in *Epithalamion*, 253–54, with respect to their sprinkling and sweating in canto xii.38. For me, the most telling parallel between the culminating events in canto xii and *Epithalamion* comes in the central stanzas of ceremony in each when time touches eternity. In canto xii, there is heard the "heauenly noise . . . Like as it had bene many an Angels voice," a song at once "heauenly" and "sweet," otherworldly and sensuous; no creature knows whence it "Proceeded, yet eachone felt secretly / Himselfe thereby refte of his sences meet, / And rauished with rare impression in his sprite" (39). These lines describe the ravishing of sense into spirit, its sublation or simultaneously its raising, cancelation, and continuation—all three, but above all here, its elevation. In *Epithalamion*, the organ notes are louder ("Open the temple gates unto my love, / Open them wide that she may enter in"); the choristers praising the Lord are human, the angels "About the sacred Altare" erotically charged by earthly beauty, and the occasion more personal than the epic's narrative, but resonance between the two occasions persists (stanzas 12–13).[71]

Subsequently, the liquid imagery at the very end of canto xii—"His heart did seeme to melt in pleasures manifold . . . Yet swimming in that sea of blisfull ioy" (40–41)—fulfills that earlier in the book, whether in Redcrosse's wet dream in Archimago's hermitage, his journey "in the wide deepe wandring," the enervating stream from which he drinks before pouring out in looseness with Duessa, or his fall into a "liuing well" in the final dragon fight.[72] An Elizabethan betrothal could extend to the rights of the marriage bed, although there was confusion regarding this rite, an issue that Shakespeare's *Measure for Measure* explores in the coupled figures of Claudio/Juliet and Angelo/Mariana.[73] Be that as it may, at the end of Spenser's first book, the liquid imagery is simultaneously fleshly and sacred, erotic and redeemed. The same holds true for the final movement of *Epithalamion*, whose penultimate stanza looks to a future perfect of children and lasting, heavenly happiness. The final truncated, imperfected stanza of Spenser's own marriage hymn then returns time to the present and its cutting off of completion; at the end of Book I, Redcrosse returns to his unfinished questing, "and *Vna* left to mourne"—either left Una behind to mourn or Una left off mourning, having been reconciled to Redcrosse's worldly task (41). Again, a self-citational, parodic comparison with Britomart is evident: when she and Artegall part in Book V, she "wisely moderated her own smart" and "tempred for the time her present heauinesse" before seeking new surroundings "her anguish to appease," again a comparison that will also come with much difference (vii.44–45). Spenser's Eden is finally more than temporally double, lost and found. It is more precisely triple, a present in the poem that encompasses past and future. In this, it recalls Augustine's threefold present, time past, time present, and time to come, and doing so, looks ahead to the similar conjunction of times in *Epithalamion*.[74]

Chapter 2

Belphoebe's "mirrours more then one": History's Interlude

LIKE UNA, BELPHOEBE IS an idealized woman-figure in *The Faerie Queene*, but she is named for a classical moon goddess, a mythologized aspect of nature, and not, like Una, christened as a metaphysical conception. She is more relentlessly virginal than Una, however, who is betrothed at the end of her book and awaits perfected union with her human lover. In sharp contrast, Belphoebe repeatedly fails to comprehend human love, even while attesting to her own mortality. Accordingly, she is never reconciled with her twin sister, Amoret, figuratively the side of her that is missing and part of her story in the poem. In further contrast to Una, Belphoebe appears in successive books of the poem and therefore in three variant contexts: temperance, chastity, and friendship, respectively, in Books II, III, and IV. Each of these books, as their titular virtues indicate, seeks some form of balanced relationship, progressively involving others. Their shifting contexts challenge the initial intimation of Belphoebe's wholeness and ultimately suggest that her figure is unbalanced, an extremity of virtue that is intemperate and, insofar as temperance is rooted in time (< Latin *tempus*), untimely. Her virtue finally belongs to some other world.

Belphoebe rushes into the third canto of Book II and promptly becomes a sustained series of perceptions—less an unfolding series, as in the instance of trouthful Una, than a shifting one, rather like a successive series of slides, or stills. Sped up, a successive series begins to look coherent and animated—moving. This initial series, a portrait that A. C. Hamilton identifies as the longest in Spenser's entire epic, foreshadows for the retrospective reader (or rereader) what will become of Belphoebe's figure in the course of the books in which she appears.[1] In this portrait, she successively takes shape in terms variously Petrarchan, courtly, mythic, biblical, classical, natural, legendary, and historical. She is both Venus and Virgo and, like the twin comparisons of her to Diana and to the Amazon Queen Penthesilea that cap her portrait, she is both mythic and human, ideal and mortal. Viewed as a portrait, like the many famous, iconic paintings of

Elizabeth, Spenser's queen, the figure of Belphoebe has seemingly unlimited potential; viewed historically, in terms of Elizabeth's actual reign, Belphoebe's initial depiction becomes an impossible contradiction, which the narrative she enters soon enough makes all too real.

Belphoebe's namesake, the moonlike goddess Phoebe—Diana in the Roman pantheon—figures in myth as both unapproachable virgin and mammary mother goddess, the latter of these instanced by Diana of Ephesus or, indeed, by Spenser's Charissa, with "A multitude of [nursing] babes" at her breasts (I.x.31). Belphoebe's genealogy, of course, also includes Artemis, goddess of the hunt, who is another multiple-breasted figure, one of whose names is Phoebe.[2] Spenser might have chosen the name *Phoebe* (Greek *phoibē*, from the feminine form of *phoibos*, "shining") in order to emphasize the lunar association of the goddess, which suits the official iconography of Elizabeth I. *Phoebe* also alludes to the name of the shining sun god, Phoebus Apollo, and in this way as well to Elizabeth as a queen.

The double nature of the moon goddess Phoebe is further embedded in the etymological relation of *moon* to Latin *mensis/menses*. Unsurprisingly, Belphoebe's extensive, all-inclusive initial portrait is full of suspended, as-yet-unresolved tensions between mythic and mortal realities, and is all the richer, more complex, and potentially more dynamic for their presence.[3] From her first appearance, her mythic, iconographic, courtly, and explicitly queenly credentials also associate her with the reigning Queen Elizabeth, most ominously by comparison of Belphoebe to Penthesilea, "that famous Queene / Of *Amazons*, whom *Pyrrhus* did destroy" (II.iii.31).[4] By the end of the proem to Book III, she explicitly becomes a figure of Elizabeth's "rare chastitee," and, in Spenser's Letter to Ralegh, which was attached to the 1590 *Faerie Queene*, she is further identified with the queen's person as "*a most vertuous and beautifull Lady*," here a figure distinguished from her person as "*a most royall Queene or Empresse*."[5] When she reappears in the third book and the fourth one, she will also be less credibly mythic and less fully ideal, compromised by her increasing involvement in the narrative with human and historical realities.[6]

The first stage of Belphoebe's portrait makes her appear more angelic than human and more conventionally rhetorical than real. Although there is cumulative movement in the poet's opening, lyrical depiction, Belphoebe herself, entering the narrative in canto iii, is stopped in her tracks. In narrative terms, her figure is now strikingly static, an emblazoned countenance, an object for gazers. At the end of her portrait, where the comparison of her to Penthesilea appears, she becomes more natural and active; she is pictured in space and historical time, moving through landscape and legend. Petrarchan hyperboles characterize the first five stanzas (cheeks "Like roses in a bed of lillies shed," fair eyes darting "fyrie beames," an "yuorie forhead," honeyed words, eyelids adorned with "many Graces"). Then, descriptions of her raiment, weapons, and hair in stanzas 26, 29, and 30 associate her with the Amazons, but stanzas 29–30 also associate her with Venus disguised as a follower of Diana, and her buskins and hunting in stanzas 27–28 further associate her with Diana.[7] These last two stanzas are mainly devoted to her legs, thus balancing those depicting her face at the beginning and following a gaze that proceeds from top to bottom. "Like two faire marble pillours," her legs "doe the temple of the Gods support / Whom all the people decke with girlands greene, / And honour in their festiuall resort." Although essentially classical and pagan in reference, and perhaps also suggesting the English folk festivals of May, this comparison and the succeeding line that virtually extends it ("Whom . . . resort") have further evoked associations as radically diverse as 1 Corinthians 6:19, Song of Solomon 5:15, and the climax of the *Romance of the Rose*. This *Romance*, known to Spenser, provides a sexual referent for Belphoebe's "marble pillours" supporting a temple that is more explicit and credible, to my mind, than the much-discussed half line that stops with the hem of her skirt (reaching to her knee or mid-calf: 26.9).[8]

The final lines of the penultimate stanza portraying Belphoebe may even imaginatively suggest such a rendering of myth as Botticelli's *Primavera* ("Spring"), a painting in which Zephyrus, the west wind, touches the nymph Chloris with the result that "flowers issue from her breath, and she is transformed into Flora, the resplendent herald of spring."[9] Early in the poet's depiction, Belphoebe has a heavenly, as well as a Petrarchan, aura ("heauenly birth," "heauenly," "Angels hew," "ambrosiall odours"); she is even said to be "Hable to heale the sicke, and to reuiue the ded" (21–22). But now, near the portrait's end, as she flees through the forest, and as flowers, leaves, and blossoms are said to enwrap themselves in her flying hair, her figure is seen instead to suggest a revival that is seasonal and thus a natural cycle of death and regeneration (30).

Incongruously, in this same canto, the poet's tour de force in portraiture is framed by the low-life figures of Braggadocchio and Trompart. A greater contrast between elevated portrait and comic encounter would be hard to imagine. A close contemporary analogy might come from the parodic juxtaposition of comic subplot with main plot in a contemporary play, such as John Lyly's *Endymion* or Christopher Marlowe's *Doctor Faustus*.[10] Belphoebe and Braggadocchio stage a debate between solitary purity and social degeneracy, ennobling desire and lustful appetite, honor and instinct that anticipates the thematic opposition in Shakespeare's *1 Henry IV* of Hotspur's extravagant idealism and Falstaff's earthy pragmatism—between Hotspur's exclamatory declamation of an "easy leap, / To pluck bright honor from the pale-fac'd moon" and Falstaff's plain, if still rhetorical, questions: "Can honor set to a leg? . . . Or take away the grief of a wound?"[11] The debate is summarily terminated when Braggadocchio offers to assault Belphoebe sexually, and, her javelin raised against him, she flees into the woods and out of Book II, leaving to others the effort to balance radical extremes in the search for temperance. At this point, she figures as a strange, sequential mixture of iconographic lyric and comic narrative, promissory inclusion and active rejection.

* * *

Before pursuing the figure of Belphoebe into Book III, I want to pause over the proem to this book, which explicitly addresses the relation of the living Queen Elizabeth to her two specified Faerie figurations, Gloriana and Belphoebe. It also introduces the theme of "mirrours more then one" already met in my previous chapter and that of the relation of art to life, which is present but suspended in Book II's long portrait of Belphoebe. But in this third proem, the poet begins to observe a distinction between truth and Faerie image that is absent from the proems to Books I and II. By comparison, these two earlier proems illuminate what is new in the third. In the first proem, the living queen, "Great Ladie of the greatest Isle," is a "Mirrour of grace and Maiestie diuine," and the poem is a reflection of "that true glorious type" of her. In the proem to Book II, despite poetic play about the location of Faerie, the queen is the living reflection of the "antique ymage," and so the Faerie image is a "fayre mirrhour" of her face and realms. Overall, the first two proems present one continuous, unbroken reflection: the queen reflects divinity; like her, the poem reflects the glorious origins, person, and reign of the living queen. The antique and Faerie images are also continuous, whereas they will increasingly diverge as the poem develops. In the first two proems, however, theirs is a continuity worthy of *Una*, yet another of the reigning queen's cultic names.[12]

Referring to the queen's face, realms, and ancestry, the final stanza of Proem II offers an apology for the antique Faerie image that is actually a confident justification of it:

> The which O pardon me thus to enfold
> In couert vele, and wrap in shadowes light,
> That feeble eyes your glory may behold,
> Which ells could not endure those beames bright,
> But would bee dazled with exceeding light
> (II.Pro.5)

The dazzling brightness of the living Queen is enfolded in shadow to enlighten feeble eyes, enabling them to behold true glory. This veil reveals a single truth instead of obscuring it, and these shadows, unlike those in the second three books, which are new in 1596, do not splinter truth or transform its character. Unlike the proem to Book VI, they do not make true glory truly fictive.[13]

In the proem to Book III, the poem continues to be the queen's mirror, and, although she is invited to view herself "In mirrours more then one"—specifically either in Gloriana or in Belphoebe—both glasses are essentially virtuous, and conceivably, at least, they could be received as an unfolding of the good queen rather than as a dispersion of her unity. But, in this proem, the present embodiment also begins to vie with the antique image, living queen with antiquity, and to challenge it. Uneasy nuances (not quite tensions) cluster around the word "liuing." In order to perceive the fairest virtue, chastity in this instance, one "Neede but behold the pourtraict of her [the queen's] hart, / If pourtrayd it might bee by any liuing art." The poet continues, "But liuing art may not least part expresse, / Nor life-resembling pencill it can paynt . . . Ne Poets witt, that passeth Painter farre." Then comes a plea for pardon that recalls the one in the second proem:

> But O dredd Soueraynе
> Thus far forth pardon, sith that choicest witt
> Cannot your glorious pourtraict figure playne
> That I in coloured showes may shadow it,
> And antique praises vnto present persons fitt.
> (III.Pro.3)

These shadows are more opaque—and, as color, significantly more material in contemporary philosophy—than the punning "shadowes light"

(light shadows, shadow's or shadows' light) of Proem II. They testify to the poet's "want of words" and wit more than they serve the purpose of revelation.[14] But the modesty topos is here a conventional mask for a more significant development. The poem is now becoming a somewhat compromised "colour show" that can merely shadow the queen's "glorious pourtraict" and tailor antique praises to present persons, a "fitt" that sounds neither so natural nor so close as the continuity of bright reflections in Proems I and II. The poem becomes the glass through which the living sovereign's true portrait is more obscurely discerned. At this point, it is difficult not to think again of Elizabeth's highly symbolic, elaborately costumed, V-waisted portraits and the conspicuous extent to which they are removed from a realistic, contemporary image of the aging queen. This sort of "fitt" exceeds any dressmaker's talents.

The lines that directly follow the poet's apology for "colour showes" and "antique praises" refer to the depiction of Queen Elizabeth in Ralegh's *Cynthia*: "But if in liuing colours, and right hew, / Thy selfe thou *couet* to see pictured, / Who can it doe more liuely, or more trew . . . ?" than Sir Walter Ralegh (my emphasis). Although the *OED* offers innocent and even positive, religious instances of *covet*, this verb is also associated strongly with sin—with envy or greed—as it is most memorably in the Ten Commandments.[15] But there is a larger point here: setting the "liuing colours" and "right hew" of the reigning queen against the "colourd showes" and "antique praises" of *The Faerie Queene*, the poet introduces a far-reaching distinction between life and antiquity, historical present and mythic past, current truth and Faerie image. This distinction does not align nicely with that between the queen's imperial and private affairs, which, in the Letter to Ralegh, are figured, respectively, in Gloriana and Belphoebe. Instead, it applies to both figures. At the same time, the explicit division of the living queen into two figures arguably compromises her unity. For a reader of Book I, the specter of Duessa hovers in the distant background. Perversely, we might even recall the contradictory, yet overlapping, images of Elizabeth and the Babylonian whore to which Claire McEachern directs our attention, as noted in chapter 1.

In stanza 4 of the third proem, when the Spenserian poet refers a true and lively picture of the queen to Ralegh's *Cynthia*, he is unlikely to have meant a picture that is merely realistic or unembellished by art. Ralegh's fragmentary *Ocean to Scinthia*, much of which relates to his imprisonment in 1592, a disgrace subsequent to Spenser's publication of Book III, is the best indication of *Cynthia*'s nature we have, and, although

Ralegh's voice in it is distinct and passionate, such highly artificial modes as the Petrarchan ("Such heat in Ize, such fier in frost") and the pastoral ("Vnfolde thy flockes and leue them to the fields") are also much in evidence.[16] The bereaved, nostalgic employment of pastoral in *Ocean to Scinthia* suggests that the earlier versions of Cynthia by her "shepherd of the Ocean," written in less desperate straits, might have been more conventional rather than less so.[17] When the poet of *The Faerie Queene* writes of the living colors and right hue of *Cynthia*, he implies a portrayal that is less hieratic, epic, and allegorical but more contemporary and personal than his own. Such a portrayal as Ralegh's might be less universal and more ephemeral, but it belongs more immediately to time.

Although Spenser's reference to Ralegh does not discredit the Faerie image, it does limit its authority unless this image can be expanded or otherwise modified to embrace life more closely. The third proem provides a particularly apt introduction to a book in which time and eternity or present age and ideal, antique image are not so smoothly continuous as indicated in the proems of Books I and II. Nothing reverberates through Book III quite like the "heauenly noise / Heard sound through all the Pallace pleasantly" at the betrothal of Redcrosse and Una—a noise like the voices of angels "Singing before th'eternall maiesty, / In their trinall triplicities on hye" (I.xii.39)—and no figure quite like the brilliantly winged angel who succors Guyon appears to rescue its knights and ladies. In fact, the closest we get to an angel in this book is Timias's illusion that Belphoebe is one when he wakens from his swoon to find her bending over him and ministering to his wounds: "Mercy deare Lord . . . what grace is this," he asks resonantly, "To send thine Angell from her bowre of blis, / To comfort me in my distressed plight?" (v.35). Then he adds, on second thought, "Angell, or Goddesse do I call thee right?" thereby echoing Vergil's famous lines from Aeneas's meeting with Venus in the guise of Diana's maiden and avouching the young squire's perception that this angelic illusion originates in a more worldly pantheon than Una's "trinall triplicities on hye." Parodically, it also recalls the same allusion to Vergil in the initial portrait of Belphoebe in Book II and, more openly and perilously, by Belphoebe's present posture—that of a pietà—the Bower of Bliss at the same book's end (II.iii.33, xii).[18]

A blushing Belphoebe disclaims the angelic or godly status Timias attributes to her and declares herself simply a maid and "mortall wight" (36). Unfortunately, her declaration is exactly what Timias might have longed, but should never have been allowed, to hear her say, for he falls irrevocably, irremediably, impossibly in love with her. Belphoebe not only denies him a reciprocal love but also fails to understand or even to recognize the erotic nature of Timias's response to her. More than once, the poet criticizes her failure as a "Madnesse" that saves "a part, and lose[s] the whole" (43, cf. 42). Oddly, an echo of his criticism will occur two books later, when another of Queen Elizabeth's avatars, Queen Mercilla, ambivalently dispenses justice to the figure of a rival queen and where justice is seen "Oft [to] spill . . . the principall, to saue the part," while trying "to preserue inuiolated right" (V.x.2). In both instances, one of the Queen's bodies is not reconciled with the other. The tensions between disparate realities that were suspended in the initial portrait of Belphoebe are increasingly coming to light.

Back in Book III, while Timias languishes in love's torments, Belphoebe spares no pains to ease him, but still not comprehending his malady, "that sweet Cordiall, which can restore / A loue-sick hart, she did to him enuy," or refuse to give (v.50).[19] Few readers or rereaders of these lines are fully prepared for those that follow, in which "that sweet Cordiall . . . that soueraine salue" is suddenly transformed to "That daintie Rose, the daughter of her Morne," whose flower, lapped in "her silken leaues," she shelters from midday sun and northern wind: "But soone as calmed was the christall ayre, / She did it fayre dispred, and let to florish fayre" (v.51). As Donald Cheney has suggested, precise equivalents for these lines do not exist. "For her," he adds, "the rose is a rose, not a euphemism."[20]

But surely not just a rose, either. Belphoebe's dainty blossom soon opens into a flower strongly redolent of myth: "Eternall God," we learn, "In Paradize whylome did plant this flowre" and thence fetched it to implant in "earthly flesh." Soon we are asked to recognize the flower as the ur-rose that flourishes "In gentle Ladies breste, and bounteous race / Of woman kind" and "beareth fruit of honour and all chast desyre" (52). A truly marvelous hybrid, this is now the *rosa moralis universalis*. Not surprisingly, one of Spenser's eighteenth-century editors compared it to Milton's "Immortal Amarant" in the third book of *Paradise Lost*, "a flow'r which once / In Paradise, fast by the Tree of Life, / Began to bloom."[21] Quite in contrast to this response to such mythologizing of the rose are medical associations between flowers and menses, specifically menstrual discharges, which Jessica Murphy has uncovered.[22] In short, here are further complications, notably involving opposite extremes—the realms of flesh and spirit.

In Belphoebe's transformation from uncomprehending nurse to vestal votaress of the rose, to antique origin and a fructifying virtue undifferentiated by time, person, or place, Timias is quite forgotten. Her specific relation to him will not align with the general moral statement into which it is translated. To echo the third proem, it will not "fitt." Honor and chaste desire, the fruit of the flower, are indeed virtuous, but Timias's love is honorable in Book III, and his erotic desire, if not virginal, appears to be decent and pure and, in these senses, to be chaste, not unlike Britomart's. Thus the general moral statement not merely transcends the particular case but wholly misses it. Timias is one person these antique praises of the flower do not suit, and, since Belphoebe's use of tobacco (v.32) to heal his wounds signals an obvious allusion to Ralegh, a reader might also think one "present person."[23]

Having glorified the rose, the poet appears in no hurry to return from antique ideal to the person of Belphoebe. Instead, he directly addresses the "Fayre ympes of beautie" and urges them to emulate their origin by adorning their garlands with "this fayre flowre . . . Of Chastity and virtue virginall." These "ympes" (shoots, scions) of beauty are preeminently the "Ladies in the Court," to judge both from the poet's present address and its resemblance to the final dedicatory sonnet of *The Faerie Queene*.[24] Timias aside, the poet opts for the general application of the antique ideal to this present world of readers. But, with the poet's final promise that the flower will not only embellish the ladies' beauty but will also crown them "with heauenly coronall, / Such as the Angels weare before Gods tribunall," the poem travels beyond even Timias's first flush of erotic illusion to a simpler, purer, less earthly vision.

The poet's address to the ladies continues in the next stanza, however, where he now commends to their attention not the beatifying rose, upon which he has spent the mythmaking of the previous stanzas, but Belphoebe herself as the true exemplar of its virtue. In effect he returns the rose, but now in its glorified form, to her person. Of particular note in this stanza are the initial recurrences of the word "faire" and the phrases "none liuing" and "ensample dead," puzzling phrases whether taken alone, together, or with the "liuing colours, and right hew" of the third Proem:

> To your faire selues a faire ensample frame,
>   Of this faire virgin, this *Belphoebe* faire,
>   To whom in perfect loue and spotlesse fame
>   Of chastitie, none liuing may compayre:
>   Ne poysnous Enuy iustly can empayre

> The prayse of her fresh flowring Maidenhead;
> For thy she standeth on the highest stayre
> Of th'honorable stage of womanhead,
> That Ladies all may follow her ensample dead.
> (III.v.54)

The repetition of "faire" is insistent, even anxiously so, but it also enforces a link between present persons and Belphoebe. This link, if only a matter of rhetoric and fair appearance, suggests a series of steps from the court Ladies' "faire selues," surely many of whom in time were bound to marry; to a generalized "ensample" of purity, to its more exclusive, or higher, form, virginity; and finally to the individual fulfillment of virginity in fair Belphoebe herself, who is found on the "highest stayre . . . of womanhead." This virginity is clearly not that of Britomart, the protagonist of Book III, whose quest is for erotic love in marriage. Notably, the stanza preceding the one just cited has slipped in the line "Of chastity and vertue virginall," in which the paired phrases are not identical, as they are not in chaste married love, the objective of Britomart's quest.

The poet's conception of a series of steps—that is, a "stayre"—becomes additionally significant on examination of the other verbal oddities in the stanza cited.[25] The first of these, the phrase "none liuing," presumably means "none of you ladies" or "no one living," since the poet here addresses his present audience, "youre faire selues," and compares them with Belphoebe, the exemplar of ideal chastity, to which "none liuing" has yet attained. Alternatively, if we take the word "liuing" to be applicable to Belphoebe, the phrase could mean "no other living lady" except Belphoebe herself. This is the meaning of a remarkably similar claim about chaste Florimell earlier in the same canto where her dwarf declares of her, "Liues none this day, that may with her compare / In stedfast chastitie" (v.8). But there are also significant differences between a claim made by a distraught dwarf within the narrative context of Faerie and one made by the Spenserian poet himself and addressed to an audience of courtly women outside the poem. We readily see that the loyal dwarf speaks loosely or hyperbolically. He really means no *other* living lady in all the realm of Faerie is chaster than Florimell or simply that she is the chastest lady imaginable. The word "liuing," however, is not so readily defused in relation to Belphoebe, who mirrors the chastity of the living queen, especially when it occurs in a direct address to the poet's living audience. If, in this context, we were to consider Belphoebe "liuing," then her figure seems at variance with the statements in the proem to Book III and downright embarrassing when we reach "her ensample dead" in the alexandrine of this same stanza. Such a radical dissolution of the fictional character of Belphoebe is entirely unexpected and would probably be wasted or, worse, misunderstood by Spenser's audience.

The natural reading of the phrase "none liuing" is, then, as suggested, the obvious one, "no one liuing" or simply "no living lady." Although this reading does not refer specifically or directly to the reigning queen, it increases the distance between Belphoebe as a mythic ideal and any living referent, including the queen, and thus the distance between antiquity and the present age. The increased distance reflects the strains between ideal exemplar and human response in the story of Belphoebe and Timias and helps to bring both their story and canto v to an appropriate conclusion in 1590, namely,

> In so great prayse of stedfast chastity,
> Nathlesse she was so courteous and kynde,
> Tempred with grace, and goodly modesty,
> That seemed those two vertues stroue to fynd
> The higher place in her Heroick mynd
> So striuing each did other more augment,
> And both encrease the prayse of woman kynde,
> And both encrease her beautie excellent;
> So all did make in her a perfect complement.
>
> (III.v.55)

The poet's depiction of Belphoebe has effectually reverted to his initial portrait of her by herself in Book II: a succession of opposites in suspended tension, potentiality but no resolution.[26] Like Timias's reference to a "bowre of blis" earlier in this same canto, the present complement of virtues that strive ("stroue . . . striuing") for supremacy glances again at Acrasia's domain, whose opposites strive "each th'other to vndermine" (II. xii.59). The strife of Belphoebe's virtues may not be that of Acrasia's, but neither is it the realized Concord of opposites figured in the emblematic figure of this name in Book IV's Temple of Venus, which is that of an assimilation, however fragile, "*above* the differences, as in the concept," to quote Paul Ricoeur. The assimilation that is Concord achieves a "level of conceptual peace and rest" and appropriately belongs to a *stationary* figure, who can withstand a threat to her equilibrium, precarious as the latter may be (IV.x.33, 36).[27]

To return again to stanza 54, if the obvious reading of "none liuing" is also the right one in its fourth line, this reading is designed to cause another, longer pause for thought when we reread the last three lines of this penultimate stanza and especially its alexandrine, juxtaposed with (or against) the stanza that concludes the canto: Belphoebe "standeth on the highest stayre . . . of womanhead, / That Ladies all may follow her ensample dead" (54). If Belphoebe is a mythic ideal who has moved farther away from a living referent in the penultimate stanza, what has she to do with death? First she seems to be mythic in stanza 54 and now to belong to history. The obvious reading of "none liuing" and the alexandrine clearly do not as yet accord. We might recall that a similar opposition arose in the initial portrait of Belphoebe in Book II, when heavenly associations and the attributes of the mythic goddess Diana were juxtaposed with Penthesilea "that famous Queene / Of *Amazons*, whom *Pyrrhus* did destroy" (II.iii.31).

The phrase "ensample dead," when glossed at all in the past, was long taken only to be an ellipsis of the clause "when she is dead,"[28] and this phrase can be referred to the occurrence of a parallel construction in Merlin's prophecy to Britomart of the child or "ymage" Artegall will leave with her when he is dead:

> With thee yet shall he leaue for memory
> Of his late puissaunce, his ymage dead,
> That liuing him in all actiuity
> To thee shall represent.
> (III.iii.29)

But the phrase "ensample dead" as readily means "her dead, or lifeless, example." Before we are startled into reassessment, this is exactly what it seems to mean, and, if this were in fact all it meant, it would be a chilling comment on the ideal Belphoebe embodies and, if at a greater remove, on that of the reigning queen as well. This alternative meaning of "ensample dead" also finds a relevant parallel in a later alexandrine of Book III. It occurs when the witch creates False Florimell, that parody of coldly sterile, lifeless Petrarchism: "and in the stead / Of life, she put a Spright to rule the carcas dead" (viii.7). Death is this carcass's present condition (dead carcass), not its future one (when dead).

The occurrence in a single stanza of two verbal cruxes as immediately and obviously related as life ("none liuing") and death ("ensample dead") is unlikely to have been adventitious. The meaning "dead example"—the more obvious reading of "ensample dead"—accords better with the more obvious reading of "none liuing," because it does not require, as does the alternative "when she is dead," an abrupt and irrational shift from mythic to historical reference and, to put it bluntly, from an ageless Belphoebe to an aging Elizabeth. There is no way to cancel the more obvious reading of "ensample dead." But perhaps we don't have to stop with its dispiriting message. In the context of Timias's highly Petrarchan adoration and idealization of Belphoebe, the alternative reading, "ensample [when she is] dead," need not refer to death as an exclusively physical event. It can also be taken in a way that makes sense of the mythic Belphoebe's connection with death and offers the positive reflection on her ideal that balances, although it cannot simply cancel, the negative one.

In its Petrarchan context, the reading "when she is dead" points to the resolution of the conflict between body and spirit that comes with the lady's physical death and spiritual transcendence. The phrase "ensample dead" therefore implies the ideal, the life-in-death, that the deadly carcass, the death-in-life, of False Florimell parodies. This reading of the phrase balances the cold reality of human loss—death, denial, lifeless example—with high praise of Belphoebe and of the queen, whose chastity, if only dimly, she still mirrors. At the same time, it continues Belphoebe's movement away from an earthly reality and suggests that the only possible solution of Timias's dilemma—and seemingly the destined conclusion of Ralegh's—is the symbolic or actual transfiguration of Belphoebe into pure spirit.[29]

Looking back at stanza 54 with the Petrarchan reading in mind, we might be struck anew by the phrase "perfect loue" and "spotlesse fame." It suddenly makes more sense that "none liuing" should be perfect or spotless in Book III, where the possibility of a living Una has receded like a setting sun, and that the "highest stayre . . . of womanhead" should be reached only with the lady's transformation through death into spirit. Presumably this is also the "stayre" on which worthy emulators of the true rose are crowned "with heauenly coronall . . . before Gods tribunall" (v.53).

It is further tempting to see a relation between the Petrarchan praise of fair Belphoebe in Book III and the first of Ralegh's commendatory sonnets to accompany *The Faerie Queene*:

> ME thought I saw the graue, where *Laura* lay,
> Within that Temple, where the vestal flame
> Was wont to burne, and passing by that way,

> To see that buried dust of liuing fame,
> Whose tumbe faire loue, and fairer vertue kept,
> All suddeinly I saw the Faery Queene:
> At whose approch the soule of *Petrarke* wept,
> And from thenceforth those graces were not seene.
> For they this Queene attended, in whose steed
> Obliuion laid him downe on *Lauras* herse.[30]

But there is also a significant distance between this vision of Laura's living successor and Spenser's fully idealized Belphoebe, whose rose opens fully only in death. Perhaps Spenser could see more clearly the temporal, human cost—to Belphoebe and Timias both—of the fully realized Petrarchan vision because he was farther removed from it personally, or perhaps just farther away in epic romance than was Ralegh in lyric. By the writing of Book III, however, he certainly knew that in time Laura's tomb could only be replaced by another's "ensample dead."[31]

The ill-fated encounter of Timias with Belphoebe occurs on the near side of the Garden of Adonis, in the canto immediately preceding it. The first stage of the Garden canto itself treats the twin birth of Amoret and Belphoebe and their adoption by Venus and Diana to be nurtured apart, Amoret in the Garden and Belphoebe in the woods. No more is heard of the figure of Belphoebe in Book III beyond the Garden canto. Yet one figure in the cantos on the far side of the Garden suggests the lingering, parodic presence of the living queen. This figure is the lascivious giantess Argante, a nightmarish distortion of chastity, born locked in incest (<*incestus*, "unchastity") with her twin brother and now roaming the countryside to capture young men to be sex-slaves in her island kingdom.[32] Besides being, like Amoret and Belphoebe, a twin, Argante's incest with her brother embodies a denial of difference in pointed contrast to the equally distorting exaggeration of difference in the separation of the twin sisters by Venus and Diana. Argante's name derives from Greek homonyms, the one, *argos*, meaning "idle" (punningly, idyll, < Latin *idyllium*, Greek *eidullion*), and the other, *argos* (cf. *arges* and *argas*), meaning "bright," "shining," "white," or "swift-footed," meanings that resonate with the name of the moon-goddess and huntress Belphoebe, insofar as *Phoebe* derives from Greek *phoibē*, or femininized *phoibos*, "shining." Still more to the point, the likeliest origin of the proper name *Argante* is found in medieval British folklore and legend, exemplified in Laȝamon's *Brut*, in which King Arthur, after the battle of Camelford, is taken to "Argante the queen, an elf most fair," in Avalon.[33] Herein lies the exemplar connecting Prince Arthur to his Faerie Queene, now a woody elf, now great Gloriana.

The figures of Lucifera and Philotime bear witness that such a distorted image—such harsh parody—as that in the figure of Argante is not alien to the poet's techniques, even in Spenser's earliest two books. Yet Lucifera and Philotime, maiden queens both, are not missing sides of the living queen but a denial of what she could and should be. In the figure of Argante, parody occurs with a difference. Where the depiction specifically of Belphoebe in Book III manages in the end to transcend—indeed, to sublate—the conflict between Belphoebe's ideal and earthly selves, the lusty Argante openly crosses the line between the royal concerns of a queen and the sexual concerns of a woman. Spenser apparently thought this to have been the case in the queen's relation to Ralegh even before 1590, when Book III was published.

Before leaving Book III for Book IV, I want briefly to connect Spenser's figures of the Queen to the narratological technique of *disnarration*, a currently popular term coined by Gerald Prince to describe a wide variety of deflective pauses, omissions, silences, absences, humility topoi (*occupationes*), cryptic allusions, lyric sublations (supersessions), allegories or dark conceits, and more (primarily post-Enlightment).[34] Prince's definitions and multiple descriptions of this technique could be stretched to encompass most of Spenser's poem, but his term is more usefully reserved to distinguish clearly disnarrative, or otherwise nameless, phenomena such as the half-line that stops with the hem of Belphoebe's skirt, the uneasy nuances of Proem III, Belphoebe's sublated rose, or anxious repetitions of "faire." Otherwise, as a general practice, more exact terms, where possible, and specific textual evidence offer fuller, more discriminating results. Even the unspoken or half-spoken phenomena for which *disnarrative* is particularly suggestive are often ambiguously or not exclusively narrative. Typically, *The Faerie Queene* eludes categorical restraints, as it does with respect to parody and epic itself.

* * *

In Book IV, Belphoebe's next and last appearance, her estrangement from Timias intersects with his relation to Amoret, Belphoebe's missing twin sister, and Belphoebe's reconciliation with Timias clashes sharply with the abandonment and slander of Amoret. With Timias's reconciliation and Amoret's revilement, duality of judgment and truth can no longer be contained in a single phrase or image, in consecutive stanzas, or even in a single character or event. Belphoebe herself—or what her figure was in Book II and perhaps even in the fifth canto of Book III, an ideal maintaining some relation to worldly reality—is fractured, a mirror now splintered. The alternatives of love and loss, of timeless and temporal truth, are no longer grasped together, no longer simultaneous and complementary dimensions of awareness, as tenuously they could still be even in the phrase "ensample dead," as well as in the juxtaposition of the last two stanzas of Belphoebe's canto in Book III (v.54–55). They have become still more sharply distinct and are in danger of becoming mutually exclusive. The distance between ideal image and present age, antique praises and living colors, is widening rapidly as history presses on the poem. Whereas antiquity was earlier continuous with the Faerie realm, it is increasingly set apart from it. At the same time, more is happening: the distance between Gloriana and Belphoebe, the imperial and personal figurations of the reigning queen, is increasingly and more openly a problem. All this is doubleness compounded.

The story of Belphoebe and Timias in Book IV is now inseparable from the last stages of Amoret's story there. Wounded and then tended by Timias, Amoret becomes the unwitting cause of Belphoebe's estrangement from him. She has become part of their story and, when she is simply abandoned by them in the middle of it, she becomes, both narratively and morally, a loose end waiting to be rewoven into some larger design. Her ties with the story of Belphoebe and Timias are symbolic and thematic as well as figural. The ruby that helps to bring Belphoebe back to Timias is "Shap'd like a heart, yet bleeding of the wound, / And with a little golden chaine about it bound" (IV.viii.6). A jeweler's replica of Amoret's heart in the Masque of Cupid, this lapidarian heart that Belphoebe once gave Timias alludes to Amoret's real one, simultaneously suggesting contrast and resemblance to it. The heart-shaped jewel also evokes the use of jewels, lockets, and limned miniatures with intimate significance in courtly culture and notably its use by Queen Elizabeth herself.[35]

The twin birth of Belphoebe and Amoret, the complementary maids of Diana and Venus, provides a richly figural backdrop to their aborted reunion, and, although Amoret arguably is, or rather becomes, a more fully human figure than merely an abstract conception of Love, or Amor, the latter is one kind of meaning she carries when she is wounded, then abandoned, and later reviled. Her abandonment resonates with Belphoebe's inability to comprehend erotic love in Book III, insofar as the wrathful Belphoebe, her trust betrayed by Timias, sees no distinction between the predations of the fantastically beastly figure of Lust and Timias's inadvertent wounding of Amoret, thinking to kill all three of them with the same arrow (IV.vii.36). But the most provocative imitation, or parody, of Amoret's thematic congruence with Belphoebe comes when the poet subsequently interrupts his narrative during Slander's revilement of the wounded Amoret to recall an Edenic age when the "glorious flowre" of beauty flourished, a time when "antique age yet in the infancie / Of time, did liue then like an innocent, / In simple truth and blamelesse chastity" (IV.viii.30). Antiquity, ideal image, mythic flower, even chastity, all previously associated with Belphoebe's rose—the poet associates them all now with Amoret. Effectually, Amoret is transported from Slander's reviling to an antique age of truth and purity, carried back, it would seem, to an "antique world" of the sort that Eden is found to be at the end of Book I, the first instance of the antique image, so specified, in the poem (xii.14). Like Belphoebe and her rose in Book III, she is translated to another place. This is a mythic place that is very "like an innocent" one (IV.viii.30). The qualification "like" is notable. Whereas the rose is finally stellified, Amoret's translation to purity remains in an antique age on earth—Edenic but also human. The intrusive timing of the poet's lyric assertion of his presence, moreover, guarantees that we notice it for itself, as well as for its content, even more than was the case with Belphoebe's rose. Little stays just the same in the still moving *Faerie Queene*.

In addition to the connections between the stories of Amoret and of Belphoebe and Timias sketched earlier, there are pointed contrasts. The reconciliation of Belphoebe and Timias is conspicuously artificial, effected through the agency of a sympathetic turtle dove and a lapidary's heart and totally removed from temporal reality. When Timias is reconciled, his condition actually anticipates Melibee's self-enclosed vulnerability in Book VI: he is "Fearlesse of fortunes chaunge or enuies dread, / And eke all mindlesse of his own deare Lord" (IV.viii.18). His Lord is Arthur, but I have never quite shaken off the intimation of a higher Lord, perhaps a memory of Arthur's role as savior in the two earliest books. Timias's condition is not made whole by his reconciliation with Belphoebe. Its divisive nature is instead reinforced by separation from Arthur and the higher calling, whatever its precise nature, that this prince represents. Timias is fixed again, frozen so to speak, in the situation he occupied with respect to Belphoebe when last seen in the preceding book.[36]

Still more noticeably, even while the estrangement of Belphoebe from Timias alludes unmistakably to Ralegh's fall from queenly favor, their reconciliation in Book IV conflicts with the real state of Ralegh's affairs in 1596, when Book IV was published.[37] After Ralegh's secret marriage to Elizabeth Throckmorton, one of the Virgin Queen's maids of honor, whom he had evidently impregnated and plausibly by marriage sought to rescue, and the consequent imprisonment of them both in 1592, he was, although released fairly quickly from prison, not in fact reconciled with the queen until 1597. His wife, left to languish in prison longer than he, never returned to favor with the queen. In the reconciliation of Timias and Belphoebe in Book IV, artificial thus means twice unreal—unreal at once in manner and in historical reference.[38] What the subtitle of this chapter, "History's Interlude," suggests now threatens the more comic, constructive stories of Una in Book I and Britomart in Books III and IV. History openly compromises the Faerie vision, as it will again in the last two books.

The plight of the abandoned Amoret contrasts sharply with the conspicuous artifice of reconciliation. When Arthur finds her in the forest, she is "almost dead and desperate," ingloriously wounded and unromantically in need (IV.viii.19). In an effort to shelter her (and her less idealized companion, Aemylia), Arthur unwittingly takes her to the House of Slander, a foul old woman "stuft with rancour and despight / Vp to the throat" (24), a description that continues the allusions to queenly attire—this time a starched ruff—begun in the proem to Book III. Once they are within Slander's house, the indignant and somewhat bitter voice of the poet, earlier noted, intrudes at length in the narrative to connect Slander to the present age ("Sith now of dayes") and to oppose this age to the ideal, antique image "in the infancie / Of time" (29–30). Slander's railings therefore have a general historicity or timeliness pointedly attributed to them for which Amoret's own adventures, apart from the topicality of her relation to Timias's estrangement from Belphoebe, would fail to account. She was captured by Lust while walking "vnwares" in the woods "for pleasure, or for need"—the latter hardly unnecessary—and by her own effort she has escaped from Lust's cave without further defilement, at least until Timias intervenes (vii.4). In short, what befalls Amoret in the two cantos she shares with Belphoebe and Timias looks very much like the other half of their story, the half muted in Belphoebe's withdrawal from Timias and suppressed in his return to her. What befalls Amoret unfolds the "inburning wrath" of Belphoebe (viii.17) and gives tongue to the revilement and infamy Ralegh's secret marriage incurred. This marriage incurred "the displeasure of the mighty . . . Then death it selfe more dread and desperate," to which the eroticized triangle of Belphoebe, Timias, and Amoret refers with startling directness (viii.1).

Writing presumably in 1592 from imprisonment in the Tower of London, Ralegh contrasted the queen's formerly gracious favor to him with his present state:

> Thos streames seeme standing puddells which, before,
> Wee saw our bewties in, so weare they cleere.
> Bellphebes course is now obserude no more,
> That faire resemblance weareth out of date.
> Our Ocean seas are but tempestius waves
> And all things base that blessed wear of late.
>
> (269–74)

If we remember Spenser's final vision of Belphoebe in 1590, with its series of "fayre" steps from living audience to the highest ideal, these words from *Ocean to Scinthia* have an added edge. But, even without this refinement, they afford a commentary on the distance that has opened between living queen and either of her Faerie images: as the imprisoned Ralegh again observes of this distance, "A Queen shee was to mee, no more Belphebe, / A Lion then, no more a milke white Dove" (327–28). As the distance widens, as an ideal Belphoebe becomes further detached from living reference, other kinds of reference to the present age build up and push intrusively into Faerie. Their violence and their ugliness, unparalleled by the more controlled images of evil in Books I, II, and even III, do not just threaten the Faerie vision but actually violate it.

The old hag who reviles Amoret, her companion Aemylia, and Arthur, their would-be rescuer, is nothing short of hideous, as extreme in her violent ugliness as conciliatory dove and ruby-heart are in their artificiality. The poet seems almost unable to put a stop to his description of her, his incursion qualifying as another instance of disnarration, refractive despite its length and violence: "A foule and loathly creature" with "filthy lockes," she sits in her house "Gnawing her nayles for felnesse and for yre, / And there out sucking venime to her parts entire" (IV.viii.23–24). The description continues for another two stanzas with a reiterative emphasis and expansiveness that partial quotation hardly conveys. She abuses all goodness, frames causeless crimes, steals away good names. Nothing can be done so well "aliue"—that is, in life—without her depriving it of "due praise" (25). As the poet continues, castigating the verbal poison

Slander spues out of her hellish inner parts, she becomes an unmistakable precursor, first of Detraction and then of that poet's nightmare, the Blatant Beast, both in Book V: "For like the stings of Aspes, that kill with smart, / Her spightfull words did pricke and wound the inner part" (26).[39]

"Such was that Hag," the poet concludes, "vnmeet to host such guests, / Whom greatest Princes court would welcome fayne" (viii.27). Then, just before the poet in his own voice breaks into the narrative for five stanzas to decry the distance between antique age and present corruption, he praises the patience of Slander's "guests," who endure every insult she can offer, "And vnto rest themselues all onely lent, / Regardlesse of that *queane* so base and vilde, / To be vniustly blamd, and bitterly reuilde" (viii.28: my emphasis). *Quean*, meaning "harlot," "hussy," or, in Spenser's instance, "hag," is not the same word as *queen*, and it might be supposed from the poet's virulent description that she is an unlikely image of the Virgin Queen Elizabeth.[40] But the word "queane" in this context is not disposed of so easily, nor is the possibility that this image of the bitter, old woman glances at the living queen.

Philologists have been reluctant to recognize the likelihood of the homonymic pun on *quean/queen* in Renaissance English that exists in modern English. Helge Kökeritz notes that contemporary philological evidence proves the possibility of such a pun in colloquial speech but doubts that polite speakers would have found the pun readily accessible. E. J. Dobson likewise notes the distinction in pronunciation of the two vowels in educated southern speech but allows for vulgar or dialectical variations in which the pun would exist.[41] The pun is therefore possible but unlikely or inappropriate in a polite context, an argument that actually might recommend it on grounds of aesthetic decorum—not to say political prudence—for the impassioned description of a discourteous hag. The historical imagination is hard pressed to picture a courtier who would be likely to explain such a pun to the queen or even willing to admit recognition of its presence.

Admitting the pun in Spenser's use of *quean*, we might regard it as one of the many signs in Book IV that in some sense the poem is becoming more private and personal, even as its topical concerns—friendship, justice, courtesy—are becoming more social. We can admit the pun, however, without having to argue that it would not have been recognized by a number of Spenser's readers. Wordplay on the combination *quean/queen* has a long history, in part because of its alliterative potential, as, for example, in these lines from Langland's *Piers Plowman*: "At churche in the charnel cheorles aren vuel to knowe, / Other a knight fro a knaue, other a queyne fro a queene."[42] In an age of printing like the Renaissance, the spelling of quean—"queen" and "queyn" in Thynne's Chaucer—was also a visual invitation to wordplay, analogous to an eye rhyme, an analogy that philology might be inclined to discount.[43] The same pun occurs as well in Middleton's *A Trick to Catch the Old One* when Witt-Good disclaims youth's follies, including "sinfull Riotts, / Queanes Evills, Doctors diets" (V.ii.185–86). The evils of queans are venereal, but highly qualified readers agree that the pun on *quean/queen* and the consequent play on *king's evil* (scrofula) are present here.[44] Contemporary, dramatic use of a pun argues its accessibility to auditors, and a play on diseases dependent on the pun urges this fact.

To my mind, the most illuminating information about Spenser's calling Slander a "queane" is that this is his sole use of the word. Occasion, Duessa, Impatience, Impotence, the witch who creates False Florimell—not a one of these hags wears this common Renaissance label, and we might almost suppose that Spenser was deliberately avoiding it. That he should suddenly have used the word "queane" accidentally or innocently in a context inseparable from Belphoebe, Timias, and the relation of Faerie ideal to present age defies credibility, and does so much more, in view of Spenser's verbal sensitivity, than does the possibility that he alludes to the reigning queen.

As with Belphoebe's rose in Book III, there are now no precise or steady equivalents for the figures gathered in Slander's House: Amoret, who has a considerable history in the poem, does not simply equal Elizabeth Throckmorton, Arthur does not equal Ralegh, Aemylia does not equal anybody, and Slander does not simply equal the queen.[45] In the moments and ways I have suggested, however, what happens to Amoret reflects the scandal, wrath, and disgrace that Ralegh's marriage unleashed, and briefly the poet again holds up to his sovereign the kind of reflection found in a hideous cartoon, as he did less realistically in the figure of Argante. Where Lucifera, Philotime, and even the much larger-than-life Argante were threats, Slander is a present reality.[46] There is nothing ludic about Slander, as there is even in the fantastic, hyperbolized lust of the giantess Argante, who bursts onto the scene with the fabliau figure of the Squire of Dames and then, snatching the mighty warrior Satyrane by his collar, plumps him athwart her horse.

* * *

Over the course of *The Faerie Queene*, Belphoebe appears in three Books, II to IV, and Amoret in two, III and IV. Belphoebe never leaves the woods during her time in the poem. Despite the promissory fullness when she is first introduced in that long, complex portrait in Book II, her persistent woodiness suggests something primitive, unsocial, and finally unfinished about her, as Braggadocchio, churlish fool though he be, alleges. In contrast, Amoret is found in Houses—more broadly in rhetorical residences, or cultural topoi, such as the Garden of Adonis, the House of Busirane, and the Temple of Venus, extending even to the House of Slander as another sociocultural site. The cave of Lust, insofar as it is a perverse reflection of the bisexed cave with the boar under the mount in the Garden of Adonis, is arguably yet another, although it might also be the exception proving the rule.[47] Although the woods—in extreme form the Wandering Wood—can be considered a topos as well, in their wilder form, indeed forms, they can also be meaningfully distinguished from the more cultivated, enclosed places of the poem.

Mainly, Amoret resides in situations set apart from the narrative of quest, if also in some sense part of it. The exception comes when she travels with Britomart (treated in the next chapter), a liberating experience that affects her figuration, and then in the sequel to these travels in Book IV: namely, her capture by Lust and escape, her inadvertent wounding by Timias, her rescue by Arthur, and her merely presumptive arrival with him to hear Scudamour recount his *raptus* of her from the Temple of Venus. Without a word from her from the time she escapes from Lust's Cave to her arrival with Arthur, and without any other closure of her story, her figure disappears from the poem, lingering only as a memory in Scudamour's narration of his Temple exploit in the tenth canto of Book IV. In Book III, Amoret's early nurture among the happy, mythic personae in the Garden of Adonis receives two stanzas of narrative in which she plays no active role. At the end of her story, she is back in the Temple of Venus, where, we now learn, her story outside the Garden began. Even in outline, it looks as though something has failed in Amoret's story and that an entrapping, unhealthy circularity has replaced narrative progress. It also looks as if the Spenserian poet explored and improvised as he went along. Certainly, with respect to the story of Amoret, by the beginning of Book IV, he professes "oftentimes" to have wished "it neuer had bene writ," although he notably continues with its further writing nonetheless (i.1). What is written, especially if then published, like what is otherwise done, belongs to history.

Does Amoret change in the course of her appearances? Does Belphoebe? Surely our perceptions of them both develop, doing so as their figures appear in different contexts and situations. Our sense of Belphoebe as the figure who fails to comprehend human love differs from our sense of her in the portrait of Book II, which includes the complexities that her figure cannot contain in subsequent narrative, and our sense of her rejection of her twin sister and Timias in Book IV differs from our sense of her earlier generosity to him in Book III. But there is no sense of her developing interiorly or consistently from one of these figurations to another. She is simply in different situations at different times, always consistently virginal—like Diana or Minerva, not Venus, even though she is perceived as Venus by Timias and her initial portrait similarly includes Venerean allusions. Her generosity to Timias, which is both qualified and inconstant, does not extend to Amoret. There is no other consistency than virginity about her. This looks like allegorical fixation rather than simply an Aristotelian subordination of character to plot.[48] At the same time, however, it is the developing narrative, or plot, that is influenced by events outside the poem and affects, or is made to affect, the situations in which the figure of Belphoebe finds herself and must function.[49] From this point of view, she is not a static figure but one who changes over time, even while she remains both virginal and in the wild woods, in an elemental and primitive environment rather than in one more fully developed. Whereas Una, another allegorical figure, learns from experience, however, Belphoebe apparently does not, and this is finally the major difference between their figurations. Whereas Una's figural being is continuous, Belphoebe's is at best paradoxical, ever imperiled by contradiction, division, and discontinuity—by shades of Duessa.

I doubt that Amoret changes much either, except in a situated, rather than an interiorized, sense. In terms of the narrative, she might have, and indeed begins to, but then she wanders away from Britomart's protection (if, ambiguously, for pleasure or for need) and discovers misery in the cave of Lust, conversing there with another pitiable woman, Aemylia, before escaping this cave to become hopelessly entangled in the affairs of Belphoebe and Timias.[50] Although Amoret is said to call out to Britomart in the House of Busirane and later, in Book IV, is said to converse intimately with her lady knight, she never speaks directly, aside from a feeble shriek, until she finds herself in Lust's cave with Aemylia, a sorry situation if ever there was one. The sad fact is that Amoret's figure, like Belphoebe's, becomes subject to the entangled narrative that is driven by its relation to contemporary history in Book IV. As a figure, she is subjected to it, and, if she is different in different situations, she too is finally discontinuously so. Adequate links and sufficient development are recurrently missing, as they are in the argument—endless for lack of enough evidence—as to whether she lands in Busirane's clutches because Scudamour is too aggressive or because she is either too fearful or, conversely, too Venereal.[51] Notably, all these too simple possibilities—even the first—would finally pin her plight on her, Busirane's object and victim.

Yet I also doubt that a dismissal of Amoret as a changing figure is sufficient in itself for several reasons. The first is that her travel with Britomart has been deferred to the next chapter, and it is her best chance for development as a figure, to which, arguably, her subsequent flight from Lust attests, even if it ends with cruel irony in the arms of Timias. This is a deferral warranted, to my mind, both because of the greater interest and importance of Britomart in the poem and because its inclusion in this chapter would require too much repetition in the next one. The second reason for deferral is that Scudamour's narrative of the Temple of Venus is a *present* reassertion of a bold, too bold beginning, at once a failed possibility within this narrative—or disnarrative—in Book IV and a testament of unfinished business. Effectually, as the latter, it is also an invitation to start the story anew or at the very least to reflect on its origin and to ponder its deep cultural roots, "yfounded strong."[52] That this retelling comes throughout in Scudamour's voice only makes it harder to assess, however. Does the irony that punctuates it signal the possibility of an expanded awareness on his part or the same old blindnesses? Analogously, in their final appearances, the figures of Amoret and Belphoebe, not unlike Shakespeare's famously inconsistent, if more fully developed, heroines, such as Desdemona, Olivia, and Lady Macbeth, who change with their situations in the plot rather than consistently, speak to us at once of lost possibilities and of still imaginable ones.[53]

Yet the best reason of all for not dismissing Amoret's change pertains to the reappearance of her dilemma in the story of Serena that occupies much of Book VI, as well as the final chapter of this book. It is in Serena's story, coupled with Mirabella's, that the misery first voiced briefly by Amoret and at greater length by Aemylia in Lust's cave—along with the nameless old woman—is fully realized. Is that old woman a recontextualized and feminized version of the biblical Old Man, or perhaps another queanly figure, a hag, whose kindness (in both senses) grimly and ironically reflects on women's plight? Be that as it may, Serena's story is where the Spenserian narrator returns to the unfinished business to which Scudamour's tale of the Temple of Venus attests. From this vantage point, the twinned stories of Amoret and Belphoebe change profoundly, involving a substantial refiguration for each that approaches and bids fair to become a new identity, as the difference in their names in Book VI clearly signals within *this* poem. The identity of each becomes at once more affective and more personal, and, to my eyes, the Spenserian poet-narrator is greatly and personally in sympathy with it. Deferring these refigurations until chapter 4 respects the unfolding of Spenser's narrative, while granting to Britomart's story in Books III to V the prominence it deserves and actualizes in *The Faerie Queene*.

Chapter 3

Britomart: Inside and Outside the Armor

THE COMPLEXITY OF THIS chapter asks for an introductory road map: its first section explores ways in which the depiction of Britomart answers to traits modern readers, notably Alan Sinfield, have found in Shakespeare's characters. The chapter next proceeds to Britomart's culminating experience in Book III, namely her adventure in the House of Busirane. Then it examines her figure through the lens of her defining armor throughout the three books in which she appears, III, IV, and V, the books of chastity, friendship, and justice. This doubled approach, occasionally looking back or forward, reflects my own interpretive history regarding Britomart and further suggests the differences that approaches themselves—critical lenses—at once reveal and create. Approaching the House of Busirane, my focus becomes increasingly rhetorical, narrower, and more detailed—largely responsive to the fact that this place, this cultural topos, is a house in the rhetorical sense—whereas, right afterward, the focus on Britomart's armor is mythic, iconological, and wider, traversing more of the narrative. My method also attempts to reflect the actual experience of reading *The Faerie Queene* for someone like me, that is, a rereader with an overview that allows for retrospection, yet one who tries to respect the forward progression of the narrative, not substituting a later stage of it for an earlier one.

Britomart is the most fully developed figure of a woman in *The Faerie Queene* and, although she could be called a character, she is also appropriately called a figure, both in order to preserve the continuum in Spenser's poem from more to less complexity of figuration and to acknowledge her symbolic dimensions. Her name most simply signifies "martial Briton"; discussion of other symbolic dimensions of her figure will occur as they become relevant to this chapter.[1] Like Britomart, the dramatis personae, or characters, in stage plays can also be considered figures, of course, and symbolic dimensions are easily enough found at once in them and in the plots in which they operate: Shakespeare's pairing of Hotspur and Falstaff,

Ariel and Caliban, Egypt and Rome afford familiar examples.[2] The proper names of Shakespeare's characters can also be suggestively symbolic, for example, those in the preceding sentence or Cordelia (Latin *cor/cordis*, "heart," and "delia" as an anagram of "ideal").[3]

Britomart and Character Effects

From Britomart's first appearance in the poem at the beginning of Book III, the narrator attributes to her an inside that differs from her outside, and he makes a point of doing so, interrupting the action in the first canto to identify her as the knight inside the armor who topples Guyon and to indicate the nature of her Faerie quest (i.8). To suggest that she has "that within which passes show" is not to claim that she has an interiority (or a lack of it) the same as Hamlet's or other representative Shakespearean characters; instead, it is only to note a certain similarity.[4] A significant difference between Hamlet and Britomart is that her interiority is subsequently exhibited at length, whereas his remains more of a mystery.

One similarity between the two is that some readers would deny interiority to them both, either not noticing it for what it is in Britomart's case, or in Hamlet's by refusing or dissolving it, whether rationalizing or materializing it, or both, into the closed terms of modern systems. Systems shed light, but they can also destroy the shadows actually present in human texts. If I had to identify one feature of Renaissance literary texts, dramatic and nondramatic, that most separates them from modern systems and, for this very reason, offers to illuminate these systems in turn, it would be their persistent, insistent resistance of such closure. Modern scientism has its virtues, but, with rare exceptions, the tendency to closure and certainty of its typical forms is deceptive when applied to creative writings, especially older ones. Hamlet's objection that his treacherous friends would "pluck out the heart of his mystery" is also his awareness that they aim to do so, his resistance of their efforts, and his determination actively and antically to frustrate these (III.ii.365–66). Centuries of criticism suggest that to a significant extent he has succeeded. He is certainly one character, moreover, for whom the designation "most Shakespearean" is also most fitting. Older writings were subject to older systems, to be sure, but typically, these were more aware of mystery and more tolerant of it. Perhaps they had to be; perhaps they chose to be; perhaps neither.

In a couple of ways, the Spenserian narrator's opening aside to readers in Book III regarding Britomart's identity and quest differs from the extensive presentation of the Renaissance inside/outside topos early in Book I, specifically in Archimago's manipulation of Redcrosse's imagination and his subsequent impersonation of his victim. First, Archimago is himself an actor in the relevant episode of Book I, rather than the third-person narrator of it as in the opening of Book III, and second, in Book III, the aside in question is the narrator's straightforward presentation of background, not his sly insinuation of his protagonist's insufficiency, an insinuation effected in Book I, for example, by his making Archimago's impersonation of Redcrosse comment on this knight. Such differences render Britomart a more autonomous figure in Book III. The narrator, so to speak, respects her difference.

Britomart's armor in the third book also differs from Una's veil in Book I by being primarily a deliberate, strategic disguise, not just protective covering or a necessary disguise for a woman in a world of woods, caves, and wild creatures, whether human or beastly. By definition, Britomart's armor, including sword and spear, is aggressive, not merely defensive. Further, insofar as Una represents Truth in this fallen world, her veil is an unavoidable reality, whereas Britomart's armor is voluntary and represents a choice. Britomart is hiding a secret; Una is not. The wimpled Una's black stole cast "ouer all" expressly suggests that she mourns "inly" (I.i.4).

As noted in chapter 1, Britomart declines to join the chase of Florimell and the forester in the first canto of Book III because she is constant to her own "*mind*," not to some other dictate.[5] At the outset, she declines the traditional role of a knight, whether to rescue or to pursue a maiden and thus typically to make love or war, as knights have done from time immemorial. Her constant quest for a specific lover is further distinguished early in canto i even from Arthur's quest, since, in chasing Florimell, Arthur moves away from his initial motivation to find his elf queen and instead seems ready to accept a substitute: later losing sight of the fleeing Florimell when night falls, "Oft did he wish, that Lady faire mote bee / His faery Queene . . . Or that his Faery Queene were such, as shee" (III.iv.54). Although his elf queen is still the gold standard, he drifts into likeness as an alternative, acceptable possibility ("such, as"). Britomart, in contrast, is steadfast. While focusing on Shakespeare, Helen Cooper describes as an inheritance of medieval romance, "the portrayal of a young woman in love from inside her own mind" and cites Britomart as a case in point; "typically feisty," the romance heroine of the Middle Ages is self-aware, passionate about "the man she chooses to love" and ready to go to great lengths to find (or "get") him.[6]

Also notable as Book III gets under way is the fact that Britomart is named almost immediately within the text as well as after first acting, rather than, for example, after a long description or first only within the argument heading a canto, as are Una and Belphoebe.[7] Her agency is foregrounded. Britomart also has a father rather than a myth of origin, a nurse, not a Palmer, and a history both inherited and destined that is set firmly on earth. In short, she looks and is more human than her most memorable predecessors in the poem, as is the potentially virtuous love for which she quests. But it is even more important that the identification of Britomart's quest at the very outset begins to be defined by her differences from and relationships to numerous other actors in the poem. Her figure has a distinctly social as well as an individualized existence. She is neither Everywoman, let alone Everyman (humankind, or in premodern usage, mankind), nor is she wholly unique. Once again such a description of her looks human.

In a perceptive discussion of character and a defense of its validity as a current critical topic, Alan Sinfield offers a "redefinition of character as continuous consciousness," while barring "establishment of the individual as a single, unified presence," as distinct from his or her enhanced subjectivity.[8] While thus rejecting the bourgeois individual of "essentialist humanism," which is post-Enlightenment anyway, Sinfield opts for more than "an intermittent, gestural, and problematic subjectivity," namely, "a continuous or developing interiority or consciousness" (62). His subsequent discussions of Shakespeare's characters make clear that such a continuous consciousness doesn't have to continue throughout a whole play: it can come and go or, once established, can afterwards simply go, leaving a resistant or unresolvable problem. From this perspective, he looks at Desdemona, Olivia, and Lady Macbeth. His list could have been extended to other problematic figures among Shakespeare's fictive women: Cressida and Isabella, for a start.[9]

My intention is not to make Britomart into a cross-dressed Shakespearean heroine, although I am not the only one long since to have remarked general similarities between her and Shakespeare's Rosalind or Viola. At the same time, however, I am struck by the number of characteristics Britomart's figure exhibits that correspond to the methods playwrights use to produce "character effects" in dramatis personae, as Sinfield enumerates them. These include self-reference and self-questioning, which might include soliloquy, and also lying, which creates distance between statement and intention, the latter indicating inwardness. I would add that *intention* is a word-concept derived etymologically from Latin *in*, "in, within," and *tendere*, "to extend, proceed, aim, direct one's self or one's course." Further included in Sinfield's enumeration are indecision, more generally the representation of decision-making, and informative conversations overheard by the audience, which raise questions about intentionality—that among Gloucester, Kent, and Edmund at the opening of *King Lear* comes to mind, for instance.[10]

Britomart lies to Redcrosse when she rides away from Malecasta's castle with him, telling him that Artegall has done "Late foule dishonour and reprochfull spight" to her, but then she waxes "inly wondrous glad" when Redcrosse tells her he is greatly surprised that Artegall should ever have done such injury to her (III.ii.8–11). Britomart's direct conversation with Redcrosse, which continues for nearly ten stanzas, including narrative framing and commentary, soon after leads in a narrative flashback to the story of her falling in love with the image of Artegall that is facilitated through a magic globe—an objectification of her waking, and awaking, pubescent imagination. The flashback then proceeds to her back-and-forth conversation about her erotic predicament with Glauce, her comic old nurse, for more than another fifteen stanzas. Not only does this conversation deliver background information and dramatize a process of decision-making, it also focuses on Britomart's inner state and reveals, in Glauce's words, that Britomart is making a "Monster of ... [her] minde"—imagining horrors and perversions, whereas she should more simply be recognizing that she is in love (40).[11] Their conversation could readily have been adapted for the Renaissance stage. It has comic features, as do the visit to Merlin and other aspects of Britomart's characterization. Notably, both women converse in terms of mythic figures, Myrrha, Biblis, Pasiphaë, Narcissus. Like the Elizabethan schoolboys Lynn Enterline has studied, they use Ovidian mirrors, types or examples, "to understand and to express" their own perceptions, which are influenced by these types, even if also reshaped and repurposed by the schoolboys (and girls) as they mature. Enterline's proof-texts are Shakespeare's Lucrece and Hamlet.[12]

Two other examples of Sinfield's character effects that produce the impression of consciousness occur in the first third of Book III. One is Britomart's much-discussed soliloquy by the seaside in canto iv, in which, now imitating a sonnet from Petrarch, she expresses the tempestuous "sea of sorrow" within her and nearly despairs of a happy outcome until

Glauce reminds her of Merlin's dynastic prophecy and a hostile knight conveniently appears to offer an immediate object on which to vent her passion (11–16). Significantly, although the ur-text here is mainly (not exclusively) Petrarchan, it is Britomart herself, not the narrator, who voices it and, within the poem, thus recreates it.[13] My other example is not the modern word "consciousness," which is just becoming available in the first half of the seventeenth century, but "awareness," or, in the form in which it recurrently occurs with respect to Britomart, a condition of being "vnwares." Her "vnwareness" is obviously based on the presumption of its opposite as the possibility to which experience leads.[14] Britomart is "vnwares" when she looks into the magic globe to see the vision of Artegall but later acutely aware of her earlier unawareness when, she tells Glauce, she swallowed this bait (III.ii.26, 38). Earlier in this book, she was also "vnwares" when Malecasta slipped into her bed, the climax in Castle Joyous of the initial stage of her initiation as an active quester into the bodily *and* sociocultural context of sexual awareness. At a later stage, she will be "vnwares" again when Busirane wounds her, a situation to which I will return (i.61, xii.33). Each of these occurrences of Britomart's lack of awareness instances an increasing development of her figure, and the correction of each leaves her more aware both of herself and of the nature of her quest. Each is a learning experience that results in growth. At the same time, there is a perceptible continuity among these experiences. This is a continuity, however, which, unlike that of the more metaphysically oriented Una—again, more oriented, not exclusively conceived—will be disrupted before the poem is finished with Britomart's figure. With this change, her figuration will be at once more problematic and more sadly, historically realistic. Still further Shakespearean?

Britomart's Awareness in the House of Busirane

When Britomart accepts a knight's plea to free Amoret from the House of Busirane, she becomes a radical challenge to the erotic culture in which she, too, has operated to this point, with the exception of her declining to rescue Florimell, the anticipatory, threshold image of Book III. Amoret, if not exactly a prop or just another exhibit in Busirane's House, has been imprisoned by the sadistic enchanter and in this way has unwillingly become his creature, another of his creations, or so his production stages her. Busirane's capture of Amoret is what we witness until Britomart ends it. We last saw Amoret only briefly in the Garden of Adonis, her former residence in Book III. Encountering Busirane's House at the end of this book, we have only the knight Scudamour's name (Shield of Love), his heraldic device (Cupid) and behavior, and his account of why Amoret is under Busirane's control, and, for six more years, from the 1590 installment of the poem until the 1596 one, Spenser's original audience lacked access to anything more.

In contrast to Amoret, Britomart reaches Busirane by actively questing and most immediately by chasing the evil Ollyphant ("destructive fantasy"), Argante's twin brother, to the sight of Scudamour "all wallowed / Vpon the grassy ground" (III.xi.7). This sequence suggests both Britomart's opposition to such fantasy and Scudamour's implication in it. Simply put, Scudamour replaces Ollyphant. Scudamour tells her that the enchanter has "pend," or through his art confined, Amoret, in effect *arresting* the very possibility of their love (xi.11)—at once imprisoning and paralyzing it. More allegorically, Scudamour, Cupid's man, has been separated by Busirane from the object of his love, Amoret, who is "*Venus* mayd," or punningly, Venus-made, ever since Venus discovered and adopted her in Cupid's "stead"—in his "place"—earlier in Book III (vi.28).[15] The possibility of the love of Scudamour and Amoret is therefore the very possibility of realizing love, not simply the love of these two figures, but, in terms of their simple allegorical natures, here Love itself.

Imprisoned in Busirane's House of perverse, rhetorical art forms, however, Amoret has become the Ovidian-Petrarchan love object. Her capture has shaped her figure, indeed, has transfigured it from what it was in the Garden. For Britomart, confrontation of Busirane is another initiation and a further education, this time with respect to Ovidian myths and Petrarchan conceits that have informed the erotic culture in which she functions and, as we have seen, have informed her own awareness. Her task is to free Amoret from Busirane's malign control and to enable the possibility of Amoret's reunion with Scudamour. Developments in Book IV subsequently make clear that both Amoret and Scudamour have to change for this possibility to be truly realized. To glance back to the last chapter and forward in the present one, in 1596 this realization fails to happen. In 1590, the lovers' reunion is greatly compromised, even dubious, a claim to which this chapter will later return.

In recent times, the House of Busirane has variously been seen as Busirane's projection, as Amoret's, as Scudamour's, as Britomart's, and, without regard for these mediating characters, as the Spenserian narrator's. This House, like the House of Holiness, the Bower of Bliss, the Garden of

Adonis, the Temple of Venus, or any other such place in *The Faerie Queene*, is a cultural site, a topos or "place." Its representation is finally the poet's, as are all the figures residing in or traveling into it, although the poet's control of it, his agency with respect to it, is mediated, limited, and compromised by his own position in language and history. He is nonetheless responsible for it insofar as he is in control of it—again, insofar as. Although the Temple of Venus in Book IV is a special case whose narration belongs to Scudamour, it, too, is finally the poet's, as he acknowledges at its very end. Like other cultural sites in *The Faerie Queene*, which have some special pertinence to the figures within them, the House of Busirane also has special pertinence to Britomart, as well as more immediately to Amoret and Scudamour, without being solely attributable to any one of them or even to them all together apart from culture and history. The nature of this pertinence—moral, theological, psychological, historical, or a combination of such—is variable, not simply formulaic, and it is subject to context when it occurs.

In Britomart's instance, aside from the general, formalized eroticism of Busirane's House, which has obvious relevance to a love quest, her progress in Book III more specifically explains why she is there: in canto i, her vulnerability to Malecasta, realized in her wounding, foreshadows her vulnerability to Busirane, and, in canto ii, the smoky, sulphurous Etna in her breast anticipates the Busiranic fire, shaking, and "stench of smoke and sulphure" (ii.32, xi.21, xii.2). Likewise, in canto ii, the perverted, mythic forms her explanation takes when she confides in Glauce foreshadow those in Busirane's tapestries. In canto iv, the "selfe-pleasing thoughts" that feed her pain, her guidance by blind Cupid, and her pendulum swing between "Love and despight," anticipations of Busirane's paired masquers, prepare for Busirane's pageant, as does her sympathetic recognition of kinship with Paridell's pain in canto ix, ominously within the perverted House of Malbecco and Hellenore.[16] Amoret, Ovidian-Petrarchan love object par excellence, is part of Busirane's pageant the first time Britomart sets eyes on her.

Once Britomart enters Busirane's enchanted House, the first room of three that she views specifically signals the inevitability of her arrival there. The tapestries on its walls share both their Ovidian source in the *Metamorphoses* and their sense of erotic compulsion with her beholding—taking in—the tapestry in the House of Malecasta that depicts the fixated, hyper-sensuous love of Venus for the boy Adonis (a foretaste of Argante's preferences) and leads in the narrative to the flashback with Glauce in which Britomart expresses her own passion as an erotic perversion in classical myth.[17] The specific Ovidian passage on which Busirane's tapestries draw is the ecphrasis of Arachne's art in her ill-fated weaving contest with Pallas Athena, the Greek Minerva. Immediately, there are ironies and crossings of gender in this situation, whose many complications must be unlayered gradually.

When Britomart initially encounters Busirane's enchanted fire, she asks Scudamour in dismay, "'What monstrous enmity prouoke we heare, / Foolhardy as th'Earthes children, which made / Batteill against the Gods? So we a God inuade'" (III.xi.22). Once again, Britomart expresses herself, and thinks, in the mythic terms studied in the grammar school texts of the period, which were read by well-educated girls, as well as by boys. Traditionally, the fire-god is Vulcan, the smith and forger of chains, as well as the figure of the jealous, overly possessive husband also evoked allusively by the netting of Acrasia and Verdant, a Venus and a Mars, in the Bower of Bliss. It is as if Britomart were again upending and improving on Guyon and his Palmer, as she was at the very outset of Book III. Her ability in her armor to pass unharmed through the fiery entrance of Busirane's House contrasts both with the disabling jealousy of Scudamour and the possessive hoarding of Busirane, throwbacks alike to Malbecco, the essence of "Gelosy" itself.[18]

Boldly invading this jealous fire-god and forger of chains, Britomart next gazes at the tapestries that recreate the one woven by Ovid's Arachne, a woman bold—perhaps too bold?—in protesting the violent excesses of the gods' passions but also one whose protest is depicted sympathetically in the eyes of the Roman poet of the *Metamorphoses*.[19] The tapestries Britomart views similarly show more than one sign of parodic protest: for example, in Mars's undignified "shreek" (comically rhyming with "eek") of passion, along "With womanish teares, and with vnwarlike smarts," or in the sequence of Neptune's undying love only for *Bisaltis* in the alexandrine of one stanza—"Ne ought but deare *Bisaltis* ay could make him glad"—followed immediately in the next stanza by the laconic statement "He loued eke *Iphimedia* deare, / And *Aeolus* faire daughter *Arne* hight" (III.xi.41–42, 44).

Yet the cross-dressed knight Britomart finds her tapestry of womanly protest within the chambers of a male enchanter, who, like herself, is also the creation of a male poet. At this point, we might well stop to ask, with Susanne Wofford, whose tapestry this is and through whose eyes we see and, more properly, "rede," or interpret it.[20] Arachne's, Ovid's, his narrator's, Britomart's, Busirane's, Spenser's as poet or narrator, the interpretive tradition's, or our own? Going beyond the possibilities Wofford endorses, I would not exclude any of these, and the ecphrasis of the tapestry itself invites them in describing Jove's rape of Leda, breaking into apostrophe in the manner of Ovid to do so:

> O wondrous skill, and sweet wit of the man,
> That her in daffadillies sleeping made,
> From scorching heat her daintie limbes to shade:
> Whiles the proud Bird ruffing his fethers wyde,
> And brushing his faire brest, did her inuade:
> She slept, yet twixt her eielids closely spyde,
> How towards her he rusht, and smiled at his pryde.
> (III.xi.32)

Considerable ambiguity of reference marks this much-discussed stanza. Is the skilled and sweet-witted man in the first line Busirane or the chameleon-like, negatively capable Spenserian narrator, or the Spenserian poet in his own voice?[21] This time, the lines cited have no direct parallel in Ovid, hence no parallel in Arachne's tapestry, and they therefore belong to the three possibilities enumerated. But are we to forget that Britomart is our gazer and that these lines could also belong to her vision or response to Arachne's?[22] In whose opinion is the man "sweet-witted"? And what do the last two lines of the stanza mean: "She slept, yet twixt her eyelids closely spyde, / How towards her he rusht, and smiled at his pryde"? Leda sleeps, like Verdant in the Bower of Bliss, and yet, also to an extent like him, between her eyelids she seems to see—to spy—the swan rushing toward her. Is she awake or in a trance or in a daydream? Each of these possibilities would imply a different kind and degree of agency. The simple adverb "closely" could indicate that her eyes are indeed shut ("closely twixt") or that she spies with close attention an object close to her ("closely spyde"). The word "spy" itself carries an insistent association with stealth or closeness—intense, secretive observation. The final clause of the line, as Katherine Eggert has noted, is also ambiguous: does Leda smile in anticipation of rapture or does the swan, as the assumed form of Jove, smile in anticipation of ravishment?[23] And is the smile one of Jovian arrogance, of pure pleasure—his, hers, or theirs—or is it an ironic smile, a self-reflexive, deflating, Ovidian possibility that the availability of the womanly perspectives of Arachne and Britomart, not to mention some other readers, enforces? The narrator's own awareness, often amazing, is not to be slighted, either.

Another passage, even more frequently remarked, expresses ambiguity of reference as well. The walls of the enchanter's House are clothed with arras,

> Wouen with gold and silke so close and nere,
> That the rich metall lurked priuily,
> As faining to be hidd from enuious eye;
> Yet here, and there, and euery where vnwares
> It shewd it selfe, and shone vnwillingly:
> Like to a discolourd Snake, whose hidden snares
> Through the greene gras his long bright burnisht backe
>   declares.
>
> (III.xi.28)

This time, the inwoven threads of metal have an explicit precedent in Ovid, although it proves as striking in its difference as in its similarity: "There, too, they [Athena and Arachne] weave in pliant threads of gold, and trace in the weft some ancient tale (*illic et lentum filis inmittitur aurum / et vetus in tela deducitur argumentum*)."[24] In Ovid's version, the gold thread, belonging to Arachne and Athena alike, lacks the last six lines of Spenserian description, which call attention—heightened attention—to the serpentine filaments. Rather than betraying the presence of art, they shout it by comparison with Ovid's text, unwilling as they may be, or rather feign to be so. The participial pun "faining"—"As faining to be hidd"—as easily supports an exhibitionist impulse as it denies one, since the homonymic pun means either pretending (feigning) or desiring (faining). The alternative of merely pretending to hide from but actually enticing the "enuious eye" would relate the serpentine threads to the gold grapes in Acrasia's Bower, which enfold themselves among the leaves "As lurking from the vew of couetous guest"—as if lurking but actually seducing (II.xii.55).

But art in the House of Busirane is not finally the same as in the Bower, where "The art, which all that wrought, appeared in no place" (II.xii.58). Here, not unlike the sonneteer's topos of inarticulateness or an elaborate declamation uttered in full erotic chase by Ovid's Apollo, art may want or pretend to hide but instead displays itself, unwillingly or not. Like the pun faining/feigning, the word "unwillingly," which specifically refers to shining or conspicuousness—"It shewed it selfe, and shone vnwillingly"—again evokes the oscillating play of visual and interpretive perspectives, along with that of inadvertency and agency. Moreover, it does so "vnwares," which is precisely the ambiguous way Malecasta earlier sneaks up on Britomart and the way Busirane's knife wounds her and the knowing and not knowing way that Leda, in all her ambiguity, awaits the rush of the swan. This is an acute, extraordinarily telling way of realizing the combination of cultural exposure and ignorance, knowing and not knowing, that characterizes Britomart's condition and observation, as indeed her youthful reading of Ovid. Britomart does not cause this cultural site, whose meaning at once precedes and exceeds her role in it, but this place of rhetorical culture bears special pertinence to her condition and quest. Again, as with Leda, she is mirrored *to an extent* in the object or site.

Britomart passes from the tapestries next to a Mammonic room overlaid with pure gold, in which the "monstrous formes" of false love are depicted and on whose glittering walls hang the trophies of love's wars and conquests (xi.51–52). Again, Busirane is a hoarder, a self-gratifying one like Spenser's Mammon, who autoerotically fingers the gold coins in his lap "to feede his eye" (II.vii.4–5). In Busirane's golden room, Britomart witnesses the procession of Cupid's masquers, figures that stage the very process of a false love which is hardly distinguishable at moments from a true one. Antiquity of origin characterizes the creations of this room, as before of the tapestries depicted. As A. C. Hamilton's gloss conveniently summarizes, the masquers draw directly on the conventions of the medieval courts of love and of Renaissance triumphs, not least Petrarch's own, as well as on those of the Renaissance masque.[25] Again, these figures are hardly Britomart's creation, although they have special relevance to her condition and quest, as they do to Amoret's and Scudamour's, and to those of other characters in Book III. The very fact, long recognized, that they can be read from either a male or female point of view indicates their basically cultural rather than exclusively personal status. Their formal artificiality also proclaims their radical—indeed, their catachrestic—constructedness. Unlike the insidious art forms in Acrasia's Bower, they make no claims on nature. On reflection, who would want such mirrors of passion as these?

Their relation to Busirane and ultimately to Britomart is worth pursuing, however. Cupid's masquers resemble the kind of form Malbecco becomes at the end of canto x, one that "Is woxen so deform'd, that he has quight / Forgot he was a man, and *Gelosy* is hight" (60). Malbecco's metamorphosis into a "passion . . . in the mind" introduces the first canto, the eleventh, in which the House of Busirane figures centrally, and, in effect, it prepares for the masquers, whose humanity, like Malbecco's, has either vanished or failed of realization.[26] Like the fixed and fixated emblem "Gelosy" that Malbecco has become, the masquers are impostors of the living and every bit as artificial, as "personified," hence metaphorized, as the "carcas dead" of the False Florimell (III.viii.7, xi.1). Malbecco makes explicit in Book III the connection between sexual and monetary hoarding that was glimpsed earlier in the figure of Mammon. Even though the masquers are in a procession—a kind of dead march—each pair in itself is a frozen stage of courtship, removed from the necessarily narrative process of allegory and quest.[27] The masquers are another product of Busirane's art, and they issue from an "inner rowme" that is his as well (xii.26).

Years since, Thomas P. Roche, Jr., glossed Busirane as *abuse* in the sixteenth-century senses of "imposture, ill-usage, delusion," or as the archaic *abusion*, meaning a "perversion of the truth, deceit, deception, imposture," and in the words of Book II, implying "fond ... illusions" (xi.11).[28] To these meanings, I would add *abusio*, the familiar Renaissance word for catachresis, here understood as a wrenching of metaphor or an extravagant use of it, in the case at hand, a violent (mis)use of language, of which the masquers' dead likenesses are a prime exhibit. In Busirane's House of rhetorical art and illusion, *abusio* reigns, or "ranes," supreme. The traditional classification of poetry as a branch of rhetoric was still common in the Renaissance, and Busirane is clearly an abuser of poetry, as well as of rhetoric.[29] By now, I imagine, it is also clear that Busirane's name puns on *abuse/abusio*—that is, A-busirane.

Another persistent association of *abusio* in the rhetorical tradition is with *audacia*, or boldness, and it offers a gloss on the strange, forward and backward, summoning and forbidding, aggressive and maidenly imperatives Britomart reads over the doors in Busirane's Mammonic second chamber: "*Be bolde, be bolde ... Be not too bold*" (xi.54).[30] In a discussion of metaphor, including *catachresis/abusio*, in *De Oratore*, Cicero's spokesman praises "paulo audaciores [translationes]," or, "somewhat bolder metaphors" that bring brilliance to a speech but do not violate "ratio"—reason, purpose, or indeed, the nature of things (*rerum natura*). Such figures are bold but not too bold.[31] Read through the lens of Ciceronian rhetoric, the writing Britomart confronts above the doors in Busirane's House of rhetoric has the Ciceronian quality of an invitation to use *audacia* and a caution against excess in doing so, as it does in *De Oratore*. The choice Britomart faces as reader of Busirane's art is edged with anxiety and danger, not unlike that faced by an orator in Cicero's Rome, as the forced deaths of so many of the speakers in *De Oratore*, as well as of Cicero himself, dramatize. Rhetoric is consequential; it is a social, legal, and political shaper, not merely a neutral ornament or tool of pedagogues. Britomart, or any other reader, would do well carefully and cautiously to heed these warnings about the boldness of rhetorical art, warnings now appearing elusive and treacherous, yet also beguiling, in the message they send "to any vnwares" in Busirane's House. They invite a decision, while undermining assurance, and the only escape from Busirane's hegemonic cultural trap here or elsewhere, then or now, starts with awareness.

Britomart's evident acceptance of the challenge to be bold, but not too bold, leads to the third chamber of the House of Busirane, where its patron, the figure or at least the first figure behind the curtains, Busirane himself, primarily represents the constructedness of the entire place. Again, this art-full place simply doesn't make the same claims as Acrasia's Bower about its nearness to or indistinguishability from nature. This is art in capital letters, and alarmingly, Amoret's life in some sense now depends on Busirane. Thus "the Lady [Amoret], which by him stood bound, / *Dernly* vnto her [Britomart] called to abstaine, / From doing him to dy" (xii.3: my emphasis). Once in Busirane's clutches, Amoret recognizes herself and is recognized as his creation, pleading for his life in order to preserve her own. Her identity as love, which is presently her whole life, depends on loving. She is, after all, "*Venus* mayd" and the complement of "*Cupids* man," as she will be described by Scudamour in Book IV (x.54). Busirane has arrested her development, both imprisoned her figure and obstructed the realization of what she could and should be.

The adverb "dernly," which conveys the tone and manner in which Amoret calls on Britomart to spare Busirane's life, means "secretly" or "privately, confidentially"; it also carries the sense "inwardly." *Dernly* is a strange but suggestive word in this context, one that in the past has often been glossed too casually in the derived senses "dismally" or "direly." More significantly, it intimates a special appeal or relationship, something understood or otherwise shared between the two women. Yet *dern(e)* also means "dark" and "secret" in the sense "done in the dark" and often has associations with craft, deceit, or evil.[32] Conceivably, if disturbingly, it could further connect Amoret with her captor, at least while in his power. Associatively, the "dark secret life" that destroys Blake's rose comes to mind.

Clearly, however, Britomart cannot destroy Busirane without destroying what Amoret now is, the cultural love object par excellence.

This Busiranic figuration underlies Amoret's development in the company of Britomart after Book III and prior to the intractable, historical entanglement of Amoret's figure with the story of Timias and Belphoebe in Book IV (vii–viii). Amoret's figuration as love object is also the reason that, although Busirane's artworks vanish, he still survives, bound by the very chain or, in further terms of traditional iconography, by the rhetorical art that he has abused.[33] Without him, there is only a vacuum, and this vacuum might also have something to do with the fact that Spenser's own *Amoretti*, written and published between Book III and the 1596 sequel, cannot wholly escape the available conventions of erotic discourse but indeed must use and try to reshape them.[34] The furnishings of Busirane's rooms may vanish at the end of canto xii, but this is hardly the last we see of their kind in Spenser's poetry.

The alternative definition of *catachresis/abusio*, namely a *necessary* extension of the signification of a word to something that lacks a word, rather than merely a willful wrenching of language, bears both on the emptiness apparent with the vanishing of the artworks in Busirane's House and on the persistence of Ovidian, Petrarchan, or otherwise Busiranic forms in Spenser's poetry. Abusive as these might have been and still might be, they are currently and culturally inescapable for a practicing poet who wants his poems read, even aside from the extent to which he is able, or is not, to get outside and to critique them. Poetry has never been written in a cultural vacuum. This is another suggestion conveyed by Spenser's ending Amoret's story with a return to the Temple of Venus in Book IV, right where her life beyond the Garden of Adonis began, as discussed in chapter 2.

Busirane represents a fantasy and, additionally, a culture of rape, as others have argued without qualification, but it should be observed as well that he is not successful. His fantasy remains exactly that, and Amoret remains a virgin under his roof: "Die had she leuer with Enchanters knife, / Then to be false in loue, profest a virgine wife"—pledged to Scudamour but not fully one with him (IV.i.6, III.xii.31). If it were otherwise, Busirane's significance as a peculiarly rhetorical form of abuse, an art with the power in actuality to arrest love, would be lost, and with it the real cultural critique of Book III. Busirane abuses figuration and the perception based on it to feign that metaphor is the same as reality, that it *is* absolutely rather than is and is not, as Paul Ricoeur would gloss this figure of perverse predication—"perverse" (from *pervertere*), "turned away, around, about" or "athwart," hence "tropic."[35] It is Busirane who feigns (and fains) rape. And his ideological legacy is the reading that believes him.

Britomart herself is wounded, although not deeply, by Busirane and therefore proves vulnerable to him. Her heart is also said to be pierced and her hair stood on end by his bloody verses, even while, her threatening sword raised above him, she controls him.[36] To my mind, this is the one moment in the scene, rather than any other one, at which Britomart experiences, or truly realizes, Amoret's condition. For a modern reader invested in psychoanalytic connections, this could be a moment when Britomart traverses, enters into, the Busiranic fantasy, even as it is the same moment in which Busirane "reuerse[s]" his spell, turning it back as when one looks at the backside of a collar, and his artworks crumble, then vanish, because there is nothing real there (III.xii.36).[37]

At one point in the immediate context of Busirane's disenchanting verses—a rhetorical spell, which like all spells, must be unbound—a truly ambiguous pronoun occurs, (con)fusing Britomart with Amoret. With "threatfull hand" unslackened, Britomart waits "[un]dismaied" (and un-dis-maided) by the quaking of this House and undeterred by "daungers dout," a phrase offering to reassume the familiar form of an actual pair of the masquers earlier seen (cf. xii.10–11, 37); thus she "Abode," occupying and inhabiting this "place,"

> to weet, what end would come of all.
> At last that mightie chaine, which round about
> Her tender waste was wound, adowne gan fall,
> And that great brasen pillour broke in peeces small.
> (III.xii.37)

The ambiguous referent of the pronoun "her" signals Britomart's *involvement*—literally her enwrapping, winding (Latin *involvere*)—in Busirane's "mightie chaine," in the toils (and coils) of his rhetoric, thus evoking the familiar iconographic identification of rhetoric with spellbound enchainment that I earlier referenced. Arguably, the first seven lines in the next stanza also encompass Britomart and Amoret, although my own awareness of the situation in the narrative just described makes me think such a reading unlikely. Be that as it may, what is significant about the one momentary identification of Britomart with Amoret in the penultimate line of the last inset is that it comes only with Amoret's freeing at Britomart's hand. It implicates Britomart in Amoret's predicament, and she could hardly not be implicated in view of the experiences that brought her to Busirane's House in the first place, but again, like Britomart's superficial wounding, in doing so it more tellingly exhibits the superiority *and* intimacy of her *derne*, or dark, secret power.

Let us briefly suppose nonetheless that the next stanza, of whose identification with Britomart I am skeptical, does continue the identification of her with Amoret, since this stanza offers the best evidence for the actual raping of Amoret and, in Susan Frye's argument, of Britomart as well:

> The cruell steele, which thrild her dying hart,
>   Fell softly forth, as of his owne accord,
>   And the wyde wound, which lately did dispart
>   Her bleeding brest, and riuen bowels gor'd,
>   Was closed vp, as it had not beene sor'd [1596,
>   1609: "bor'd"],
>   And euery part to safety full sownd,
>   As she were neuer hurt, was soone restor'd:
>   Tho when she felt her selfe to be vnbownd,
> And perfect hole, prostrate she fell vnto the grownd.
> (III.xii.38)

The crucial words occur in the lines describing the wound in "Her bleeding brest, and riuen bowels" that "Was closed vp, as it [the wound] had not beene sor'd." Although these lines are about as transgressively suggestive as *The Faerie Queene* gets, I would reject a reading that swallows catachresis whole, actualizing the radical metaphors present here. The meaning of the lines depends heavily on that of the words "bowels" and "as" in them. Contrary to the popular modern understanding of *bowels* exclusively as "guts," in the sixteenth century this word commonly referred to "the seat of the tender and sympathetic emotions" or the "heart, centre," and in Spenser's writing it frequently, although not always, carries the latter meaning, as is also true of English translations of the Bible in this period.[38] Doublets, such as "bleeding brest" and "riuen bowels" in the first of the crucial lines, are rife in Spenser, and the prominence in canto xii of Amoret's transfixed heart also favors the meanings, now archaic, that I have cited. Use of a singular verb ("was") and singular pronoun ("it") with reference to the single wound in "brest" and "bowels" further enforces identification of this alliterating doublet as a single unit.

The other word, *as*, in the phrase "as it had not been sor'd," could be read "as if," but it need not be. This word can also mean "inasmuch as" or "since," and this is what I take it to mean here: "inasmuch as it had not been sor'd."[39] I would not reject the other possible reading out of hand either, although in context I find it a stretch—"far-fet," indeed an *abusio*, and notably Busiranic in viewpoint. But metaphor, even abusive, catachrestic metaphor, *is*, as well as is not. Ricoeur, for one, insists on such "split reference," a meaning that is there and not there, and Pierre Bourdieu similarly speaks of the ambivalence of sublation, of a lifting or raising that "simultaneously denies and maintains both the repression and the repressed" and thus "allows for a doubling of profits: the profit of saying and the profit of denying what is said by the way of saying it."[40]

In the Spenserian passage in question, however, the possibility of the counterfactual reading "as if," like the former possibility of reading "bowels" as "guts," hence "belly" or reproductive organs, would only return us to the multiple perspectives of the participants in this canto—here specifically those of Amoret, Britomart, Busirane, the sometimes unreliable narrator, and the Spenserian poet himself. The pun on "whole" in the final line of the stanza is equally undisturbed by the reading I have advanced or by the one that *chooses* Busirane's perspective on it: Amoret, representative love object, is rendered "whole and wanting," at once perfected, or completed, for the passion of Cupid's man and both lacking and desiring him. Freely now, her responses, like Britomart's, are holistic in every sense of the hopeful or disheartening pun, as the reader will have it.

We hear or half hear submerged, or (im)possible, puns of the sort just addressed even when prolonged attention to syntax and context indicates that they are far-fetched or grammatically irrational. They are plentiful in the literature of the period, in Shakespeare and Donne, for obvious instances, and notably in Spenser as well. Studying the mental processes by which we select and comprehend words, the psycho-linguist Jean Aitchison has found evidence that I see supporting the viability of such puns: readers or listeners "briefly activate both meanings of a homonym, even in cases where one of them is inappropriate"; in fact, according to one model, "A whole army of words, it seems, marches up for consideration each time a word begins."[41] Aitchison's explanation of homonymic punning is readily extended to a syntactical construction or to any alternative signification of a single word.

Whatever the precise workings of our mental circuitry, a third Spenserian example of (im)possible punning is ready to hand slightly earlier in Britomart's confrontation with Busirane, and it raises similar issues of reading, thus contributing to this significant interpretive pattern in Busirane's third chamber. When Busirane's knife wounds Britomart,

"Exceeding wroth therewith the virgin grew, / Albe the wound were nothing deepe imprest" (xii.33). In an examination of Spenser's puns on the word "nothing," Eggert has suggested that *nothing* here might be a noun and therefore a sexual pun, the familiar Shakespearean equivalent of "hole," or "vagina, genitalia": in this reading "nothing [is] deepe imprest."[42] Once again, though surely prematurely, the "virgin" Britomart is presumed to have been raped. But, as Eggert has agreed, the concessive "Albe" (meaning "albeit, although") preceding "nothing" syntactically negates such a pun and indicates instead that "nothing" is an adverb—that is, "nothing [or not at all] deepe imprest"—with the result that Britomart is far from having been violated except in a superficial sense. Once the grammatical reading dominates, the (im)possible pun spectrally present serves to insinuate a more threatening potential in the situation—one submerged and unrealized—and it may intimate as well the precariousness of Britomart's control at this moment, a control, by drawing her sword, that she quickly asserts and maintains (33–34). Once again, the abusive reading is finally meaningful only as an expression of the threat and indeed of the projected fantasy of Busirane. The (im)possible pun would nominalize the word "nothing," insisting on its literal sense "no thing"; this is the sense that negates the male member, or "thing," in a common Elizabethan sense of the word *thing*, while also evoking it, and thus motivates the sexual pun. In this way, the "abusive," Busiranic reader deconstructs the more abstractive (supersessive) adverb to find the material root that makes it a noun and a metaphor. At the heart of this practice is debate about the viability of dead metaphors, appropriately mentioned in passing here.[43]

In both the 1590 and 1596 editions of *The Faerie Queene*, Busirane's artworks disappear once he is captured, and in the 1596 edition Britomart and Amoret leave his House, only to find that Scudamour and Glauce have departed, fearing the worst. In the 1590 edition, however, Amoret is reunited with Scudamour outside Busirane's House. Hamilton's gloss on their embrace is hardly alone in suggesting that the embrace is orgasmic, and I suppose it might be, but Britomart's presence as an observer gives me pause. Certainly their embrace is passionate: Amoret melts in pleasure and pours out her spirit in "sweete ravishment"; the embracing lovers are "like two senceless stocks," and, as if grown together, they resemble the marble statue of a hermaphrodite (xi.45–46). The fact that Spenser cancelled this ending in 1596 is the strongest sign that something is wrong with it, however, and the "senceless stocks" and marble hermaphrodite are two others. A stock is a tree stub or a block of wood, both lifeless, as is the marble statue, fixed in its place.[44] The image of the hermaphrodite in this context is at best ambivalent—grotesquely double-limbed, motionless, and dubiously human. That Britomart is said to half-envy the lovers' embrace half-suggests that she does not embrace it herself without reservation and half-suggests that she does and therefore that she has more learning to do.

Understood sequentially as resulting from Britomart's victory, the conclusive image of the hermaphroditic statue reflects ironically on her triumph. Amoret has been freed, but she remains to an extent Busirane's creature, a figure bound to his erotics, even as she is bound to Cupid's man Scudamour, whose identifying shield, which is emblazoned with the figure of Cupid, results from his conquest of unwilling womanhood in the Temple of Venus (see III.7, IV.x.55, 57). Even in Book III, his name and blazon identify him as Cupid's surrogate. Aside from the Temple of Venus, which only appears in the tenth canto of Book IV, Amoret's sociocultural shaping preeminently has been at Busirane's cruel hands. The hermaphrodite is what survives Busirane's cultural site when all his other erotic forms have vanished, and its survival will be further apparent when, after a hiatus of six years, the second installment of *The Faerie Queene* is published—Books IV to VI. Of course Busirane, like Archimago and Acrasia before him, survives, too, although we see no more of his figure. The poet of Faerie may be an idealist, but he is hardly unaware of the real world, as we call it and as these survivals testify.

As if to observe the hiatus between the first installment of *The Faerie Queene* and the poet's reflections on it in the proem to Book IV, I want first to review Britomart's role to this point and then in the next section to begin anew with another, different approach to it, through something at first glance purely external, her armor. This approach will thus use a new lens, which the 1596 installment does not inaugurate but makes further significant. Republishing Spenser's first installment together with his second, with heightened emphasis on Britomart's armor, the 1596 *Faerie Queene* itself invites a review of Book III.

Although Britomart is repeatedly developed at length in relation to others in the first four cantos of Book III, she still remains focal. Her quest provides the main story line: Malecasta, the flashback with Glauce, the visit to Merlin, her complaint by the seaside, which is mirrored by Cymoent's and Arthur's in the same canto (iv). Admittedly, Merlin's history lesson over twenty-plus stanzas stretches this point, yet his history is centered on Britomart's progeny. In the second four cantos—Belphoebe and Timias, the Garden of Adonis, Florimell, the witch and old fisherman,

Argante, Satyrane, the Squire of Dames—Britomart is absent as a figure in the action. Then, in canto ix, she shares a role at and in the castle of Malbecco, there discovering her genealogical connection with Paridell. The metamorphosis of Malbecco into the emblem of jealous fixation in canto x, a story from which Britomart is again absent, introduces the first of the cantos of Busirane. That Britomart's absence from nearly half the cantos in Book III conforms to the structure of romance is important, but, in a poem that everywhere makes form and structure meaningful, it means more.

When Britomart reappears for the last two cantos, which are situated in Busirane's House of Rhetoric, she looks once more like the major representative of the story line, yet her primary function for stanza after stanza is to tour the artworks that dominate the scene, and to participate in the multiple points of view explored through them. When she acts to save Amoret, the heightened, layered ambiguity of what actually transpires, albeit comprehendible, conspicuously leaves the final decision to others—viewers and readers as participants. In short, the dominant subject now looks cultural, and the primary focus thematic rather than characterological. Whereas the characterological features of the first four cantos might have invited the view that Britomart is in herself the subject, the final eight cantos, including the adventure of Busirane, have readjusted it. *The Faerie Queene* is never static, let alone formulaic. In Book IV, Britomart's figure will become less conventionally cross-dressed, and, in accordance with the more generally experimental nature of this book, her figure will also become more experimentally so. This is the development that I intend to trace next by considering Britomart's armor, from Book III through Book V, where her story shifts again before ending.

Britomart's Armor

Throughout Book III, Britomart has been vested in armor that forms and masks, expresses and veils, defends and contains her. She has been further invested in finding Artegall, whose identity is known to her by his own vesting in the conquered arms of Achilles. By the opening of Book IV, Britomart, the armed but nubile virgin, not only Venus-Virgo but more radically Venus within Mars, has become a complicated cultural signifier implicated in cultural conceptions of gender. Riding into Book IV, Britomart and Amoret share a single horse, a traditional symbol of passion, as well as a single saddle, unless Amoret perches on the horse's rump—a passing, parodic thought. Since Britomart wears a full suit of armor, their combined silhouette on the horse recalls the hermaphrodite in the original ending of Book III. This transposed, catachrestic, hermaphroditic form at the outset of Book IV, which replaces the one in the original ending, is in effect a continuation of unfinished business. Their silhouette also anticipates the statue of Venus with "both kinds in one, / Both male and female, both vnder one name" that presides over the Temple of Venus in the tenth canto of this fourth book (41).

A fixed, emblematic statue is not a figure developing in figured narrative, however, and sex need not be equated with gender. Nonetheless, by Book IV it is clear that a binaristic conception of gender is inadequate.[45] Clearly now, there are four terms in play, and, with the benefit of retrospection, at least two in each of the major amatory players of the books featuring Britomart. The play of these terms with respect to Britomart is my major focus in what follows, but, with respect to Artegall, it bears mention, precisely because four terms, not just Britomart's two, are vital to it. When Artegall appears at a tournament in Book IV of the poem, his first appearance as an actor rather than merely as an image, he is "the saluage knight" with "Saluagesse sans finesse"—artless, uncivilized savagery—emblazoned on his shield (IV.39, 42). Encountering Britomart's spear after toppling all other knightly contestants, he is summarily knocked from his horse. A poor loser who harbors a grudge, he still sports his savage identity when he next meets Britomart and engages in hand-to-hand combat with her, an episode that I will subsequently examine in detail. Its result is Artegall's assumption of his true identity as he yields to Britomart.

Both armed encounters of Artegall with Britomart dramatize that his savagery needs softening, refining, civilizing. As the loaded term *softening* signals in a context of gender and sexuality, softening suggests his need of the Venerean principle, ranging from love to courtesy, gentleness, generosity, and compassion, a principle that has been hidden, indeed absent, from his actions as the savage knight. In mythological terms, this principle might be dubbed his inner Venus. It will moderate and civilize his hyper-masculinity, his exclusive maleness. Much more happens in Artegall's own book, the fifth, although its complexities exceed my present focus. Yet briefly, in a parody of Artegall's yielding to Britomart in Book IV, he yields again to a woman, the wrong one, in Book V, and his doing so results in his punitive cross-dressing as a woman. He is humiliated and effeminized but simultaneously humanized—once again civilized—by this fall, and with it, for the first time in Book V, he recalls his betrothal to

Britomart in Book IV. His regressive, brutal figuration as Justice earlier in Book V effectually enters a Venerean world of romance in which love can redeem him.[46] His quest as both knight and justicer thereafter is beyond my present concern with Britomart, since she, having saved Artegall, disappears from the poem.

A major problem with the fusing of Scudamour with Amoret, Cupid's man with Venus's maid, at the end of Book III in 1590 is precisely that only two terms, opposite ones, male and female, are involved. Venus-Virgo does not sufficiently represent the doubled perception that four terms require either, no matter whether Virgo is perceived as Diana or Minerva/Athena. Unless seen as a cultural inflection of the composite Venus-Mars, Venus-Virgo masks the truly Martian, martial, masculine nature of Brito*mart*'s figure—her "manly terror," as the poem puts it early in Book III (i.46). Venus-Virgo elides the hard questions that her armor presents, those involving combinations of nubility and firm resistance, incorporation and active, assertive agency, the kinds of questions involving degrees, kinds, and causes of what the early modern period perceived as masculinity, whose relation to maleness per se was not well defined or neatly separated from other spheres and aspects of life. Edgar Wind's familiar reflections on Venus as Mars, Mars as Venus, are informative for their stress on the compounding of the nature of each of them: "Dressed in armour ... the *Venus victrix* or *Venus armata* signifies the warfare of love; she is a *compound* of attraction and rejection, fostering her gracious aims by cruel methods.... Even Virgil's Diana-like Venus ... is but a variant of the *Venus armata*: a bellicose Venus who has donned the weapons that normally belong to her opponent—either Diana, Minerva, or Mars." Wind's conception might be analogized to a compound sentence, which connects two independent clauses. Pertinent to "Venus as a Mars," James Nohrnberg further observes that "All Amazons are ... 'daughters of Mars,'" to which I would add emphatically with respect to Britomart, even Venus manifested as Jove's daughter Minerva and vice versa.[47]

In what follows, my intention is to work with Spenser's poem without imposing on it a clarity it does not have or, perhaps, want. Although acknowledging the relation of Venus-Virgo to Britomart, I find that its exclusive use figures a woman apart from a man without pressing specifically enough the nature of this a-partness—this compounding—or pressing it to the extent that the poem does.[48] Accordingly, I plan to highlight the *Venus armata* composite as Venus-Mars and to trace how a doubled perception of Britomart's gender develops. As before, my approach will continue to engage the process of figuration in Britomart's story. Britomart is an evolving figure, and her armor conspicuously participates in—indeed figures—both the development of her integrity and its loss.

My method reflects what happens to mythological sources in their creative revision within the movement of metaphorical narrative and, in the focal instance at hand, to Britomart. In this respect it differs, while benefiting, from the central concerns of an art historian such as Wind, whose work is primarily grounded in paintings, medals, sculptures, and other more stationary forms. Instead, it seeks to approach a process of figural thinking that overlaps with allegory but also loosens it.[49] This process produces figures that are considerably fuller and less simply abstract, perhaps closer to the figuration of the gods and goddesses of ancient myth themselves, who have sometimes been classed with allegory or subjected to reductive allegoresis and sometimes have not been. Basically, however, this process of thinking is yet another, further extension of continued or moving metaphor, as classical and early modern rhetoricians have described allegory itself. In Cicero's immensely influential *De Oratore*, for example, Crassus, one of two major spokesmen, considers allegory an extension of metaphor in "a chain of words linked together: ex pluribus [verbis] continuatis connectitur" and thus, in modern terms, in the contiguous relationship that characterizes narrative (II:130: Bk III.xli.166). On this note, furnished with immediately relevant principles of gendering and reflections on method, I would return to Britomart herself in the early cantos of Book III.

The Briton Princess Britomart wears the armor of the Saxon Queen Angela, but armor itself is coded male in Spenser's culture, as is evident whenever Britomart encounters a knight with her visor down and, in the Castle of Malecasta, even with her visor up.[50] Britomart's vesting herself in this armor narratively follows on, and causally results from, her visit to Merlin, who has been Arthur's armorer and therefore in some sense his maker, and Britomart's use of her armor not surprisingly remakes her as well.[51] Her arming is also a process that her motherly nurse Glauce first suggests and then facilitates following their crucial visit to Merlin, which is itself Glauce's womanly conception. So vested, Britomart is no longer the merely frustrated and enclosed pubescent child, the sheltered girl, of the second canto, but suddenly refigured as a knight "trained vp in warlike stowre, / To tossen speare and shield, and to affrap / The warlike ryder to his most mishap." These lines, spoken by Britomart to

Redcrosse (erroneously printed Guyon) would have sufficed to explain her quest, but gratuitously she adds,

> Sithence I loathed haue my life to lead,
> As Ladies wont, in pleasures wanton lap,
> To finger the fine needle and nyce thread;
> Me leuer were with point of foemans speare be dead.
> (III.ii.6)

Ostensibly, Britomart here rejects the weaving, spinning, and other crafts of "needle and nyce thread" especially associated with Minerva (not to mention Arachne). She is not simply dressed but is vested in her armor and the knightly role it represents. Although she feigns in the lines just cited, she is also describing the way she actually behaves once she is in Faerie Land, where all figures are feigned and defined by what they do. Like all the young men in *The Faerie Queene* who seem to have some future—Arthur, Redcrosse, Artegall, and Tristram, for example—Britomart is here separated from her family, significantly armed, and thereby reinvented. In order to survive or to find the possibility of a future—purpose, being, or justice—escape to Faerie appears as necessary in this epic romance as to Arden in Shakespeare's *As You Like It*.[52] Aside from this constructive reading of Britomart's *enabling* armor, the last line cited in the inset could be taken with comic irony as Britomart's inadvertent expression of a desire to find her "foeman" Artegall's spear and thereby to consummate her love quest. More than once, the representation of Britomart in Books III and IV is touched by parody or comic wit. This is another humanizing touch in her figuration, as it recurrently is in that of Spenser's Arthur and Una.[53]

Like Artegall's armor, a sign of his Trojan and British lineage, Britomart's Saxon armor also has a dynastic function.[54] Since Britomart is a Briton princess, it figures the eventual joining of Briton with Saxon, as predicted by Merlin, who, as maker of the magic globe belonging to King Ryence, Britomart's father, is not surprisingly the expositor of Britomart's "heuenly destiny," which her deliberate, conscious speculation, as distinguished from her initially empty, passive viewing in the self-reflective globe, first intimates (III.iii.22–24). King Ryence never appears in the poem, and his shadowy presence serves mainly to validate Britomart's dynastic role, which is more directly scripted by Merlin, the wizard with a sense of humor whose comic ancestry includes a "Lady Nonne" (lady none, or nun), Matilda (Teutonic: battle-maid, or battle-made), and Pubidius, a historical nonentity with a name glancing at Latin *pubes/pubis*, "puberty" (iii.13).[55] Such ancestors could hardly better befit Britomart's condition: they are made for her, and the same is true of Merlin's dynastic prophecy, which at once reflects and guides her wishes. Although the male/female cooperation here has been read as compromising her agency, I see it as potentially further empowering her—again, potentially. On the one hand, in "this man's world," as too common a saying of the twentieth century went, she has to start somewhere if she is to have a viable quest. On the other hand, if she really is, or is to become, a composite of Mars and Venus, the male/female cooperation expresses rather than compromises her integrity.

Britomart's Saxon armor was acquired by a band of Britons on a "forray"—a raiding party bent on pillage—a "Few dayes before" when they "had gotten a great pray / Of Saxon goods, emongst the which was seene / A goodly Armour" belonging to Queen Angela (iii.58). This account highlights the fortuitous, even casual, quality of the armor's acquisition. Angela was not defeated by the Briton king in battle; in fact, the account suggests that the pillagers might have broken into one of Angela's storehouses or, perhaps more ingloriously, into her country house in her absence.

Angela herself and Britomart's father, King Ryence, do not even seem directly involved, and the fact that Ryence's acquisition of the armor is subsequently termed a "gladfull victory" renders it about as glorious as Artegall's winning the arms of Achilles is actual (59). As Ryence's "onely daughter and his hayre" from whom "nothing he . . . reseru'd apart," Britomart might actually be thought to have a right to the captured armor—in legal terminology a vested right (III.ii.22): in English law, women had full rights to inheritance when sons were lacking. In this connection, two attributes of Minerva, as identified with Athena, come to mind, namely her unique possession of her father Jove's thunderbolt and aegis with the Gorgon's head.[56] In sum, Britomart's robbery of her armor from a church is on the transgressive scale of her later white lies to Redcrosse, who is himself Saxon-born. In Faerie, Saxons and Britons such as Redcrosse and Arthur mingle readily.

Britomart's martial accoutrements actually combine Saxon with Briton. Although her Saxon armor is not magical, her ebony spear, made by Bladud, a Briton king, has been produced by magic and has magical powers that an opposing rider cannot withstand.[57] Although Britomart also has a sword, the spear is her ultimate weapon, and it is alike an attribute of Mars and Minerva. The spear has been stored in King Ryence's church, which begins to sound like an armory or virtual history museum. Even Glauce finds her nondescript suit of armor there. Since Britomart's shield, emblazoned with Brutus's lion passant, is simply said to be beside the spear, it too could be associated with Bladud or with her dynastic genealogy. When Britomart sets off for Faerie immediately after her arming, the hunched figure of old Glauce trails her: the lady knight brings with her, so to speak, her own gently comic visual parody.

Variously glossing *Glauce*, the name of Britomart's nurse, A. C. Hamilton suggests Greek "owl," a bird traditionally associated with Minerva, as well as Greek "grey" (that is, old Glauce), and the mother of Diana in Cicero's *De natura deorum*.[58] As a combination of Venus and Mars, the amorously motivated Britomart is as much a parody of the fiercely, eternally virginal Minerva herself as is Glauce of Minerva's owl. Notably, Glauce as a visual form of parody trailing Britomart disappears by the end of Book III, although then she ludicrously trails Scudamour instead. Given Hamilton's glosses of Glauce's name, a more appropriate verb for her presence with respect to him might be "shadows" or, better still, "haunts." When Britomart finds Artegall in Book IV, Glauce briefly reappears in the conventional role of complicit nursely matchmaker, a version of Fair Welcome (Bialacoyle, in Chaucer's rendering of *Le Roman de la Rose*), after which point she vanishes from the poem (IV.vi.25: "belaccoyle").[59] With significant figural difference, in Book V an armed Britomart will resume her Faerie quest accompanied by the iron man Talus.

Momentarily excepting the sojourn with Malecasta, Britomart removes either her helmet or all her armor twice in Book III: first at the seashore and then in the castle of Malbecco. In both instances, the danger of containment by the protective armor in the negative sense of suppression and self-enclosure becomes evident. Both witness an outpouring of what is inside this armored and self-contained figure—frustrated desire, patriotic affection, a kind of figural voice, since she, not the narrator, is the speaker. In Philip Sidney's term, at these moments she is literally and memorably a speaking picture.[60] Sitting unhelmeted beside the seashore, she utters her passionate love-longing in a notably Petrarchan form, but then she suits up again in the enabling armor to get on with the quest and to topple "loues enimy," the aggressor Marinell, who has rashly advised her to retreat (III.iv.26).[61] Later, within the Castle of Malbecco, and now fully divested of her armor, she discovers and reveals her kinship to Paridell, not only as a Trojan descendant but also, in a phrase that refuses containment, as "another partner of . . . [his] payne" and of his "pitifull complaint" of his lost homeland (III.ix.40). The inner Britomart, so to speak, takes surprising cultural forms, not merely borrowing those of males but truly vesting herself in them. The cultural alternative for her in the poem would appear to be silence, and the cultural challenge to modify or to exceed these inherited forms in some way.

In the Castle of Malecasta, Britomart remains fully suited, although, to her mischance, she has her visor up, thus projecting "amiable grace," along with her "manly terror" (III.i.46). She later unsuits in private; her bed is invaded by the deluded and delusional Malecasta; and, as a result, she is slightly wounded by Gardante (Looking), who leers at her when she is clad only in a smock. Punningly, she is further vulnerable as well for having let her guard down, whether by having a look around Malecasta's domain or by "dissembl[ing]" her disapproval of the temptress's outrageously open advances "with ignoraunce" (i.e., playing dumb) and by "entertayn[ing]" her instead with "faire countenaunce" (i.50, 55). *Delude*, incidentally, is another word deriving from *ludere*, "play," and surely there is something parodic about this incident in Castle Joyous. (Intertextually, the plight of Sir Gawain comes to mind.)[62] Britomart, as we know, will also be wounded, although again not deeply, in the House of Busirane, but this later time, with significant difference, through her full suit of armor. Here the wound will signify her vulnerability to Busirane despite the armor, but this is not all. The armor, including shield and sword, its phallic "point direct[ed] . . . forward right," has helped her through the flames of Busirane's porch, which divide themselves, allowing her to pass through, "as a thonder bolt / Perceth the yielding ayre" (III.xi.25).[63] The image is distinctively Jovian; that Jove's cerebral offspring Minerva can also be represented hurling the thunderbolt makes it no less so. Like father, like son; is it really like daughter, too? Britomart will be wearing the same armor when she meets and crucially engages Artegall in Book IV, where the thunderbolt will be his.

When Britomart is wounded through the armor by Busirane and yet is victorious, it is as if the armor had become more fully a part of her in some way, at least while she is in the condition of possibility and creative figuration that Faerie affords. An analogy to the shifting relation of Christian armor to what is inside it at various points in Book I is available, as is the implication of such shifts for the broader relation of surface to substance in the poem.[64] This developing relation may be a constructive reason, in addition to the deceptive and abusive ones, the throwbacks to

Busirane, why Britomart stays safely within her armor at the beginning of Book IV where, rather than reveal herself to Amoret, she "fain[s]"—ambiguously pretends, desires, or both—her sex male and thereby "maske[s] her wounded mind" (i.7). She has, after all, been thrice wounded by love—first by her vision of Artegall in the magic globe and twice by love's perversion at the hands of Malecasta/Gardante and Busirane. All these wounds were painful.

Along with the narrator's word "abuse" characterizing Britomart's deception of Amoret, the other words I have just quoted from the first appearance of the two women together in Book IV, namely "fain" and "maske," enforce the specter of Busirane. Britomart's masking her female sex from the anxious, defenseless Amoret, while feigning and faining to be a man, both reflects Busirane's abusive masking and ironically suggests that Britomart is at once the heir of his art and of Amoret, its ultimate object.[65] Surely cruel, not merely comic, Britomart's abusive playing with and upon Amoret's responses suggests both curiosity and resentment—an openness to experience and a resistance to the stock-in-trade of conventional womanhood, to something of what Shakespeare's Angelo calls the "destin'd livery" of woman.[66] Yet it also enables her exploratory performance of manhood, an alternative and possibly liberating identity. This is another point at which her figuration as Mars clashes more noticeably with her figuration as Minerva, both figural possibilities present in the *Venus armata* composite. For a modern reader, it is also a point at which the Renaissance figure of Britomart strongly suggests Judith Butler's emphasis on the performativity of a gendered identity.[67]

Like Britomart's momentary identification with Amoret in the House of Busirane, her "abusion" of her charge at the beginning of Book IV might again suggest a Lacanian traversal of the fantasy, a completing or an experiencing of both (or all) sides of it—earlier of victimhood, this time of Busiranic abuse.[68] Accordingly, Britomart might turn from a projected identification of herself as the object of desire, that is, an identification with Amoret in the House of Busirane, to an introjected identification of herself as the agent of desire, or Busirane himself, at the beginning of Book IV. As signaled by the similarity of the word *traverse* ("turn across, athwart") to *translate* ("carry across"), the latter a term specifically for metaphor and alternatively for tropicality in general, this notion is allegorical, whether metonymic and substitutive or more properly metaphorical, the latter being at once constructive and differential, never just the same.[69] Such traversal offers a useful connection and insight, since it further highlights Britomart's characterological features, as long as it does not produce sameness at the expense of difference—the difference between identification and Britomart's sustained control over Busirane in his House, despite her momentary vulnerability, and the difference between mere *abusion* of Amoret and Britomart's constructive, experimental performance of manhood.[70] This is also the difference between armor that is merely alienating and armor that is constructively enabling.

In sum, at the outset of Book IV, the true Britomart is no longer simply within the armor, if, once armed, she could ever have been characterized this way. Her figure continues to exhibit characteristics of interiority and awareness—Sinfield's "consciousness"—but even so, as this book begins, she is more fully invested in armored form and expression than ever before. The potential of her figure as at once Mars and Venus, aggressive boar and sensuous flower, male and female, hard-edged form and melting passion has increasingly been realized in Book III, yet, when her own book ends and Book IV opens, her armored form and her per*form*ance of manhood are further definitive.[71] In view of her final adventure in Book III in which the armor is already so much a part of her, this is less a deepening revelation, a word I used with respect to Una, than a further development, a broadening of her figure—a greater comprehension. Subjected to friendship, the form of love thematic in Book IV, Britomart's figure will be at once different and still continuous by Book IV's end. Both Una and Britomart learn from experience in their own Books (I and III), but the shaping of Britomart in the course of Books III to V is more extensive, prolonged, and remarkable with respect to her awareness and, be it added in a glance forward to Book V, with respect to her unawareness, as well.

* * *

Further discussing composite forms in Renaissance art, Edgar Wind offers the images of a closed fist and an unfolded palm to illustrate how a composite image, such as Venus and Mars or amiable Concordia and martial Constantia, might be represented: "Normally, Constantia would hold a lance or lean on a column. . . . But the lance is replaced by an arrow of love which she swings in a defiant bellicose manner, and the column on which she leans is formed by a bundle of arrows, the traditional symbol of Concordia. The visibly fierce, unassailable Constantia is therefore a concealed Concordia; like a closed fist withholding an open palm. . . . [Thus] Constantia is represented as an 'infolded' Concordia—Concordia as an 'unfolded' Constantia" (76). In a variation on Wind's image, at the beginning of Book IV, mounted on that single horse with Britomart, the Venerean Amoret is this knight's love outfolded, the best outward, unfolded expression presently available, while Britomart herself remains the outfolded form of Mars, whom the enabling armor expresses. Ideally, the Venerean Amoret, as a generative symbol of Britomart's love, will be incorporated—perhaps more accurately reincorporated—into Britomart, and Amoret herself, as a separate figure, will somehow find a viable external form and reformed cultural expression.[72] The alternative to such constructive, figural reformation will be Amoret's discarding, not entirely unlike the disappearing Fool in *King Lear*, whose role Lear subsumes in the storm and whose figure he replaces with Poor Tom's. Realism of plot and character in the modern quotidian sense is foreign to the constructive, bold process that Spenser's fourth book undertakes, as well as more broadly to his culture.[73] Form, too, has a cultural history that remains conspicuously significant in *The Faerie Queene*, where Amoret as a figure differs formally from the relatively greater complexity and awareness of Britomart. Both the conventions of narrative and of symbolism in the Renaissance bear on Book IV, and the conflict between them becomes focal as the book develops.

More than once, Book IV refers suggestively to Amoret as Britomart's love. A telling example occurs in Satyrane's tournament in canto v, when the lady knight will not forgo "her owne Amoret" for False Florimell (20). The possessive adjective "owne" accentuates Amoret's figural signification as Love: Britomart's own Amoret is both her friend and the love she possesses and continues to nurture. Earlier in this book, Britomart's abusive deception of Amoret ceases once she meets and overcomes the nameless, faceless knight outside the nameless castle in canto i, subsequently unhelmeting herself to reveal her womanhood and thus enabling all three of them (Britomart, Amoret, and the young male knight) to enter the castle, each as a pair (IV.i.10–13). The young knight's namelessness has particular significance in an allegory, one of whose characteristics is significant naming. His anonymity facilitates his interchangeability with Britomart, and hers with Amoret as well—a triangulation of the three, with the lady knight performing as Venus and Mars, simultaneously man and woman, and thus conceived as at once a mean point and a moving one. The mathematical diction seems appropriate. There is an abstract logic to the plot at this moment.

This new Britomart behaves differently from the one in Book III; she reveals her erotic beauty voluntarily and for a socially constructive purpose, not simply in response to discomfort within her armor, whether from a surge of emotion at the sight of the surging sea or a downpour outside the Castle of Malbecco, as happened in the third book. Britomart's self-revelation now comes while she still wears the rest of her armor, and it is actually more wondrous for combining the armor with her cascading golden hair. The narrator celebrates the occasion with rhetoric that at once recalls Acrasia's Venerean veil in the Bower of Bliss and the comet-like appearance of Florimell at the outset of Book III.[74] The imagery of fire and light rather than of showers or cloudbursts predominates:

> With that her glistring helmet she vnlaced:
>   Which doft, her golden lockes, that were vp bound
>   Still in a knot, vnto her heeles downe traced,
>   And like a silken veile in compasse round
>   About her backe and all her bodie wound:
>   Like as the shining skie in summers night,
>   What time the dayes with scorching heat abound,
>   Is creasted all with lines of firie light,
> That it prodigious seemes in common peoples sight.
>   (IV.i.13)[75]

All glistening, golden, fiery, and bright, there is nothing abstract about the cascading hair. With this unfolding of Venus from within Mars, the Venerean figure of Amoret draws "freely" and naturally to Britomart's bed in another memory of Book III, where Malecasta, free in the licentious sense, has earlier done so. This all makes figural sense. Amoret's attraction necessarily derives from her figural nature as "*Venus* mayd" (IV.x.54).

"All that night" the two women, inside the castle and together in bed, as old Glauce and Britomart were in Book III, "of their loues did treat" (1.16). In Spenser's time beds were valuable commodities, and it was common to share one. Notable are the plural "loues," the information in the immediately following lines that the two women "priuately bemone" one another's plight with "griefull pittie," and especially the conspicuous figural dimension of both women from the outset of Book IV, which here is singularly affected by Britomart's being divested of the armor that has increasingly become a part of her. These considerations noted, the phrase "their loues" remains susceptible to a homoerotic reading, which history justifies and others have observed. That this, and more, is Ate's reading later in the same canto ensures rather than erases its textual existence.[76] Without her armor, Britomart is more simply female, like Amoret.

The women's treating of their loves lasts all of four lines. At dawn, Britomart is revested (and reinvested) in armor, and she and Amoret ride again on a single horse, together a hermaphroditic silhouette atop that traditional symbol of passion. Again in an exteriorized, exposed, and less private landscape, they are not long on the horse before the fickle knight Blandamour challenges Britomart for possession of Amoret. Now occurs the strange but crucial stanza in which perspectives repeatedly oscillate between Britomart's and Blandamour's points of view and simultaneously between chivalric and erotic, outer and inner, and narrative and symbolic values. (All these pairs, especially the last pair, are not simply and synonymously exchangeable with each other, though all are in play.) Although familiar to Spenserians, the stanza bears citing:

> The warlike Britonesse her soone addrest,
>   And with such vncouth welcome did receaue
>   Her fayned Paramour, her forced guest,
>   That being forst his saddle soone to leaue,
>   Him selfe he did of his new loue deceaue
>   And made him selfe thensample of his follie.
>   Which done, she passed forth not taking leaue,
>   And left him now as sad, as whilome iollie,
> Well warned to beware with whom he dar'd to dallie.
>   (IV.i.36)

The combination of Britomart's armed form with the outward possession and expression of her own Amoret—*Amor*, her love—causes still further confusion between merely fleshed and more inclusively figural meanings—again, genuine confusion, not the simple fusion of both terms of a single binary. The combination is problematical: whether Blandamour is Britomart's or Amoret's "fayned Paramour" is uncertain, as are the location and identity of "his new loue"—inner or outer, Britomart or her Amoret. The motivations, erotic or chivalric, of Britomart and Blandamour are similarly uncertain, as are narrative and symbolic dimensions more broadly. A reader might even wonder whether the assault of the fickle Blandamour, the object of whose loves is ever shifting, is a further comment on the night Britomart and Amoret have spent together, an accusation of infidelity like Ate's, only eleven stanzas later (47–49). The result of the encounter of Blandamour with Britomart and Amoret is a blur, but a *meaningful* blur, analogous to—that is, like and unlike—the endless, undefined (formless), regressive, and chaotic fighting of the false friends in Book IV's first and ninth cantos. It is also a situation in a single stanza that is momentary; it cannot be lasting without signaling poetic negligence rather than poetic significance. Clearly significant, it participates in a recurrent pattern in the experimentally figured narrative of Book IV.

Amoret accompanies armed Britomart in the rest of Book IV only until Amoret walks off "for pleasure, or for need" while Britomart is sleeping, as Britomart recounts much later (vii.4). Said to be "vnwares" and, though in a forest, "of nought affeard," Amoret may suppose herself free of courtly danger, the only sort she knows, when she wanders off, or she may even fancy herself back with Pleasure, her youthful companion amid the myrtle trees in the Garden of Adonis. Then the figure of beastly Lust seizes her. Thereafter, abandoned by Belphoebe and Timias and found in the woods by Arthur, she returns to her former status as a separate figure with her own story line, such as it now is. She is now a desperately wounded figure who seems to have nowhere to go and no story to fit into. Arthur feels only pity for her, and she is a fifth wheel in the story of the look-alike squires and their morally compromised ladies, which comes next.[77]

It makes a kind of figural sense that Amoret should have to withdraw from Britomart's company before Britomart can achieve loving "accord"—heartfelt harmony—with Artegall (IV.vi.41). Yet even in this "accord," Amoret's presence lingers punningly: the word with which Spenser thus characterizes it plays etymologically on Latin *ad*, "to, toward," and *cor/cordis*, "heart," and phonologically on English *chord* and *cord*. English *chord* enriches the harmony signaled by the word *accord* itself, but resonant in the homonymous *cord* there is also a memory of the chain Busirane used to bind Amoret. Is the tie that binds creatively revised in the accord of Britomart and Artegall, or is this transformation merely apparent? Could the tie that binds still be enchainment? Submerged in a pun in Book IV, this question emerges openly in Book V, whose time, to paraphrase Merlin's prophetic words, is not yet. Puns can work this way in *The Faerie Queene*, as memorably in other writers of the period.

Earlier in Book IV, Britomart, fully suited and still with Amoret, fights Artegall in Satyrane's tournament and again later on foot, when her armor is breached as Artegall shears off her ventail, the first step toward a truce between them. When she and Artegall subsequently retire to solace and feasting, reach their "accord," consent to marriage, and are privately betrothed, Britomart is presumably unarmored, but this is a point the poem passes over in silence, perhaps signaling its lack of significance now

(IV.vi.39, 41).[78] When she and Artegall separate again—specifically and importantly with her assent (vi.43: "wonne her will")—and, promisingly, she now accompanies Scudamour in his search for Amoret, she is again armored and committed to "vertues onely sake, which doth beget / True loue and faithfull friendship" rather than to the marital love quest that initially led to her arming (vi.46). Clearly, Amoret no longer belongs to Britomart in the same sense as when Amoret was "her owne" in Satyrane's tournament (IV.v.20). Although in Book IV we never see Britomart without her armor after her accord with Artegall, the armor now appears more practical than significant. This situation will change again in Book V.

* * *

Before moving on to Book V, however, I want to look again at developments in the fourth book over which I have just skimmed—briefly to recapitulate Amoret's capture by Lust, along with her subsequent history in Book IV, and then more closely to examine the combat that leads to Britomart's and Artegall's accord, insofar as Britomart's armor plays a notably figural role in the latter and, doing so, provokes a nagging question: why does Spenser, the poet of the *Amoretti* and *Epithalamion*, deny the principal couple of the poem a conciliation less steely (and likely off-putting) than clashing and clanging armor? The mix of genres in Book IV hardly accounts for this denial. To my mind, the significance of Britomart's armor to this point is again the major reason for it, the inescapable specter of Busiranic art forms continuing to be another, as was evidenced in the hermaphroditic figure concluding the 1590 edition and as it will be again by Scudamour's *raptus* in the Temple of Venus.[79] A third reason is the persistent, recurrent, significantly thematized disjunction and confusion of the merely fleshly and the more inclusive figural, of the inner and outer, and of the narrative and the symbolic in Book IV that is at once exemplified and crystalized in the early encounter of Blandamour with Britomart and Amoret that I recently examined.

Achieving accord, Britomart's battle with Artegall surmounts these thematized problems, at least as much as is possible in Book IV. Seen retrospectively through the same problematized, thematic lenses, the poem then cedes Amoret to genital Lust, a bisexual, hence hermaphroditic, figure that could hardly be depicted in more explicitly physical, fleshy terms and one whose cave alludes parodically in its bisexuality to that beneath the Garden of Adonis.[80] Although Amoret escapes from Lust, as my last chapter indicated, she continues to be compromised in the narrative, which answers to events outside it, even while her figure is once and forever idealized by the sublating lyric voice of the Spenserian poet, who, for this purpose, abruptly and impulsively interrupts his bleak narrative of a night with Slander during the eighth canto, as also treated in chapter 2 (65, 67–69). In other words, in Amoret's story, apart from Britomart's, disjunction merely increases. Her reappearance in the Temple of Venus then becomes at once a discouraging memory of the forms that led to the House of Busirane in the first place and, perhaps, as I tentatively suggested, the defiant intimation of a rebeginning. Understandably, the figure of Amoret nonetheless disappears from the poem, evidently having become a property too hot for the poet to handle.

In contrast, for better or worse, the accord of Britomart and Artegall, the latter masking as the Salvage Knight, represents in armed combat the principle of erotic coupling in *The Faerie Queene*. Their combat, which simultaneously climaxes both their relationship and the first half of Book IV, is both focal and distinctive. Its position in a central canto of this book corresponds to that of the Garden of Adonis in Book III. In terms that I variously derive from Jean-François Lyotard on the figurality of the dream-work and from Ricoeur on iconic metaphor, their combat is highly figural—embodied but not simply fleshly—and, in the main, its contours are cognitive, imaginative, and affective, rather than directly emotional or passionate.[81] As a battle, the ur-conflict of epic romance, it is also a narrative moment in the poem that belongs to the quest, rather than to a statue, an extended emblem, or a lyric. It is full of mutual, developmental action.

In Ricoeur's theory, the iconic dimension of metaphor, which, like other figures of speech, has a "quasi-bodily externalization," also carries feeling (as distinguished from raw emotion). Ricoeur describes this feeling as a complex form of affection, intentionality, "interiorized thoughts," "felt participation," and the like (142, 154–55). Lyotard, opposing the Lacanian view that dream-work is a form of discourse, argues instead for its less abstract, more Freudian figurality; for Lyotard, "An imaged text is a discourse that is very close to the figure." Its proximity inheres in "the figurative power of a word, of course, but also the rhythmic power of syntax, and at an even deeper level, the matrix of narrative rhythm."[82] Addressing this matrix, Lyotard explains that, "The great linguistic figures, of discourse, of style, are the expression, right in the heart of language, of a general disposition of experience, and the phantasm is the *matrix* of that ordering, that *rhythm*, which will henceforth be imposed on everything that happens on the levels of 'reality' and expression" (245: my emphasis). As form, matrix, and rhythm, the figure "jam[s]" the communicative constraints inscribed in "any *language*. . . . By virtue of the fact that it sets up a closed circuit intercom system of the work with itself." Lyotard concludes that, "language, at least in its poetic usage, is possessed, haunted by the figure" (246).

Characterized by elemental and animal imagery, by reference to religious forms, by wounds, sweat, and blood, the combat of Britomart with Artegall is violent and erotic as well as figurative. It is sexually suggestive, for example, when Artegall "Thrust[s]" at Britomart from below as if "an eger hound" were thrusting "to an Hynd within some couert glade"; Artegall has a couchant hound on the crest of his helmet (presently masked by "woody mosse"), and a hind is a female deer.[83] Similarly suggestive, he next deeply wounds the "hinder parts" of Britomart's horse, that conventional symbol of bodily passion earlier shared by Britomart with Amoret (vi.13). But the combat of Britomart and the (still) Salvage Knight is not directly and immediately genital the way Lust's fleshy figure is, instead being relatively and significantly more masked, sublimated, and, in a word, civilized. Their combat is not merely chaotic and endless as is the initial and later battling of Blandamour, Paridell, and the like (e.g., ix.20–33). Rather, it has a kind of form and pattern, a rhythm and, crucially, a progression. It is at once Typhonic-Chthonic and dance-like— both explosive and generative, both Hate and Love, in terms I take from the Temple of Venus. This is the sort of figuration that Lyotard intends when he refers to the matrix of narrative rhythm.

In the heat of their encounter the knights exchange the roles of hunter and hunted recurrently—either of them "Sometimes pursewing, and sometimes pursewed" (vi.18).[84] Britomart wounds Artegall directly despite his armor: his "mayle [punningly male] yriv'd, and plates yrent," his blood pours to the ground (vi.15). In contrast, Britomart's armor twice deflects the force of Artegall's blows, his first consequential stroke glancing down her back to light on her horse:

> Like as the lightning brond from riuen skie,
>   Throwne out by angry *Ioue* in his vengeance,
>   With dreadfull force falles on some steeple hie,
>   Which battring, downe it on the church doth
>   glance,
>   And teares it all with terrible mischance.
>   (IV.vi.14)

With this imagery Scudamour's less violently graphic church-robbery later in the Temple of Venus comes to a rereader's mind, as does the earlier, bizarre containment of chaotic urge and violent desire in the religious idolatry and ritual battle of Satyrane's tournament, which, with all its primitive and parodic limitations, is a relatively civilizing form, greatly superior to the still more formless, endless fighting at the outset of this book (Blandamour, Paridell, etc.). The limitations termed primitive and parodic in the preceding sentence include Florimell's girdle enshrined within an ark, insistent images of animality and elemental force, and knightly figures named Bruncheval, Sangliere, Brianor, and Ferramont (Brown Horse, Wild Boar, Bear, and, ludically, Iron Mount). Similarly in the present combat, Artegall's lightning is significantly Jovian, formed into myth, as well as elemental. The steeple on which it falls is as pointedly phallic, moreover, as is Britomart's magic spear, which Artegall's Jovian blow to her horse renders ineffectual.[85]

Artegall's second crucial stroke lights on Britomart's helmet and glances harmlessly down the front of her body armor, yet it shears away her ventail en route and exposes her face, framed by wisps of golden hair, which is culturally coded female. This partial breach of her armor is an unmasking rather than a total divesting, however. The difference is vital for a poem in which masking, with its Busiranic potential for abuse, has been thematically recurrent and specifically vital for the figure of Britomart, whose armor is integral to her quest and whose outfolded figural *integrity* is armored. Now without her spear, Britomart crucially retains her raised sword, exactly as she did in her vulnerability both within Malecasta's bedroom and the House of Busirane. Yet no more than Artegall is simply lightning, hail, hound, Jove, or an idolator is Britomart simply her horse's animality, a church, an angel, an artwork, a goddess, priestess, or even her own armor. The armor itself, moreover, cannot be translated simply as her chastity, as Hamilton's second edition might suggest (e.g., 453n13.4). The armor is at once multivalent and responsive to specific context. By this point in the poem, it signals her agency and specifically her will to resist and act freely.[86] It further represents the force of her virtue, not merely its moral form but also its Machiavellian *virtù*, control and ability to effect, and Latin *virtus*, "power, strength, value."[87] *Virtus*, of course, derives from *vir*, "man." Most striking of all, Britomart's armor signifies her hardness and even her hate, again, as this concept appears in the Temple of Venus, as a cosmic force harmoniously, concordantly balanced by love, and finally, her armor signifies her masculinity, if not her maleness per se.[88]

Tellingly, Britomart's armor, though culturally coded male, has been a queen's from the start—a good "fitt," in the punning, physical sense of this word in the third proem.[89] Although her figure wears a habergeon, or coat of mail, it has never explicitly received the descriptor "mayle" (or male), a recurrent Spenserian pun applied to other knights. This is merely a negative piece of evidence about her, minuscule yet still notable. By the end of her battle with Artegall, her integrity has been *figured* not as anatomically doubled like the hermaphroditic statue imaged in 1590 but as truly, integrally both Martian and Venerean in effectual, psychological, and agential terms. In these telling respects, her figure is androgenous. The distinction between an adjectival and a nominal form, here between *androgenous* and *androgyne*, is relevantly significant, comparable to that between *allegorical* and *allegory*, distinctive property and defining literary form, for example. Distinguishing such verbal forms in terms of their grammatical and semantic functions, as in traditional logics and rhetorics, simultaneously enables preservation of relation and acknowledgment of difference: an allegorical figure, like one on a shield or in a tableau, is not just by virtue of the adjective a literary allegory if an allegory is a moving metaphor, that is, a narrative or dramatic one.[90] The adjectival form also sits more comfortably with mythic forms creatively revised within a moving, metaphorical narrative of the sort that is found in *The Faerie Queene* and most complexly exemplified by the story of Britomart. When Britomart finds Artegall, the difference between her evolving role as an actor and the function of an emblematic statue such as the bisexual Venus of canto x, not to mention the one that survives the capture of Busirane, becomes quite definite.

In a useful discussion of intellectual sources for Spenser's Garden of Adonis, Jon Quitslund highlights some aspects of Leone Ebreo's influential *Dialoghi d'Amore* of 1535, which bears on imaginative writing in England from Spenser through Donne and Milton.[91] Leone reverses the amorous roles our own age still considers conventional, not to say hegemonic or "normal." His male lover is maternal, and his engendering female beloved is paternal—the true father of love. Here, the woman's fatherhood occurs within a culture and context that still attribute originary potency to men, yet it is nonetheless striking that for Leone this fathering resides in the woman. As Quitslund summarizes Leone, "each sex or gender is not an autonomous entity but an aspect of mankind ('*l' homme*' in Tyard's translation).... 'Each of them has a masculine part, perfect and active, which is the intellect, and a feminine part, imperfect and passive, which is the body and matter'" (235). Clearly these parts are not reducible to genital differences, and they both underwrite human eros.[92] Suggestively in Leone's statement, sex and gender are also not differentiated from one another as fully or neatly as our age still tends to think of them.[93] The potential for their confusion is evident and often occurs in *The Faerie Queene*, whether in comic, threatening, or constructive modes, or in varied combinations of them.

In the combat of Britomart and Artegall, he is overcome by her beauty, available to him only in her flushed and sweating face, framed by wisps of hair. Once his phallic sword has fallen from his correspondingly "slacke" fingers, Britomart's long-lost nurse Glauce intervenes to persuade Britomart to offer Artegall a truce, which eventually turns out to be a mutual recognition of love or overwhelming attraction (vi.21). This enabling truce extends to Scudamour, still the totally conventional bearer of Cupid's shield. Glauce salutes Britomart with "seemely belaccoyle" and here, in effect, is transformed to a figure straight from *The Romance of the Rose* who helps the Lover gain access to the Rose, or nubile Woman (vi.25). This *Romance* (and its tradition) is another source at once underlying the Temple of Venus and Busirane's masquers. Not long after these pronounced inclusions of convention, Britomart accepts the unmasked Artegall as her future "Lord," or husband, another glance at conventional, sociocultural assumptions (vi.41).[94] Recognizing all these as shadows of the ever present Busiranic forms, I look again to Britomart's armor, still encasing her, as the sign of her strength—her virtue—even while her experience incorporates these reminders of contemporary erotic culture, including and subordinating them in what could be or become a better possibility. In this way, the accord of Britomart and Artegall is not simply a fiction opposed to contemporary culture and denying it. Instead, like metaphor and allegory, as a form of metaphor, whose "as if" is and is not, it doubles what we know and reaches beyond it.[95]

Any inclusion in the poem of the unreformed sociocultural past, which remains alive and well in Elizabethan England, brings subversive ironies and huge future risks, however. Relevantly and realistically, the concluding stanza of Book IV will reaffirm these, remarking ambivalently of Florimell's affection for Marinell: "Ne lesse was she in secret hart affected, / But that she *masked* it with modestie, / For feare she should of lightnesse be detected" (xii.35: my emphasis). The specter of Busiranic form is persistent.

Reversing Britomart's Figuration

As earlier indicated, Britomart's amor, having made its point, has little import in the rest of Book IV, but Book V is another matter. In this book, the armor is so undistinctive that Britomart's pairing with Talus leads to misrecognition of her armed figure as a substitute—merely a metonym—for Artegall. This new effort to transform her figure and willfully to unmake its complex wholeness is the more significant insofar as she does not participate voluntarily in it. To invoke my earlier pun, she does not per-*form* it. Instead, her figure is passively subjected to this change. Still more importantly, this process *openly* occurs *despite* her feelings and intentions. In other words, the poem makes sure that we notice it. It is as if figure and fated plot, figure and ongoing narrative—for Britomart, developed character and prophesied marriage—were somehow separate or separating, as memorably happens at times in Shakespearean drama, notably in *Hamlet*, wherein the prince resists his narrative fate, the familiar revenge plot. As William Morse has suggested, one word for such Shakespearean separation is *irony*, which might more broadly be glossed for my purpose as double vision.[96]

For Britomart, the first stage of this ironic process comes in the episode of misrecognition by Dolon and his sons, who mistake her for Artegall mainly because she has the iron man Talus with her. In the second stage, the authoritative priestly interpretation of her experience in Isis Church (i.e., the Temple of Isis), it comes in an emphatically ideological simplification of her figural integrity to this point.[97] Whereas in Book III, Merlin, together with Glauce, could offer the pubescent Britomart a future beyond herself that purposed her feelings without denying them, Isis's chief priest simply displaces them. Britomart, at this stage, is not the same uninitiated, "vnwares" girl she was early in Book III, and the distance between her experience in Isis Church and what the priest would make of it is glaring. A character's growth has consequences for her author, a developing creature for her creator, as any reader of *Paradise Lost* comes to see with respect to Eve, as well as to Adam and Satan. The more developed a character is, the harder it is to repurpose or reverse our awareness of her being.

The first and second stages, Dolon and Isis Church, are further comparable with respect to Britomart's armor. In Dolon's chamber, Britomart utters an impassioned complaint while fully armored, and, her helmet only unlaced, in Isis Church nonetheless experiences "troublous passion," "fearfull fright," and doubtful "dismay," all of which are justified by what is happening to her figural integrity, indeed, to her very being.[98] In the Temple, the flames that grow outrageously "vnwares," along with the rest of her visionary experience, recapitulate the course of her fearful fall into love, then her finding and fighting Artegall, his surrender, their accord, and Merlin's earlier prophecy of their future progeny, in short her history through Books III and IV (vii.14–16). Venus and Mars, infolded and unfolded opposites, her own inside and outside, are not at variance in the Dolon and Temple episodes, but her mature, composite figure is now quite at odds with the readings conspicuously imposed on it by others in the poem. The Merlin ploy, so to speak, is no longer enough. Britomart's being is no longer so simple.

The first of these misreaders is the deceitful Dolon, named for a Trojan spy who betrays his own side, ironically a side from whom the figure of Britomart is descended. The crow of a cock, "The Bird, that warned *Peter* of his fall," right before Dolon activates the would-be entrapping bed, suggests that Britomart's figure is experiencing some form, or forms, of self-betrayal—her jealousy, yes, but much more (vi.27, cf. 25). Who besides Dolon is betraying her self—Britomart, Artegall, the Spenserian narrator? Who is unclear, but Dolon is not alone. When Dolon misrecognizes Britomart, the narrator intervenes to let us know what is going on, but makes a point of telling us that Britomart does not know—"Now mote ye know (that which to *Britomart* / Vnknowen was)" (vi.31)—and that she will never know. He now treats Britomart the way he treated Guyon at the outset of Book III (i.8), whereas, at that earlier point, in contrast to this one, he respected her figural integrity. Now he seems to want us to notice that he no longer does. The next day Britomart meets two of Dolon's sons, who misrecognize her again and accuse her of killing the third son, but "Strange were the words in Britomartis eare," the narrator tells us, before she summarily dispatches the brothers (38).

Britomart's next misreader, her third, is Isis's chief priest, a celibate ascetic, and his interpretation smothers her richly mythopoeic vision of sexuality, birth, and death into wooden exegesis and legal-dynastic anodyne. Her fourth reinterpreter will again be the narrator himself, whose rendering of her final acts in canto vii, the battle with Radigund and its sequel, produces comparable reduction, then stasis.[99] This development is the final stage of her transformation. If we were to take the effectual disabling of Britomart's armor *only* to signal that her passionate response to Artegall's capture is excessive, that she must sacrifice herself to save

Artegall, or that the figure of Artegall has simply replaced hers through legal coverture, which could suspend a woman's "very being"—all readings to which her figure has been subjected by critics—we would have to overlook the fact that the poet appears to have written her journey precisely to make us notice this process of denial and suppression and to heighten our awareness of its ugly cost.[100] We might also notice in passing that coverture is absent actual marriage in Britomart's instance unless it is off stage, or page—that is, simply not there. We even assume her earlier betrothal, rather than witnessing it as we do Una's. Given opposition in Spenser's *Shepheardes Calender* and *Mother Hubberds Tale* to a marriage by the queen, the compromising of Britomart's identity as she travels toward Artegall adds a political dimension to our awareness of its personal cost. The poet has had further opportunity over time to reflect on these costs, and doing so has apparently affected his own awareness.[101] The recurrent confusion of the queen's two bodies in the poem has also made the danger to a woman's agency, indeed to her "very being," more threatening.

Britomart's climactic fight with Radigund reopens the issue of the armor's signification with a vengeance. Strikingly, the two women do not first fight with spears on horseback but on foot with curved swords, whose semicircularity qualifies their phallic potency. Like "a Tygre and a Lionesse" fighting to possess the carcass of some prey, they "hack" and "hew" each other, not sparing their breasts or other "dainty parts," the latter a coy phrase even without the whiff of Victorian priggery sensed by a modern reader (vii.29–30): "so dainty they say maketh derth," as the Spenserian sage once wryly forewarned us (I.ii.27). Furious, both women forget their martial skill and fight to maim and spoil as much as to win. There is a chaotic, disturbing excess to this battle that is wasteful specifically in sexual and generative terms: blood flows from their sides and gushes through their armor; they tread "in gore ... and on the ground their liues did strow, / Like fruitles seede, of which vntimely death should grow" (V.vii.31). As the whole encounter suggests, their battle is the undoing of Mars and Venus, tiger and lionesse, both.[102] Like the misrecognitions and misreadings of Britomart's figure earlier in Book V, battle and battlers participate in her figure's undoing. This narrator is now more than Dolon. He is Busirane, abusing and reversing his own forms.

The blood gushing from multiple wounds blazons Britomart's vulnerability to Radigund, but it is the blow glancing from Britomart's shoulder-plate to bite deeply to the bone instead of glancing harmlessly down her armor that signals most sharply the difference between the present encounter and her earlier combat with Artegall. Clearly the armor is now mere armor, finally and fully drained of its potency and multivalence. Of all the violations Britomart's figure receives in *The Faerie Queene*, this is the one that seals her figural fate, despite her summary dispatch of Radigund right after. Redcrosse's Pyrrhic victories over Error, Sans Foy, and Sans Joy come analogously and worrisomely to mind.

As the destructive wastefulness of the battle with Radigund has certainly suggested, killing Radigund, Britomart has lost too much of herself. Radegone, the city Radigund has named after herself, is the state of a selfish woman, enclosed upon itself, a mirror of self-regard. Yet if the only alternative to it is Britomart's repeal of the "liberty of women," this is also blatantly the repeal of her own figure as we have seen it developing in earlier books (vii.42).[103] In these books, she is self-centered in productive senses, and she has to be so. Otherwise she is a suit of armor with nothing at all within it, and certainly not a version of Venus. Like but also unlike Jove's brain child Athena, born after the god has swallowed the nymph Metis, Venus is born from the foamy sea-sperm outside and beyond a male god: Gaea (Earth) has brought this sea forth of herself; the sperm is that of castrated Uranus, son and husband of Gaea. "Male and female through commixture joynd" in this way, Venus quickly becomes a various, multiple, material other and a distinct form, who will only join Mars as an equal.[104]

* * *

When Book IV makes an issue of interpretive readings, it chiefly does so obliquely through modes and cumulative patterns of meaning. In comparison, Book V makes an outright and eventually blatant issue of such readings, to be followed in this kind of questioning still more blatantly and thematically in Book VI. The arch-villain of Book VI, the Blatant Beast, like his predecessors Ate, Slander, Envy, and Detraction, is ostensibly, at least, a vicious misreader. Put simply, in the interpretive context of Book V and of the books on either side of it, and especially in that of the conspicuously imposed misreadings that have accompanied Britomart to Radegone, I do not trust the narrative voice that tells me Britomart's replacement of women's liberty with their subjection to men is true justice, "That all they [the women?] as a Goddesse her adoring, / Her wisedome did admire, and hearkned to her loring" (vii.42). This voice is similar to, if still more excessive than, that of the priestly interpreter in the Temple of Isis. It does not belong to the poet of Book IV or Book III. From the beginning, Book V has more openly than ever before advertised its narrator as a persona, himself a mask, now to be trusted, now not, now within the fiction, now apart from it, as even a casual reading of the fifth proem makes clear.[105] The chaff of this persona's misreading comes home in Britomart's last appearance. Almost nothing is left of her figure, Venus within Mars, the richly valent figure of Books III and IV.

Although in Book III Merlin prophesied a son for Britomart and Artegall, the fulfillment of his prophecy defies belief in Book V. Now alone, Britomart leaves the poem in sorrow and anguish, seeking some other place, and Artegall, who earlier won the legendary armor of Achilles and whose name once intimated equality with the legendary Prince Arthur, rides off at last to become the equal of Arthur, Lord Grey de Wilton, chased out of Ireland by the Blatant Beast of Envy and Detraction.[106] Effectually, Artegall's figure enters present time, from which there will be no credible return to Faerie for him. Protesting his innocence of the charges against him, he appears just long enough in the restorative Faerie context of Book VI to pass the baton to Calidore and then, like Britomart, to vanish.

Whether the unnamed "Goddesse" to whom Britomart is assimilated at the end of her mission to subdue the liberty of women should be imagined as equitable Isis or as wise Minerva hardly matters. In either case, her divinity offers a substitute for Britomart's former figural integrity. As earlier in Britomart's progress through Book V, this assimilative process is basically metonymic and therefore substitutive, but with a final difference: the figure of Britomart now cooperates in it.[107] Her integrity bled out of her, so to speak, in the battle with Radigund, the process of her incremental figuration is finished by being undone. She is immobilized and effectually outside further narrative process. Now, she is properly statuesque. As a modern film-goer, I am reminded of the startling, disturbing transformation of a once lively face, that of Cate Blanchett's Elizabeth I, into the white grease-paint mask of Elizabeth's court portraits, the frozen mask-face on which the camera fixes at the end of Shekhar Kapur's 1998 depiction of this queen.[108]

* * *

Honoring the fact that an epic romance is by virtue of its structure potentially endless, I have two more observations about Britomart's figure in *The Faerie Queene*. I would stress again that the process by which her figure is reduced is *made* obvious to us in Book V. It is something that the Spenserian poet-narrator wants us to see. The only escape from an otherwise enveloping ideology is awareness of it and the agency this awareness makes possible. Awareness crucially comes first. This is what Britomart's progress through Books III and IV most importantly shows a reader, and in a different, more disturbing way, Book V does as well. But what is done to her figure in Book V, the Book of Justice, which by definition has no respect of persons, subjects her awareness to her function as a vehicle of merciful redemption for Artegall, after which she is effectually discarded, like Amoret. In both characterological and allegorical terms, her figure becomes subject to a changed context, a different surround, another lens, that of justice. But is this justice? This is the question Book V repeatedly asks about all its episodes. Again those inconsistent, problematical women in Shakespeare's plays also come back into view. In Britomart's instance, however, a narrator is openly involved at the end, in addition to a thematized change of context. We might ask what happens to the narrator or replaces a narrator's role when shifted to drama, as in the related instances of Shakespeare's figures of women, and conversely, what happens to dramatized silence (or silencing) when shifted to narrative. With respect to *The Faerie Queene*'s narrative in the books added in 1596, the role of the narrator, or poet-narrator, which has recurrently been self-reflexive, becomes outspokenly so regarding the ethics of his own culture. This fact makes the very end of Britomart's story, like the silencing of women at the end of Shakespeare plays, even more troubling. This could be precisely its point.

Chapter 4

Phantasies, Pains, and Punishments: A Still-Moving Coda

THE MAIN TITLE OF this chapter comes from the end of Busirane's pageant, where the narrator describes the "many moe like maladies" that he can neither count nor name, "So many moe, as there be phantasies / In wauering wemens witt, that none can tell, / Or paines in loue, or punishments in hell."[1] All these march in symbolic attire and accoutrements—"in masking wise"—as did the pairs that the narrator earlier named. They include mind-made and emotional disorders and their consequences. Moving from Spenser's major figures of women in *The Faerie Queene*, namely Una, Belphoebe, Britomart, and, to a related extent, Amoret and Florimell, to the rest, I newly appreciate the narrator's sense of inadequacy. The rest at this point seem endless. Writing in the early 1960s, Anne Paolucci compared Dante's women in *The Divine Comedy* to Spenser's in *The Faerie Queene*; her work was not published until 2005.[2] It includes brief chapters on the "Spectrum of Female Types," "Dress and Physical Features," "General Properties," "Techniques of Characterization" (figurative language, parallels, and the like), and, finally, "Allegorical Significance." Paolucci's book is relatively short and, in the main, her approach is general and taxonomic. Other, more recently conceived approaches, many included in my text and notes to this point, have valuably and more narrowly focused on a single topic or on one or more aspects of the women in Spenser's poem, such as Amazons or erotic politics, as well as on selected episodes, such as the initial portrait of Belphoebe or the Marriage of Rivers.[3] For the purpose of this final chapter, an approach between the all-inclusive and the highly selective looks like the best option. I derive it from my preceding chapters.

In them, a recurrent drumbeat has been the opposition or the paradoxical conjuncture of stillness and movement, constancy and change. Negatively, in further expansion of these terms, *stillness* suggests fixation and death; positively, it suggests inclusion, for example as conceptualization and lyric sublation (cancelation, continuity, and transcendence, each of which is partial). *Movement* positively suggests life, temporal development, and narrative; negatively, it suggests instability, shapelessness, inconstancy: in the *Mutabilitie Cantos*, "all that moueth, doth mutation loue," a resonant line that plays on the Renaissance commonplace that whatever lives moves and therefore changes (VII.vii.55). Stillness and movement hardly constitute the only binary relevant to figuration in *The Faerie Queene*, but they are a recurrent one, as noted, for example, in the description of Florimell "Still as she fledd," which anticipates the focal punning on still movement, "still moouing," in the *Mutabilitie Cantos*, as well as elsewhere in Spenser and other poets of the period, such as Jonson and Shakespeare (VII.vii.13).[4] Cosmic love and hate, attraction and repulsion, centripetal and centrifugal forces, for instance, are variations of another relevant binary, one that bears on the decisive battle between Britomart and Artegall in Book IV, yet this binary has proved less useful to my specific concern with the figurations of women that remain to be considered than has the relation of stillness and movement.

Among these are Duessa, Hellenore, Aemylia and Poeana, and Mirabella and Serena, most importantly this last pair in Book VI. As earlier suggested, it is in Serena's story, intersecting with Mirabella's, that the twinned stories of Amoret and Belphoebe both recognizably reappear and change profoundly. This recurrence involves a substantial refiguration—stillness and movement for each—that entails a new identity, as their new names in Book VI unmistakably indicate within this poem. The identity of each figure becomes at once more affective and more personal, signaling as well the Spenserian poet-narrator's sympathy for each. Deferring these refigurations until the present chapter, rather than trying to treat them in Belphoebe's, has respected the unfolding of Spenser's narrative and the crucial temporality of its movement, indeed, its still movement, in *The Faerie Queene*. This is a movement that includes sameness and difference, still points and changes, a memorable past and a present newness. It realizes a developing process of creative thought and exploration. Before turning to Serena and Mirabella, however, I want to account in a general way for the numerous figures of women I do not treat in detail and thereby at least to gesture toward the taxonomy that Paolucci offers. Stillness and movement are my organizing principles in what follows, or, more exactly, still movement is.

* * *

Figures of women found in a single location and condition in *The Faerie Queene* are situated—placed—in both these senses. They may move within their site but not beyond it: Alma moves within the body, for example, and Lucifera moves from her throne to a coach for a drive around her estate. Coelia's movement within the House of Holiness is implicit in the other figures dwelling there. This situated sort of figure is the good or evil genius presiding over a place: Lucifera, Coelia, Medina, Alma, Acrasia, Malecasta, Isis, Radigund, Mercilla, and, together, Nature and Mutability, who share Arlo Hill.[5] That the presiding figure in these rhetorical places, or cultural topoi, is a womanly figure is largely conventional, although the figures of Acrasia and Malecasta also have a specifically sexual and gendered charge, as do the figures of Radigund and Isis. Given that a queen reigned from the English throne for nearly the entirety of Spenser's lifetime, we generally recognize that many of the presiding figures glance at her in some way: for example, the maiden Queen Lucifera as a warning, and Queen Mercilla, her throne embossed with the royal arms of England, as a more direct representation. Radigund, Acrasia, and others have also been thought to allude to her.[6]

Acrasia, whose seductive figure occurs at the end of Book II, which, excepting only Amavia, otherwise features strumpets and virgins, has proved the most engaging and challenging of these figures of women for contemporary readers. Her figure is central to questions of sex and gender in *The Faerie Queene*. Accordingly, although I have treated her and her Bower of Bliss elsewhere in detail, I want to pause over her image at least in a truncated version here, before returning to further enumerations and distinctions.[7] My pause starts with the second view of Acrasia that readers get. This view begins where the first left off, with the captivated Verdant's "sleepie head" softly positioned in her lap, following sexual intercourse. (II.xii.76). The stanzas describing her, this time without intrusive moralizing, speak affectively and effectively for themselues:

> Vpon a bed of Roses she was layd,
>   As faint through heat, or dight to pleasant sin,
> And was arayd, or rather disarayd,
>   All in a vele of silke and siluer thin,
>   That hid no whit her alabaster skin,
> But rather shewd more white, if more might bee:
>   More subtile web *Arachne* cannot spin,
>   Nor the fine nets, which oft we wouen see,
> Of scorched deaw, do not in th'ayre more lightly flee.

> Her snowy brest was bare to ready spoyle
>   Of hungry eies, which n'ote therewith be fild,
>   And yet through languour of her late sweet toyle,
>   Few drops, more cleare then Nectar, forth distild,
>   That like pure Orient perles adowne it trild,
>   And her faire eyes sweet smyling in delight,
>   Moystened their fierie beames, with which she thrild
>   Fraile harts, yet quenched not; like starry light
> Which sparckling on the silent waues, does seeme more bright.
>
> (II.xii.77–78)

The audible attraction of the words and rhythm in these lines, reinforced by visual, tactile, and other sensuous and associative suggestions, is amazing. Like the word "crime" at the end of the Song of the Rose in Acrasia's Bower, the word "sin," rhyming with "thin," "skin," and "spin," is barely distinguished in this context.[8] By the outset of the second stanza, it has effectually been forgotten, and, if we actually read and listen without presuming misogyny, the narrator sounds as eager to enjoy this "snowy brest" as either to scorn "hungry eies" that greedily seek "spoyle" or to decry Acrasia's readiness. The appeal of the stanzas exceeds sharply defined barriers of gender and other rational determinants. At moments, the landscapes and soundscapes of Acrasia's Bower, which further express her, evoke a sense of wondrous pleasure that together with her own image has often been likened to the description of Shakespeare's Cleopatra at Cydnus (and elsewhere), who, where "Other women cloy / The appetites they feed, . . . makes hungry / Where most she satisfies."[9]

Jean-Luc Nancy's philosophy of the image, primarily the painted image but also the literary one, is here suggestive for its use of such terms as *reflection*, or mere mirroring; of *form* as essential surface and force, and of affective participation and contagion. Nancy observes that, "Even when the image is mimetic, it must fundamentally by itself and for itself, count for more than an image; otherwise, it will tend toward being nothing but a shadow or a reflection [a mirroring]." For Nancy, who addresses both Renaissance and modern images, the "*mimesis* [of the image] encompasses *methexis*, a participation or a contagion through which the image seizes us." The surface of the image is "Not an 'idea' (*idea* or *eidolon*), which is an intelligible form, but a force that forces form to touch itself."[10] Similarly, an image in allegory Acrasia may be, but, as image, she, like her garden, nonetheless exceeds and surpasses rationality, or even intelligibility, alone.

That an image in an allegory of temperance should do so is in some way a greater expression of artistic power than that one less morally contextualized should. Acrasia's image compels participation—perhaps contagion—and serves to suggest the power Spenser's situated figures of women can project.

Acrasia's veil, spun as subtly as, or even more subtly than, a web by Arachne, suggests arachnidan entrapment, of course, but as a woven fabric, or text (Latin *textum*: "web, fabric, text"), it also associates Acrasia with Book II's Palmer, since he, like her—or is it she like him?—is a fabricator, a maker of nets, and, elsewhere in Book II, a spinner of landscapes and stories. In short, Acrasia, like the Palmer and also like the Spenserian poet, is an artist.[11] Ovid's Arachne, last discussed as a presence in Busirane's tapestry and here implicit in Acrasia's art, is a woman bold (too bold as her tale eventuates) in protesting the violent excesses of the gods' passions and one whose protest is depicted with positive sympathy and possible ambivalence by the male Roman poet.[12] As Ovid depicts Arachne's weaving, it is deeply subversive, and reference to it in describing Acrasia conveys this suggestion as well. Arachne's eyes gaze defiantly, intertextually back from her image, and, whether they are beside or within Acrasia's, they are ostensibly, disturbingly those of a woman for viewers with eyes to see them. Like the figures in Busirane's pageant, including his figuration of Amoret, and like Leda in his tapestry, Acrasia can be read from both a man's and a woman's point of view, and appropriately so, insofar as she inhabits a cultural site.

Listing the major, situated figures of women, and illustrating the potency of their roles by its most powerful example, Acrasia, I have set aside the figure of Venus in the Garden and Temple of Books III and IV, respectively, first because Venus is a mythic goddess and second because, in Book III, her avatar is seen outside as well as inside the Garden, of which Adonis, not she, is the eponymous figure.[13] In the Temple, Venus is a statue, albeit one to whom Scudamour attributes sexes, gender, assent, and thus animation; her spirit certainly animates the place. Isis is a goddess and a statue, too, and perhaps I should have set her aside with Venus, but the historical origin (among others) that Plutarch attributes to her was well known in Spenser's time, and her relation to Britomart leads me to keep her within my present list. A sea nymph, such as Cymoent, and Chrysogonee, daughter of a faerie, belong to another order of figural being—earthly and natural, yet nonetheless mythic. My concern in this chapter is primarily with more distinctly human figures.

Reviewing my list of the major, situated figures of women to this point, and excepting traditional figures of myth, I note that the romance Books, III, IV, and VI, do not have as pronounced a centering figure of this type or as many of these as to be found in Books I, II, and V. In the romance books, the womanly figure (or figures) is less centripetal and contained (in both senses), another suggestive change reflecting the romance form. In these books, the extremes of woman on a pedestal or in the brothel, woman as either virgin or strumpet, are likewise loosened. In the Renaissance, romance was traditionally and not surprisingly associated with women as readers. Of course, there are additional, minor Spenserian instances of womanly figures who remain in a single location and condition, such as Corceca (and her daughter) and the witch and her son (another incidental alignment of Una's experiences with Florimell's). Also memorably situated are Amavia, Phaedria, Slander, Poeana, Lady Munera, and Briana, the last together with a number of other figures of women in Book VI. As here, my examples are exemplary rather than exhaustive, and my groupings include localized figures in other respects quite disparate.[14] A poem as massive and various as Spenser's invites provisional groupings that attend to differences and exceptions, while resisting tight categorization.

Most often, the quest of a protagonist leads into the houses, or situations, of centering woman-figures such as Lucifera, Coelia, Alma, and Acrasia, and the condition encountered there bears in some way on the quest itself. That is, the landscape of quest effectually includes these places, even while they are set apart from it, and the resident woman-figure who presides over each place is for a time (or time-out) its focal expression. But it is the visitor who is changed, informed, tempted, initiated, imperiled, or otherwise affected, not the tutelary denizen of the place or topos. Even the capture of Acrasia or the death of Radigund effects no change in what either figurally is, although it violently arrests the former's spell and it claims, at great cost, to eliminate the latter's injustice. The presiding figure is basically fixed and isomorphic with her location, whether she is good or evil, whether she is depicted with psychic depth like the glittering, discontented, joyless Lucifera, beneath whose House is a hell, or whether she is depicted more simply like the bead-bidding, physically aged yet spiritually joyful Coelia.[15] She might be fascinating for imagistic, historical, theological, or other sociocultural reasons, but not primarily in herself, so to speak. That is, not primarily as a person with her own story, or narrative. This difference strikes me again as important, and it is a narrative difference, as the preceding chapters have shown.

* * *

Other Spenserian figures of women besides the major ones move into different places and contexts, and at least one, Duessa, has a role in four different books: I, II, IV, and V. She is Arthur's nearest competitor in this respect. Like Acrasia's, her womanly figure, the radical enemy of Una's figure, as treated in chapter 1, asks for additional attention. Duessa's thematic and historical manifestations change in the course of the poem, but she remains at bottom the same—fundamentally wicked and duplicitous, in this regard a constant that is minimally affected by her changing situations. (Compare Belphoebe's more virtuous fixation?) If Duessa's condition is still moving, it is so in a perverse sense. Movement and stillness are for her little more than illusions, as they are for her sidekick in Book IV, namely Ate, or hellish discord, "raised," presumably by Duessa, "from below / Out of the dwellings of the damned sprights" (IV.i.19). Like the walking dead in Busirane's pageant and the "carcas dead" of False Florimell, neither Duessa nor Ate is capable of changing. Theirs is a negative life that feeds on the living like a necrotic disease, thus realizing the traditional sense of evil as negation. This is why Duessa pleads for Redcrosse's life in Book I when Orgoglio threatens to destroy him (vii.14): she *needs* him to live. Like Archimago, Duessa assumes various guises in the poem, some comic, others debatably so, but none leads to good. Evil lacks dignity—human worth, as defined in chapter 1. It is fissiparous, seeking incoherence, formlessness, disorder, cosmic hatred, dis-creation as its end and, in personified form, doing so on purpose. (As Milton discovered in *Paradise Lost*, the sense in which Evil, literally the personified abstraction Satan slips into, is free remains at best a knotty conundrum.) Unmasked in Book I, Duessa is monstrous, and her escape into the wilderness recalls her earlier passage in Night's chariot to Hell, via a parodic allusion to the wooded entrance into the *Aeneid*'s underworld—in the traditional interpretation, thus entering the nether world through matter (*hyle, silva*).[16] Although she returns to the poem in various guises thereafter, she remains fundamentally wicked and duplicitous, *Duo-esse*.

The last of Duessa's appearances, which occurs in Mercilla's court in Book V, might appear to challenge her figuration in the first two and fourth books, though I doubt it.[17] Her figure participates in the vexed problem of justice that Book V explores. In the episode at issue, the figure of Mercilla barely, only nominally, masks reference to the living Queen Elizabeth, as do Duessa to Mary Stuart and Duessa's trial to Mary's. To say that this episode has been much discussed would be an understatement; the poem makes the issues involved in the trial unavoidable.[18] The problem is that Duessa's figuration comes too close to history, bringing with it the complexities of human life and justice in a real-life world. At the same time, her figure, nominally a fictional one, has become oddly attenuated—again hardly more than a name—and effectually abstracted from movement, as well as subjected to one near-bodiless abstraction after another: Zeal, Kingdom's Care, Authority, Religion, Pity, Regard of Womanhead, Danger, Nobility, Grief. Even Ate is now said to testify against Duessa/Mary, her brief testimony suggesting that of a co-conspirator turned witness for the prosecution and furthering the discord on which she thrives. Ate, like Duessa, has a body to match her intent, a "lying tongue ... in two parts diuided" and feet that simultaneously move in opposite directions, one going backwards, one forwards (IV.i.27). Reminding us of Duessa's misdeeds in earlier books, the narrator makes specific mention of Ate's mischief in Book IV, where this hag was introduced into the action by Duessa, raised from hell as we heard.[19] Ate's testimony adds another flurry of charges, this time including several more personal ones—Incontinence, Adultery, and Impiety, along with Murder and Sedition. Seemingly a collective noun for all social, political, and personal ills and thus a common name, Duessa has little other figural substance in Book V. She remains wicked and duplicitous, nominally figured still as a woman, even while her figuration signals, not to say screams, that something is wrong here, perhaps in this way also figuring the voice of the poet whose tongue is nailed to a post at the very entrance to Mercilla's court. If so, the poet has effectually, startlingly become another cross-gendered figure in this same episode, as well as a self-reflexive one.

Joan Copjec offers a Lacanian description of Vergil's Fama (rumor or report) as a paranoid image of the dismembered body that casts a suggestive light on Spenser's silenced and immobilized poet and its self-reflexive cross-gendering. This paranoid image of dismemberment "appears at a point where the narration has reason to doubt its own omniscience, its own position as source of knowledge"; it is at this point that "a cry [in the form of Fama] is torn from the throat of the narrative which [forcefully] reattaches it to the events of the world."[20] Like Fama, Spenser's poet, tongue nailed to a post, can be seen as "a "hypostasized image of speech, an intrusion that is simultaneously the very substance of the narrative"—indeed, in my terms, its own self-reflexive commentary (44).

This silenced, immobilized poet, dubbed Malfont, inescapably recalls the figure of another womanly figure in Book V, Lady Munera, whose hands and feet are nailed to a post to become an emblem of the brutal miscarriage of true justice. Munera is duplicitous in more than a moral sense, her figure being double-sided and having, with utter equivocation, hands and feet of precious metal or else of human flesh, that is, figurative or real ones.[21] In Book V, Duessa, the very agent of division, similarly lacks *figural integrity* in a way she earlier did not. Earlier, she was herself single-mindedly wicked and divisive, with a monstrously misshapen body, once she is unmasked in Book I, to match her evil intent. Nominally, in her final appearance in Mercilla's court, she has a past in the poem that her name signals, but her attenuated, nigh-bodiless, abstracted presence explicitly, overwhelmingly also signals her dubiously just transfiguration into a woman once actually living—Mary Stuart. As in the episode involving Artegall and Burbon, which soon follows the trial of Duessa/Mary, here Faerie fiction temporarily collapses into history.[22] (A Spenserian pun on the derivation of *temporarily* from *tempus*, "time," is welcome.)

Aside from Duessa, the more interesting figures in the mobile grouping of relatively minor figures of women are those with some degree of movement within a canto or between cantos within a single book. Although lacking the prominence of the mobile figures of women treated in my first three chapters, who either play a central role in one book or play significant roles in several books or do both, such figures are more than features of the landscape and often are problematical or puzzling with respect to it. They appear after the tightly structured Books I and II and especially in the books with romance structures. Among them are Pastorella, Aemylia, Mirabella, and Serena, on the four of whom I will spend the rest of this chapter. Each of them has narrative life—a story. I shall consider Hellenore here as well, in part for lack of somewhere else to put her and also in part because her husband Malbecco usually gets all the coverage, despite the fact that she, too, has a notable story.[23] She is also thematically relevant.

Malbecco becomes a fixated form, Hellenore a form of natural mutability. Curiously, only Una and Hellenore get to spend time in the woods with satyrs. Both episodes are comic, one high, the other low, and both also celebrate nature. In Una's experience, this is mainly kindness conceived as generosity, in Hellenore's as hyperbolized sexuality—merely animal as portrayed, but also vital, alive by contrast with Malbecco's fixated fate as Jealousy, and, indeed, a kind of *energeia*. Instead of expressing surprise at the relatively sympathetic, if also ironic, tone of the narrator's treatment of Hellenore, we might look at Spenser's fabliaux elements in Book III through a Chaucerian rather than a Victorian lens and see this tone for what it is. As his narrator comically remarks of Hellenore, "not for nought" she "loued [the satyrs] so well / When one so oft a night did ring his matins bell" (III.x.48). The punning, bawdy, double negative is tonally telling, as is that irreverent moment of sacred parody in the matins bell. Hellenore's mobility and mutability enable her escape from what Malbecco is: an unnatural, frozen, deathly being, comparable to the figure of Despair in Book I, as well as to Busirane's masquers. When Hellenore chooses ("chose") "emongst the iolly *Satyres* still to wonne," she freely and parodically embraces a form of still movement—always (still) moving—but a vital, living one in this instance (x.51).

In chapter two, in connection with Amoret, I described Aemylia and Poeana, both found in Book IV, as morally compromised figures insofar as they have been marked by lust. The look-alike squires they are to marry are similarly marked, although one of them is lustful, gigolowise; he is so on behalf of friendship in order to free his look-alike from the dungeon of Corflambo, another figure of lust, who has separately seized the imprisoned look-alike, namely, Aemylia's lover. But this is multi-figured romance, and I get ahead of the complicated story. Aemylia, daughter of a "Lord of high degree," encounters Amoret in the cave of Lust and tells her how she was seized by this cave-creature when she attempted, against her father's and "all her friends" wishes, to meet her lover Amyas, a squire of low degree, and "away to flit" with him (IV.vii.16–17). Hardly by coincidence, this failed tryst happened the same night Corflambo seized Amyas, before the actualization of the lovers' tryst and apparently as a substitute for it. The rest of Aemylia's story includes her rescue, in sequential order, as a result of Amoret's flight from Lust, Belphoebe's killing this cave-creature, Arthur's aiding the abandoned Aemylia and Amoret in the forest and his night with these two women and Slander, then Arthur's killing Corflambo, and finally Aemylia's happy reunion with her lover Amyas. This reunion apparently countenances Aemylia's violation of her father's and friends' wishes, although only after hardships and the death of mutual lust (the figures Lust and Corflambo).[24] Viewed in this light, so far the story of Aemylia and Amyas bears witness at once to suffering and to reform, that is, to change for the better. In this respect, it looks ahead to Book VI.

Yet the imprisoned Amyas, whom Poeana wants as her lover, has already granted her wishes, though coldly, we hear, in the hope of winning his freedom. He is only freed, however, when Placydas, his look-alike friend, intervenes, an effort that unexpectedly leads to the death of Corflambo at Arthur's hands and then to the liberation of his castle. Again, I am ahead of the story and need to fill in the parts of Poeana and Placydas, as I shall after pausing to offer a mnemonic assist with the confusion of names and roles in this foursome. That it is needed (as I hope by now to have demonstrated) strategically underscores the extent to which they are relatively attenuated figures, simple in striking contrast to Una, Belphoebe, and especially Britomart. The foursome's tangled story is a bare exemplum, so much so as to enable a reader to recognize that it actually parodies the interlaced complications of the romance form, even as it accentuates sociable interlinkages in this, the Book of Friendship.

Conveniently, the alliterating A-names, the coupled Aemylia and Amyas, both phonically suggest love and friendship, Latin *amo* and French *ami*, and the P-names, Poeana and Placydas, also go together. The latter two suggest Latin *poeana*, "punishment, satisfaction" on the one hand and, on the other, Latin *placeo*, "to please, satisfy." In short, together the P-names signal pain and pleasure. A. C. Hamilton notices that, twice in the 1596 edition, Poeana's name is later spelled "Paeana," from *paean*, "a shout of joy," and he takes the new spelling to reflect her changed condition—in my terms, formerly pain but now pleasure for both lovers (473n49.4–7). Hamilton also takes Poeana's punishment as the pain and grief of her rejection, that is, as the coldness of the love, or rather lust, that Amyas nonetheless grants her.[25] But it might better refer to the death of her father and her surrender of control to Placydas in the end, and I take it to do so. She pays for her pleasure.

Placydas, having learned of his friend Amyas's imprisonment by Corflambo and his daughter, manages to insert himself into the prison and to pose as his look-alike friend. Coming to Poeana without the restraint of a former erotic commitment to another woman, he satisfies her lust and eventually abducts the keeper of the keys to her prison, absconding with both keeper and keys. This is the point at which Corflambo, Poeana's father, follows in wrathful pursuit, meets Arthur, and is duly beheaded.

Poeana's castle is then liberated through a ruse, the requisite scene of recognition occurs, and Placydas accepts Poeana "to his wedded wife," along with "all her land and lordship during life" (ix.15). The happy foursome, Amyas, Aemylia, Placydas, and Poeana, all formerly lustful and all now reformed, look like a parodic, more imperfect, and arguably more human version of the idealized foursome Canacee, Triamond, Campbell, and Cambina met earlier in the same book (IV).

Substitution, extending even to the old woman's substituting for Aemylia in the cave of Lust, is so conspicuous in the story of the present foursome as to become itself an issue, as Jonathan Goldberg noticed long since.[26] Perhaps through substitution with Aemylia, Poeana, whose two names (Poeana, Paeana) fit Aemylia's story along with her own, might also be considered a mobile figure: even though Poeana remains in her castle, her father extends their range outside it, and, far more significant, she reforms, even getting a new name or at least a meaningful new spelling of her old name, as if she had actually changed her location together with her condition.[27] This would be yet another strange variant of still movement, one that complements Aemylia's and Amyas's constancy in the course of changed locations.

Yet, with all this substituting, it is remarkable that Aemylia does not for a moment take Placydas for Amyas when she first sees him. She recognizes Placydas as Amyas's friend: embracing him, she inquires, "And liues yet *Amyas*?" to which Placydas immediately responds in the third person as well, "He liues . . . and his *Aemylia* loues" (viii.63). Continuing the same stanza, she replies, after reference to her own trials, in the present tense, "what mishap thus long him fro my selfe remoues?" and Placydas again recounts the tale of his effort to free Amyas that he has already told Arthur. (That he has already done so further enforces our awareness that he is Placydas.) Only Poeana, her perception weakened by lust, is wholly fooled by the look-alike squires, as is Lust in the dark cave by the old woman. Evidently, likeness is not identity, and difference still matters, except to Lust. But the more significant takeaway in the present story is the possibility of reform among the compromised and fallen, apparently after or through suffering of some sort. Amoret alone seems excluded (by Belphoebe) from this ethic of forgiveness in Book IV. She escapes Lust's cave only to be actually wounded by Lust.

In Book VI, Serena's story, which resonates variously and recurrently with Amoret's, spans six cantos (iii–viii) and overlaps with Mirabella's in two of these (vii–viii, although Mirabella is briefly mentioned in vi).

Mirabella's story resonates at first distantly and then more closely with that of Belphoebe, as it alludes unmistakably to the reigning queen. Notably, Belphoebe and Mirabella even share part of their names, Bel/bella (beautiful, beauty). Both Serena's and Mirabella's stories also concern choice, fortune, and responsibility, which are interlocked thematically throughout Book VI, and thereby they serve to introduce the more localized stories of Melibee and Pastorella in cantos ix–x (and with a difference in cantos xi–xii).[28] Agency is a major theme in Book VI, and Serena's and Mirabella's participation in it goes a long way emotionally to deepen and personalize their figures, especially Serena's.

Synoptically, Serena moves from dalliance with Calepine, to the venomous bite of the Blatant Beast, to rescue by the Salvage Man, to a second rescue by Arthur and then, together only with Timias, to ministration by the old hermit. Later, she flees the prospect of Mirabella, her torturers, and their captives, now including Timias, and finally, she is captured by cannibals, from whom Calepine saves her, if anyone really can. This overview makes a point: no other character in *The Faerie Queene* has a story that less fits her name than does Serena (from Latin *serenus/-a*, "fair, serene," usually in reference to the weather, but tropologically, "glad, joyous, tranquil"). Serena keeps moving from one location to another, apparently constant to Calepine, although her stillness in this respect is not emphasized to the extent that his is. Whereas he searches actively for her, she seems only to move from place to place. What comes to the fore is her constant misery and finally her total lack of serenity, which looks as much like self-cancellation as does Turpine's total ignominy—his ultimate namelessness (< Latin *in*, "not," and *nomen/-inis*, "name")—his fate of inverted, degraded, dis-figured knighthood in this same book. Further pertinent to self-cancellation is Timias's shaming, or loss of honor (Greek *timē*, "honor," "dignity," "worth"), the source of his name, at the hands of Mirabella's tormentors.[29] His having caused, if accidentally, the wounding of Amoret by Lust in Book IV might be seen in this loss to catch up with him.

Defeat of the Blatant Beast is the objective of the nominal protagonist of Book VI, Calidore, knight of Courtesy. This Beast serves Envy and Detraction; he specifically wounds human names, that is, human identity and dignity, thus specifically human being: no other kind of wound "so sore doth light, / As doth the poysnous sting, which infamy / Infixeth in the name of noble wight" (VI.vi.i). Names, though not always in the same way, have been highly significant throughout the poem. Serena's story, which meaningfully intersects with those of multiple others in Book VI—Calidore, Turpine, the Salvage Man, Arthur, the hermit, Timias, Mirabella, the cannibals, and, of course, her lover Calepine and the Blatant Beast[30]—also presses and probes hard questions about the relation of responsibility to fortune and of agency to suffering and in doing so bears some relation, not only to Amoret's story, but also to Florimell's, as remarked on several occasions in chapter 1. Serena's story presses this relation to a degree and an extent that Florimell's does not in Books III and IV, however.

Spanning six cantos in Book VI, Serena's story indicates a thematic importance at once continuous and developing that is not usually attributed to her figure. Converting it into economic, colonial, political, religious, and other ideological dimensions in selected incidents can be illuminating (and has been), but tropicality, especially discontinuous tropicality, cannot replace or displace her figural basis, which is distinctly that of a woman and which I mean to reaffirm.[31] At its most pronounced, such tropic conversion itself becomes the cancelation of her own identity as a womanly figure. Ironically, with the destruction of her serenity, this has proved, not surprisingly, indeed her fate. In her figure, the violence of tropic extremity finally takes over. Although I do not share the view that allegory is ipso facto violent, its abuse can be.[32] *The Faerie Queene* examines and brutally exposes this fact—this catachrestic, Busiranic allegory—in the story of Serena, as it does less affectively and complexly in the trial of Duessa/Mary Stuart. Significantly, this fuller exposure occurs in Book VI, not in earlier books and certainly not in Book I, in which the dominant figure of a woman is Una, or even in the relatively more symbolic and sublated—artistic and civilized—horrors of Busirane in Book III, in which the dominant figure is Britomart. Book VI, whose arch-villain is a blatant and beastly misuser of language, is still more fundamentally and insistently about words, names, interpretations, and poetic forms, and Serena is its major figure of a woman.

If Serena's trials are not treated in detail, as they regularly are not, what matters in her story, which is also the story of her figuration, gets lost. What follows will accordingly be detailed. Serena's trials begin when Calidore happens upon her together with Calepine, enjoying "their quiet loues delight" in the shade of a covert (VI.iii.21). Mutual abashment overcome, the two knights pleasure themselves with knight-talk, and Serena, both shut out of the conversation and

> Allur'd with myldnesse of the gentle wether
> And pleasaunce of the place, the which was dight
> With diuers flowres distinct with rare delight,
> Wandred about the fields, as liking led
> Her wauering lust after her wandering sight,
> To make a garland to adorne her hed,
> Without suspect of ill or daungers hidden dred.
>   (VI.iii.23)

This is the point at which the Blatant Beast catches her "vnaware . . . thus loosely wandring here and there" (24). Even without the last five words of narrative commentary, which feature the third use of *wander* within seven lines, now modified by the adverb "loosely," Serena's aimless movement, led only by her fluctuating, wavelike pleasure, is clearly narrated as too heedless for so pleasurable a place, a *locus amoenus* and implicitly an idyllically pastoral one to boot. Her occupying herself with her own adornment, a garland of flowers for her head, mindless of danger the while, is as ominous a note as the distance beat of approaching danger heard in a melodrama. The culling of flowers is a common figure of "proper choice."[33] Yet the "myldnesse of the gentle wether" is naturally alluring to her precisely because she is *Serena*, "fair, serene," usually in reference to mild and gentle weather and, tropically, to a condition of gladness, joy, tranquility. She is where she naturally belongs, allured by nature herself, here the springlike weather. Her "lust," which ranges in meaning from "pleasure, to delight, to desire," is hardly unnatural or wicked, and (*pace* Hamilton), she is not seized and wounded simply by monstrous Lust, as Amoret was, but by the vicious mouth of the Blatant Beast, a venomous attack from without. The Beast's venom soon spreads within, however, going beyond the vicious social offense of gossip or slander that first wounds Serena, to eat away at her self-respect—her self-worth, as we took to calling it in the twentieth century, according to the *OED*.

Later in this same book, Melibee will spend "all the night in siluer sleepe" and attend all day to whatever he pleases, to what he "listes," that is, "lustes" in a variant spelling; carelessly, he will also lay his "limbes in euery shade . . . And drinke of euery brooke" (ix.22–23). The vulnerability of either figure, Serena or Melibee, a woman or a man, results from self-indulgent imprudence, once we accept an invitation to read allegorically and, more exactly here, morally: prudence is a cardinal virtue. In Serena's instance, however, the failing is far less deliberated and less willful than in Melibee's.[34] She appears to be young and is certainly "vnaware" and inexperienced, as we have been told. Moreover, Serena's plight implicates Calepine's inattentive thoughtlessness as much as her own. Calepine and Calidore are discourteous in their self-centered knight-talk, and the result, exceeding any offense, is the serious wounding of the vulnerable Serena,

> Crying aloud in vaine, to shew her sad misfare
> Vnto the Knights, and calling oft for ayde,
> Who with the horrour of her haplesse care
> Hastily starting vp, like men dismayd,
> Ran after fast to reskue the distressed mayde.
> (VI.iii.24)

The rhyming play on "mayde" in the last two of these lines mocks the knights' manhood, their humiliating failure to protect a vulnerable woman, and the rhyme word "misfare" virtually becomes Serena's motto from this time forward. From a prefix meaning "badly, mistakenly, amiss" and a noun (or verb) meaning "journey," *misfare* is "The action or process of going wrong or astray; a mishap, misfortune, ill-fate."[35] Hamilton glosses the phrase "haplesse care" in the same passage simply as "trouble," but "haplesse" more likely means "unfortunate," a meaning that evokes the word "fortune," which, as we know, together with responsibility, is thematic in this book; besides "trouble," "care" indicates "mental suffering, sorrow, grief."[36] In passing, I note again that Serena is here a "mayde," her dalliance with Calepine notwithstanding. Indeed, the Beast's intention is to drag her into the woods and to "spoyl" her, that is, "to destroy, injure bodily, ravish," or otherwise "violate" her.[37] The instability of figurative and physical dimensions in her plight is conspicuous. They are coextensive. The Beast's malice endangers her whole being.

Having forced the Beast to drop his victim, Calidore pursues him, disappearing from sight until canto ix, and the story of Calepine and Serena, now together, now apart, becomes the Book's major thread. Calepine, on foot, with the badly wounded Serena on his horse—imagined in silhouette, the three an emblem of passion's wound—seeks assistance and shelter from Turpine, who first denies these and then assaults and seriously wounds the unmounted, disadvantaged knightly protector of the wounded Serena.[38] At this point, the Salvage Man, another figure of natural compassion, appears, chases Turpine off, and takes the wounded knight and lady to his forest dwelling in a "gloomy shade" (iv.13). Under the kindly Salvage Man's care, Calepine recovers, but the Salvage finds no herb able to heal Serena's wound, "for it was inwardly vnsound" (iv.16). The Beast's bite is venomous, but again, as with Serena's wandering and wavering through the flowery fields, a persistent intimation of immorality, this time present in that single word "inwardly," is becoming harder to escape. Or is it just easier to hear a second time? Has the process of reading itself been affected? Could the Beast's poison be spreading? In the opening episode of *The Faerie Queene*, it was the maple tree that was "seldom inward sound," phrasing whose signal of corruption few readers miss (I.i.9). In poetry that is incredibly self-conscious, the Beast's bite is affecting the figuration of Serena and simultaneously our reading of it. This development exceeds the impact of history on the triangle of Belphoebe, Amoret, and Timias in Book IV because it comes from within the poem itself. It now does so noticeably, moreover.

At this juncture, Calepine, wending "abrode . . . To take the ayre, and heare the thrushes song"—whispers of pastoral again—encounters a bear with a baby in his jaws, gives chase, and rescues the baby, but in the course of doing so loses himself in the forest (iv.17).[39] Unable to find the knight, the Salvage conveys his loss to Serena, who for the first time loses control, tearing her hair, rending her garments, beating her breast, tormenting herself (v.4):

> Vpon the ground her selfe she fiercely threw,
>   Regardlesse of her wounds, yet bleeding rife,
>   That with their bloud did all the flore imbrew,
>   As if her breast new launcht with murdrous knife,
>   Would streight dislodge the wretched wearie life.
>   There she long groueling, and deepe groning lay,
>   As if her vitall powers were at strife
>   With stronger death, and feared their decay,
> Such were this Ladies pangs and dolorous assay.
>   (VI.v.5)[40]

Another, similar stanza follows as the Salvage tries to help her, "But day and night did [she] vexe her carefull thought, / And euer more and more her owne affliction wrought" (6). She is feeding on her own misery, much as did Scudamour in Books III and IV, not to mention Redcrosse in Book I. When any hope of Calepine's return has faded, however, she arises (like Una) and sets out for help, mounted on Calepine's horse and accompanied by the Salvage, now in Calepine's armor and on foot. They encounter Arthur and Timias, who has also been bitten by the Blatant Beast. By now, we read, Serena's "wounds corruption gan to breed; / And eke this Squire, who likewise wounded was / Of that same Monster late, for lacke of heed, / Now gan to faint" (v.31). "Corruption" is now out in the open, not just intimated by wandering or inward unsoundness, and it is directly Serena's but only Timias's in "like" manner: a hair's breadth of difference, but nonetheless evident. Timias's wound, moreover, is specifically the result of a "lacke of heed," together with entrapment, whereas Serena's, which heedlessness also occasions, is intimated to be more culpable. What is progressively exposed to view in Serena's story is the way meaning and its consequences get attached to an event and indeed to a figure—the figure of a woman, as it happens, and not without the narrator's awareness, arguably both sympathetic *and* realistic—truthful.

Serena, who has not spoken since her cry for help when the Beast seized her and then her futile plea to Turpine to spare Calepine, intervenes when Arthur and Timias first find her with the kindly Salvage, whom Timias tries to subdue. She calls on Arthur to separate the combatants, and he, significantly having first asked whether she is freely with the Salvage, or not, for nearly three stanzas hears her sad story. That she is herself the teller bears emphasis, as does her awareness of what has happened to her. Discerningly, she characterizes herself as a dame "Who both in minde, the which most grieueth me, / And body haue receiu'd a mortall wound," and she characterizes her companion as "a saluage wight, of brutish kind" who has been bred among forest beasts, yet one in whom "It is most straunge and wonderfull to fynd / So milde humanity, and perfect mynd" (v.28–29).[41] From this point forward, we recognize that Serena, no merely passive object, appreciates what is going on. She seems more fully human, particularly in her awareness of her mental suffering and in her grateful wonder at the Salvage's "straunge," or unaccustomed, kindness. Notably, however, she has been wounded in body as well as in mind.

Arthur commits Serena and Timias to the care of the holy old hermit, who treats their wounds, now festering "pruily," "rankling inward" with bouts of pain, and putrifying the "inner parts"—in short, quite desperate (vi.5). The hermit's "counsell to the minde" by means of artful words is well known: "For in your selfe, your onely helpe doth lie, / To heale your selues, and must proceed alone / From your owne will, to cure your maladie" (5–7). It would be hard to imagine a more emphatic emphasis on the word *self*, which in this period is acquiring its modern meaning as "that which in a person is really and intrinsically [s]he (in contradistinction to what is adventitious)."[42] Selfhood is associated with self-awareness and vice versa, as well as with responsibility and agency—with "your owne will," as the hermit puts it. He also counsels self-restraint and avoidance of "things, that stirre vp fraile affection" (7). His discipline is stern; "affection" indicates not simply passion (in the popular modern sense) but anything that affects the sensible soul. Whether "fraile" applies to all passion or only to its corrupting forms is open to interpretation. The hermit is an elderly ascetic who would be at home in the House of Holiness, were it not for its formal features, which are not *merely* formal. This hermit, in contrast, has also had a long and active life of worldly experiences. What seems quite clear is that the sickened plight of Timias and Serena has reached a need for desperate measures.

The hermit further explains that the Blatant Beast bites "both good and bad, both most and least," thereby injecting doubt back into the question of his patients' responsibility for the extremity of their conditions (12). Serena, like many a modern patient, comically wishes for a salve that might magically cure her malady, instead of the harsh, therapeutic discipline the hermit prescribes, but then she joins Timias in accepting the hermit's more detailed remedy:

> Abstaine from pleasure, and restraine your will,
> Subdue desire, and bridle loose delight,
> Vse scanted diet, and forbeare your fill,
> Shun secresie, and talke in open sight.
> (VI.vi.14)

Thus fortified, Timias and Serena again set forth and promptly see Mirabella and her two tormentors, whose story I defer until done with Serena's, treating only Serena's response to Timias's capture. Seeing Timias clubbed to earth by Mirabella's Giant Disdain, Serena flees "away with all the speede she mought [might]," just as Una fled from the battle of Satyrane and Sans Loy in Book I (VI.vii.50, I.vi.90). Both women flee anticipated capture with good reason, but, whereas Una next finds the dwarf traveling toward her with Redcrosse's abandoned armor, to which she transfers her attention, Serena is not so fortunate. Serena flees at once into and away from herself, "afeard"

> Of villany to be to her inferd:
> So fresh the image of her former dread,
> Yet dwelling in her eye, to her appeard,
> That euery foote did tremble, which did tread,
> And euery body two, and two she foure did read.
> (VI.viii.31)

In the first line of the inset, the word "inferd" signals Serena's fear of being judged vicious, or depraved in character, a fear that results from the vivid memory—indeed the image "Yet dwelling in her eye"—of her seizure and near-spoliation by the Blatant Beast.[43] She is haunted, traumatized in modern terms, by a flashback to that experience and by the inference drawn from it, the inference of culpability and inner corruption that I have traced. The hermit's counsel, supposedly her cure, has only increased her terror of regression or the mere inference of it by others. The sight of Mirabella and the capture of Timias by Disdain and Scorn have triggered the terrifying flashback.

Flying "Through hils and dales, through bushes and through breres . . . till that at last she thought / Her selfe now past the perill of her feares," Serena dismounts and utters a complaint about Calepine's disloyalty in abandoning her in the forest, unaware that he has spent the intervening cantos trying to find her (32).[44] (Even Una, on the basis of abandonment, entertained a passing contrast between the kind lion that protects her and her unfaithful knight: I.iii.7.) Serena, now thinking herself safe and worn out by travel and sorrow, falls asleep. This is when the savage cannibals, who are not only sexual predators but conspicuously also Petrarchan sonneteers, hence eroticized makers of cultural meaning, discover her. Unlike the artist Busirane, however, they are first and foremost—literally, as we say—eaters of human flesh. By further translation, of course, the cannibals turn out also to be Catholic idolators, exploitative colonizers, mercantilists, natives of the New World or of Ireland, and more.[45] Such extraordinarily pronounced tropic conversion, I would reemphasize, has a cost. It becomes itself the cancelation of Serena's identity as a womanly figure, together, ironically, with the destruction of her serenity and, in short, of Serena herself. By such tropic interpretation, her figure becomes as multiple as that of Duessa, the other figure of a woman in the poem who is stripped (I.viii.45–50). But surely with a difference. Beneath her clothing, Duessa is a monstrous cartoon of misshapen matter. Serena is undeniably a woman. And a beautiful one, at that. In further contrast to Duessa, this time as Mary Stuart in Book V, Serena is not essentially reduced just to her name as a common noun in the poem. She has, instead, quite a story.

With the cannibals' voyeuristic, wishful dismemberment of Serena's nakedness and their plan for her ritual sacrifice, to be followed by a feast on her flesh, we are well beyond Busirane's feigning. This time the performance is more than a little too real. Given what Serena has been through—especially "the image of her former dread / Yet dwelling in her eye" that has been so recently renewed, together with "the villany . . . to her inferd"—it is surely tempting to suppose that the cannibals are her fantasy, fueled by fear and guilt.[46] They are this, but by no means only or simply so. The text is clear on this matter: Serena wakes to a real nightmare, not simply from one:

> The damsel wakes, then all attonce vpstart,
>   And round about her flocke, like many flies,
> Whooping, and hallowing on euery part,
> As if they would have rent the brazen skies.
> Which when she sees with ghastly griefull eies,
> Her heart does quake, and deadly pallid hew
> Benumbes her cheekes: Then out aloud she cries,
> Where none is nigh to heare, that will her rew.
> 			(VI.viii.40)

This looks like, *and is*, isolation, desperation, and sheer terror. Evidently there really are "paines in loue" and "punishments in hell," together with the "phantasies / In wauering wemens witt." They can superimpose themselves on each other inextricably.[47]

Even as the savage priest lowers his sacrificial knife toward Serena's "*brest*,"—notably not, like Busirane's Amoret, her breast and bowels—Calepine arrives on the scene "by chaunce, *more* then by choyce" and saves her (viii.46, 48: my emphases). Because it is night and she does not speak—"So inward shame of her vncomely case / She did conceiue"—he fails to recognize her (51). Three of the most elusive lines in the entire poem then follow: "So all that night to him vnknowen she past. / But day, that doth discouer bad and good, / Ensewing, made her knowen to him at last" (51).[48] The poet promises a continuation at another time, but never gets to it. This is the last we see of Serena. Whether what is discovered is good, bad, or both and what "knowen" means in the last line are left hanging, apparently left up to readers in another strong instance of what I termed disnarration in chapter 2.[49] What we do know, however, is that Serena can never again be serene—cheerful, tranquil, carefree as a day in June.

Unlike Amoret near the end of Book III, moreover, Serena indubitably does not feel "her selfe . . . perfect hole" when she is finally rescued (III.xii.38). A modern comment about forgiveness, which in Spenser's Book VI is a version of courtesy that is evident from its earliest cantos, seems more appropriate at this moment than a sexual pun on "knowen," not to mention another on "case" in the same stanza. This comment resonates with what we know of Serena's story to this point.[50] It encompasses both fortune and agency: "Without being forgiven, released from the consequences of what we have done, our capacity to act would, as it were, be confined to one single deed from which we could never recover; we would remain the victims of its consequences forever, not unlike the sorcerer's apprentice who lacked the magic formula to break [or, like Busirane, to reverse?] the spell. . . . no one can forgive herself."[51] This challenge to interpretation, also resonating with challenges in Florimell's flight in Book III and more loudly with Amoret's plight in Book IV, is an appropriate note on which to turn next to the story of Mirabella, whose sight precipitates Serena's headlong flight, unwittingly, as it turns out, into torment by the savages.

Mirabella's story interlinks with Serena's, as earlier noticed, and, like hers, recurrently recalls the story of Amoret and the history of Ralegh's wife that informs it. Ralegh referred to his wife as Serena.[52] Another reason that the story of Mirabella occurs between Serena's cure by the hermit and her headlong flight from the sight of Timias's capture by Mirabella's tormentors is that the figure of Mirabella, a representation of the conventional Cruel Beauty of the Middle Ages and the Tudor sonnet tradition, also glances unmistakably at England's Virgin Queen, who long refused parliamentary requests that she marry and about whose love life cultural fantasies proliferated.[53] The opening stanzas of the eighth canto of Book VI, which intervene between the initial report of Serena's terrified flight and Mirabella's full tale, issue a warning to the queen. The first of these starts by addressing "gentle Ladies, in whose soueraine powre / Loue hath the glory of his kingdome left" and then cautions them,

> Be well aware, how ye the same doe vse,
> That pride doe not to tyranny you lift;
> Least if men you of cruelty accuse,
> He from you take that chiefedome, which ye doe abuse."
> (VI.viii.1)

Critical analyses of Elizabethan sonnet sequences have long accustomed us to the subtleties of their political nuances, but there is little subtlety about the language of royalty in the present context: "soueraine powere," "tyranny," and "chiefedome" require little effort of the readerly imagination.[54]

Somewhat gentler, the next stanza recalls the advice in the proem to Book IV that Cupid "chase imperious feare" from the queen's "high spirit . . . And vse of awful Maiestie remoue," sprinkling her heart with drops of love and softening her "haughtie courage . . . That she may hearke to loue, and reade this lesson often" (5). This stanza directly introduces the full story of Mirabella by suggesting the fall from high to low estate that Fortune's wheel produces. It continues the address to court ladies, urging the practice of kindness (natural goodness, generosity) that is further thematic in Book VI and then the banishing of "cruelty and hardnesse"

> That all your other praises will deface,
> And from you turne the loue of men to hate.
> Ensample take of *Mirabellaes* case,
> Who from the high degree of happy state,
> Fell into wretched woes, which she repented late.
> (VI.viii.2)

Aside from reference to the queen, Mirabella is another, profoundly psychological study of womanly misery, as well as a kind of emblematic road show—a "Ladie free," who rides "an Asse / Led by a Carle and foole, which by her side did passe" (VI.vii.27). Guided, or led, as is Mirabella, by her Giant Disdain and with her Fool Scorn beside her, the sense in which she is "free" is in question from the very start. The word "free," reinforced by the word "libertie," occurs twice in the four stanzas depicting her here. As Hamilton notes in his edition, "free" is a stock epithet for a lady of noble birth, and he further suggests that the initial use of the word at this point carries "the sense of being wilful," a quality, I would add, that, if pertinent, is hardly evident this soon (648n27.7). A beauty, "deckt with wondrous giftes of natures grace," Mirabella scorns and disdains scores of languishing lovers, until eventually she is haled before Cupid as judge, and this love god imposes a penance on her (vii.28). Until she saves as many lovers as she has destroyed, she is to wander with the Fool and the Giant, who also happens to be the sib of Orgoglio (Book I's Giant Pride). As this threesome travels, the Giant cruelly demeans Mirabella, and the Fool occasionally whips her, along with her horse. She is also furnished with a backpack for her repentance that has a torn bottom and with a leaky bottle for her contrite tears. The figure of Mirabella, embodying futility as well as misery, looks like yet another expression of despair. She is a far cry from the earlier cartoons implicating the queen, such as Argante and Slander, insofar as her story includes some appreciation of her unhappy plight.

When Timias, traveling with Serena, tries to rescue Mirabella from the Giant and Fool, he is instead captured by them, as is the knight who next tries to intervene. Mirabella's tormentors lead Timias, bound like a dog, and then threaten to yoke the two captured knights together as if they were oxen. They degrade and dehumanize the men they control. Mirabella herself, whose aggressive behavior they embody, is their prisoner, too, and, seen this way, she is to be pitied. Everything about her signals hopeless self-enclosure. Her name suggests not only beauty (*bella*) to be admired but also, in view of her life-long behavior, a mirror: like Latin *mira* and *miror/-ari*, which derive from *miro*, "to wonder," these Latin roots underlie the English word *mirror*, which sound alone would suggest as a play on Mirabella's name. If Mirabella's Giant Pride is Orgoglio's brother, her sister is Lucifera, the joyless Queen of Pride's House, who holds in her hand "a mirrhour bright" and "in her selfe-lou'd semblance" takes delight (I.iv.10).[55] The difference between these two queenly figures, however, is Mirabella's awareness of her guilt as well as her misery, evident in her confessing to Prince Arthur the damage to others her self-loving denial of true love has done and its painful consequences for herself (viii.19–22).

Like Amoret in Book III, however, Mirabella pleads self-destructively for the life of her own oppressors, her Giant Disdain and Fool Scorn. Yet, having heard Mirabella's pleas to spare her tormentors and then having "wisely" attended to her own account of her plight, Arthur suddenly and surprisingly offers her redemption:

> Now Lady sith your fortunes thus dispose,
> That if ye list haue liberty, ye may,
> Vnto your selfe I freely leaue to chose,
> Whether I shall you leaue, or from these villaines lose.
> (VI.viii.25, 29)

Arthur clearly puts no stock in Mirabella's hopeless understanding of her present plight. But her reply to his offer is simply that "it may not be" because she has to fulfill the penance enjoined by Cupid, which she cannot fulfill, not least because of the bottomless bag of repentance and the leaking bottle of contrition, which mock a religious doctrine of meritorious works—that is, self-help. This is the point, not earlier, at which Mirabella's freedom ironically becomes, by her own choice, its lack. The repeated word "free" in her initial portrait only now becomes clearly ironic by virtue of retrospection, at once with respect to her will and to her

Chaucerian "fredom and curtesye," generosity and its social expression in courtesy, forms of love and forgiveness.[56]

Mirabella has been self-loving, and Cupid has sentenced her to herself. The disdain and scorn with which she hurt others have turned in guilt and penance back upon herself. They lash out at any, such as Timias, who would rescue her. They are still her masters and, indeed, have become her gods. Led by them, she finally refuses her own right to redemption when Arthur offers it to her. From one point of view, she is willful but, from another, quite will-less and lacking not only in kindness but also in faith. Mirabella and her tormentors keep moving, but they get nowhere. Effectually, she is stuck in one place and condition, an effect that sheds light on her initial depiction in so strikingly emblematic a form. Her refusal of Arthur's offer, his "good will," as with unwitting irony she calls it, immediately gives way in the same canto to the episode of Serena and the cannibals (30). Whereas Serena is depicted essentially as a victim of fortune, however, Mirabella is depicted as a victim at once by choice and its lack. In this, she bears an odd resemblance to Acrasia, as Harry Berger has glossed this witch's name, which alludes at once to power and to powerlessness.[57]

Discussing the stories of Belphoebe and Amoret in chapter 2, I suggested that Spenser explored and improvised as he went along; at this point, I would add that, as time passed, he re-envisioned his massive project with respect to its figuration of women. The figuration of Serena and Mirabella, an extensive transformation of Amoret and Belphoebe, extends not only to their names but even to the prioritizing of their respective stories within the poem, and it does so conclusively. Whereas poor Amoret just keeps falling into lustful hands—Busirane's, Lust's, then Lust's again (with Timias's help), then seemingly once more Scudamour's—Serena's story is not primarily about lust but more complexly about pleasure, detraction, agency, trauma, and the poetic and readerly generation of sociocultural and personal meaning. As for Belphoebe and Mirabella, whereas Belphoebe's figure suggests fixation, Mirabella's more sympathetically and starkly explores its sociocultural and personal sources, or mechanisms— including choice and fortune, *virtù* and *fortuna*.

Yet simply to make contrasting exempla of the linked stories of Serena and Mirabella, the one too free with her favors, the other too stingy, would be, although not wrong, morally reductive. It would violate the human contours, the emotional insight and complexity, of their figures and stories, that is, of their narrativized figuration. Like Una, Serena and Mirabella are offered real, salvific help by Arthur, not just the pity he feels for Amoret in Book IV. Serena, in fact, gets the same help as Timias, although their plights diverge once they leave the hermit, and the help both women get in Book VI involves the human dignity of responsible choice. In short, this book brings not only a return to romance after the epic form that dominates Book V but also a profound conceptual shift in the figuration of its major woman, Serena, with whom Mirabella is still meaningfully twinned.

The interlinked episodes of Serena and Mirabella lead into the pastoral cantos of Melibee and Pastorella, the old shepherd's foster child and a foundling, with whom Calidore, the nominal protagonist of Book VI, falls in love. He first sees her "placed" on a hillock, "Environ'd with a girland, goodly graced, / Of louely lasses," a sight that anticipates his later vision of the Graces (ix.8). Charmed both by Melibee's way of life and Pastorella's beauty, Calidore dons the garb of a shepherd, and a pastoral courtship ensues. Little distinguishes Pastorella from many another pastoral queen, and here she exists only in the narrator's brief accounts of Calidore's courtship and her response to it. Essentially, she belongs to Melibee's idyllic situation, his place and condition, as her name signals. When, in Calidore's absence, brigands capture Melibee and "all his people," including Pastorella, they effectually destroy the place of pastoral (x.40). Pastorella's situation becomes the brigands' cave, where "darkenesse dred and daily night did houer / Through all the inner parts" and where "continuall candlelight . . . delt / A doubtfull sense of things, not so well seene, as felt" (x.42). In this situation, Pastorella exercises some ingenuity, pretending to favor the brigand's captain, who is attracted to her, and feigning sickness to escape his attentions. In short, she lies, one of the character effects discussed in chapter 3. The narrator also reports that she suffers in mind and body but is constant in virtue and troth. By and large, however, she remains a stock figure of romance. When Calidore rescues her from the brigands and restores her to "joyous light," he takes her to a castle, which turns out to belong to the parents who lost her as an infant (xi.50). He thus takes her home, her third and final situation. Here, Pastorella's mother recognizes her long-lost daughter by a birthmark in the shape of a rose on Pastorella's breast (VI.xii.7). This birthmark recalls and reembodies Belphoebe's rose, which was formerly recalled in the poet's lyric sublation of Amoret's "flowre" (IV.viii. 32–33). Yet, in all Pastorella's differing locations—pastoral fields, hellish cave, true origin—she never speaks directly or otherwise exhibits much awareness or depth.

If our sense of who she is changes, it does so mainly because her situation does. She remains largely a function of the plot and, for this reason, usefully sets off the figures of Serena and Mirabella in this book, both of whom are effectually psychological studies with multiple historical and cultural dimensions.

To end a discussion of Spenser's figures of women with Pastorella is in one sense to end with a whimper. Yet Pastorella on the pastoral hillock prefigures the "countrey lasse" at the center of the vision on Mount Acidale, and her joyous redemption from what is termed the "hell" of her capture by the diabolical brigands also participates in the reaffirmation of *trouthe*, fidelity and truth—her own, Colin's, and Calidore's—close to the end of Book VI (x.25, 43). The language of this redemption, especially Calidore's breaking open the "dores" and "locks" of the brigands' cave, is laden with distant memories of the harrowing of hell, more insistently recalled in the debate between Duessa's emissary Archimago with Redcrosse and Una at the end of Book I, which I examined in chapter 1 (VI.xi.43, 50).[58] Of course, in the final stanzas of canto xii, on the other side of the Acidalian vision and this further reaffirmation of redemptive *trouthe*, the Blatant Beast continues to rage and spread poison, a process studied so acutely in the story of Serena's figuration and, like it, never ending. At the end of Book I, we similarly realized that Archimago would escape his prison. The difference involves tone and emphasis: a hopeful promise at the close of the opening book but, at the close of the final book, a bitter complaint. If Books IV to VI witness a massive refiguration, barring the *Mutabilitie Cantos*, which reflect on time and change, they also witness the end of *The Faerie Queene*.

* * *

The major figures of women examined in this study—especially Una, Belphoebe, and Britomart, but also Amoret, Florimell, Mirabella, and Serena—depict the status of women with a greater sensitivity to their problems and experiences than is the sociocultural norm in the Elizabethan period, even while staying largely within it. They push meaningfully against it, although only so far. Una's truth, her "trouthe," finds fulfillment only in Eden; Belphoebe's early promise turns into haggish cartoons; Britomart's approach to selfhood is suppressed in the end; Amoret is abandoned; Mirabella is arrested in misery; and Serena seems damaged for good. Only Florimell enters wedlock, yet the culturally normative happiness of her wedding day with her long-sought Marinell, which has been taken to symbolize the coming of spring, the return of Persephone to earth, the fruitful conjunction of heaven and earth, and more, turns out at best to be nostalgic, "taking *vsurie* of time forepast," as the narrator remarks of it (V.iii.40: my emphasis). The term *usury* suggests a self-indulgent and dubiously ethical exploitation of what belongs to the past. Nostalgia is what Pastorella's happy ending offers as well, in this instance for the homecoming that concludes Book I, yet there remains in her restoration a present memory of Una's achievement and, with it, a still lingering reaffirmation of renewal as well. Spenser's figuration of the women of Faerie does not end in ways to content most modern readers, but the explorations of possibility in his figured narratives are still complex, impressive, and promising. As one of my former graduate students, a committed feminist, memorably asked a harsher reader of Spenser's poem, "Don't you get credit for trying?" Awareness is where still movement starts.

Notes

Introduction: Spenser's Narrative Figuration of Women

¹ On "enabled," see Penelope Anderson, *Friendship's Shadows: Women's Friendship and the Politics of Betrayal in England, 1640–1705* (Edinburgh: Edinburgh University Press, 2012), for example. Anderson focuses on a later period, but her argument has significance for the friendships of women in Spenser, Sidney, and Shakespeare. Another enabling example is the well-recognized use Elizabeth I made of her womanhood in order to rule when the rule of a woman was thought to be "unnatural." For a review of contentious debates regarding sexual identities, which have long borne on their relation (or not) to gender, see Valerie Traub, *Thinking Sex with the Early Moderns* (Philadelphia: University of Pennsylvania Press, 2016), 1–34, e.g., 18. Spenser is outside Traub's purview.

² *Rethinking Feminism in Early Modern Studies: Gender, Race, and Sexuality* (London: Taylor & Francis, 2016), Ania Loomba and Melissa E. Sanchez, ed., introduction to *Rethinking Feminism in Early Modern Studies: Gender, Race, and Sexuality* (London: Taylor & Francis, 2016), 1-12 at 2. Idem., see esp. Loomba's and Sanchez's "Feminism and the Burdens of History," 15–41; Coppélia Kahn, "Family Quarrels: Feminist Criticism, Queer Studies, and Shakespeare in the Twenty-First Century," 43–57; Kathryn Schwarz, "Whose Body?" 213–28; Valerie Traub, "Afterword: Early Modern (Feminist) Methods," 229–45. Loomba's and Sanchez's collection lacks an essay on Spenser.

³ On the usefulness and necessity of history, see Loomba and Sanchez, *Rethinking Feminism,* 3; Kahn, 55; Valerie Traub, "The New Unhistoricism in Queer Studies," *PMLA* 128.1 (2013): 21–39.

⁴ Kathy Eden, *Poetic and Legal Fiction in the Aristotelian Tradition* (Princeton, NJ: Princeton University Press, 1986); Andrew Zurcher, *Spenser's Legal Language: Law and Poetry in Early Modern England* (Woodbridge, UK: D. S. Brewer, 2007); Lorna Hutson, *The Invention of Suspicion: Law and Mimesis in Shakespeare and Renaissance Drama* (Oxford: Oxford University Press, 2007).

⁵ As the word "broad" in the next sentence signals, I refer to the familiar knowledge that common law and casuistry (< Latin *casus*, "case") generally reason from precedent instances to present ones.

[6] See James J. Paxson, *The Poetics of Personification* (Cambridge: Cambridge University Press, 1994), esp. chap. 1, "A history of personification theory." Also James E. Berg, "Wopsle's Revenge, or, Reading Hamlet as a Character in *Great Expectations*," in *Shakespeare's Sense of Character: On the Page and From the Stage*, ed. Yu Jin Ko and Michael W. Shurgot (Farnham, UK: Ashgate, 2012), 65–82, at 67, on the difference between the modern character, "a complex, 'three-dimensional,' 'inward psyche' who undergoes 'growth' and 'change,' who seems to have a presence above the page or between the lines," and the Theophrastan character, the word *character* now implying "a rigid and unchanging signifying mark, or stamp, or seal, or handwriting expressive of some unchanging readable aspect of a person." See also my use of Alan Sinfield's argument about Shakespearean character in my introduction and chapter 3, including endnotes. André G. Bourassa, "*Personnage*: History, Philology, Performance," trans. Jennifer Drouin, in *Shakespeare and Character: Theory, History, Performance, and Theatrical Persons*, ed. Paul Yachnin and Jessica Slights (Houndmills, UK: Palgrave Macmillan, 2009), 83–97, observes that Shakespeare used *character* thirty-seven times, giving it, around 1590–91, "the sense of inscription, of a material sign, extended metaphorically to a moral sign." He adds, "once in *Coriolanus*, 1607–8, we recognize a meaning close to personage" (85). The present book was in production when Andrew Escobedo's *Volition's Face: Personification and the Will in Renaissance Literature* (Notre Dame, IN: University of Notre Dame Press, 2017) appeared, but I have reviewed it for the online *Spenser Review*, 2017 (fall).

[7] George Puttenham, *The Arte of English Poesie* (London: Richard Field, 1589; repr. 1988), 246.

[8] *Edmund Spenser: The Faerie Queene*, ed. A. C. Hamilton, text edited by Hiroshi Yamashita, Toshiyuki Suzuki, and Shohachi Fukuda, rev. second ed. (Harlow, UK: Pearson, 2007): IV.xii.35.

[9] On figuration, including its history, see the editors' introduction to *Go Figure: Energies, Forms, and Institutions in the Early Modern World*, ed. Judith H. Anderson and Joan Pong Linton (New York: Fordham University Press, 2011), 1–18; also Erich Auerbach, "Figura," trans. Ralph Manheim, in *Scenes from the Drama of European Literature: Six Essays* (New York: Meridian, 1959 [1944]), 11–76.

[10] *Online OED*, s.v. *figure, n.*: I. 3, 5a; II. 9.b., 10.a. 11.a–b, 12.; IV. 18.; V. 21.a–b (accessed April 21, 2016).

[11] Judith H. Anderson, *The Growth of a Personal Voice: "Piers Plowman" and "The Faerie Queene"* (New Haven, CT: Yale University Press, 1976), esp. 114–21, 221n23.

[12] Judith H. Anderson, *Reading the Allegorical Intertext: Chaucer, Spenser, Shakespeare, Milton* (New York: Fordham University Press, 2008), chaps. 1–2; other chapters are relevant.

[13] For Dryden's report that Milton acknowledged Spenser as his "Original," see Barbara K. Lewalski, *The Life of John Milton: A Critical Biography* (Oxford: Blackwell, 2000), 508. The Milton chapters to which I refer are in Judith H.

Anderson, *Light and Death: Figuration in Spenser, Kepler, Donne, Milton* (New York: Fordham University Press, 2017).

[14] I do not focus on Duessa because her figure has been perceptively done and overdone. Stripped of her disguise(s), she is primarily a hideous cartoon, and I have little to add to existing criticism of her stripping in the first book. I attend to other hideous cartoons of women, specifically of the reigning queen. To make Duessa the primary or typical representation of Spenser's figuration of women in the poem is distorting, unbalanced by (and sometimes ignorant of) the equal-opportunity sexism of a figure such as Lust in Book IV, not to mention the depiction of Una in Book I and other important figures of women in other books of the poem. The problems of matter, the body, and representation in the period include Duessa (and Charissa!) in Book I, but are larger than Duessa, especially in Spenser's ever-interconnecting allegory. The pairing of Una and Duessa is also more complex than the contrast of virgin to whore, nowadays a truism. The *details* of similarity *and* contrast in Spenser's still-moving narrative are what make it interesting and engaging. But see my discussion of Duessa, especially masked as Mary Stuart, in chapter 4.

[15] Margaret A. Rose, *Parody: Ancient, Modern, and Post-Modern* (Cambridge: Cambridge University Press, 1993), 6.

[16] Alan Sinfield, *Faultlines: Cultural Materialism and the Politics of Dissident Reading* (Berkeley: University of California Press, 1992), 52–79. See also the notes to my chapter 3 regarding debates about character in Shakespeare's plays.

[17] For a taxonomy of women in *The Faerie Queene*, try Anne Paolucci, *The Women in Dante's "Divine Comedy" and Spenser's "Faerie Queene"* (Dover, DE: Griffon House, 2005), and my comments early in chapter 4.

[18] This sentence and the preceding one account for my not including Venus in the Garden of Adonis, on whose figure see my *Allegorical Intertext*, 214–23; see 135–53 for another chapter on Spenser's figures of Venus.

[19] The *Mutabilitie Cantos* are yet another story: for a variety of perspectives, see *Celebrating Mutabilitie: Essays on Edmund Spenser's Mutabilie Cantos*, ed. Jane Grogan (Manchester, UK: Manchester University Press, 2010).

1 Parody and Perfection

[1] Quotations from *Edmund Spenser: The Faerie Queene*, ed. A. C. Hamilton, text edited by Hiroshi Yamashita, Toshiyuki Suzuki, and Shohachi Fukuda, rev. second ed. (Harlow, UK: Pearson, 2007), here III.Pro.5. Notes are cited as Hamilton, ed. (2007), unless otherwise indicated.

[2] *The Works of Edmund Spenser: A Variorum Edition*, ed. Edwin Greenlaw, Charles Osgood, and Frederick Morgan Padelford, 11 vols. (Baltimore, MD: Johns Hopkins Press, 1949), 10:472 (Appendix I).

[3] Margaret A. Rose, *Parody: Ancient, Modern, and Post-Modern* (Cambridge: Cambridge University Press, 1993), 6. Anne Lake Prescott associates Rabelais with

"Cyniquized, and Menippized" satire: *Imagining Rabelais in Renaissance England* (New Haven, CT: Yale University Press, 1998), 59. She cites many another influence as well, momentarily including Aristophanes (87). See also note 4 below.

[4] In "Spenser's Parody" in *The Faerie Queene*, Donald Cheney focuses on Spenser's "sympathetic parody" of Ariosto: *Connotations* 12.1 (2002/03): 1–13. Citing Charles Ross ("Boiardo and the Derangement of Epic," *Renaissance Papers* [1988]: 77–97), who cites Fredric Jameson (96), Cheney suggests that romance parodies epic, "deforming and reforming" it (13). Lawrence F. Rhu responds to Cheney's essay ("On Cheney on Spenser's Ariosto," "*Connotations*" 15.1-3 [2005/06]: 91–96), as does Richard A. McCabe, concentrating attention on definitions later than Spenser before enumerating instances of Spenserian parody: "Parody, Sympathy, and Self: A Response to Donald Cheney," *Connotations* 13.2 (2003/04): 5–22.

[5] Rose, 10–11, excepting Walkington, cited in *OED*, s.v. *parody n.*^{2}, 1.a (accessed online July 28, 2015); Aristotle, *Poetics*, trans. Richard Janko (Indianapolis, IN: Hackett, 1987), I.ii:48a, 10–15.

[6] *The Institutio Oratoria of Quintilian*, ed. and trans. H. E. Butler, 4 vols. (Cambridge, MA: Harvard University Press, 1920), 3:Bk. IX.ii.35. Describing a (legal) will, Quintilian finds in it a *figure* that "borders"—"Incipit esse quodammodo"—on parody and does so abusively, likening it to the trope/figure catachresis.

[7] John Milton, *Paradise Lost*, ed. Barbara K. Lewalski (Oxford: Blackwell, 2007), IV.310.

[8] Miri Rubin, *Corpus Christi: The Eucharist in Late Medieval Culture* (Cambridge: Cambridge University Press, 1991), 345–46 (subsection titled "Parody").

[9] George Puttenham, *The Arte of English Poesie* (London: Richard Field, 1589; repr. 1988), 199–200.

[10] See, for example, Alastair Fowler, *Kinds of Literature: An Introduction to the Theory of Genres and Modes* (Cambridge, MA: Harvard University Press, 1982), 18, 23: "the character of genres is that they change"; they "are continuously undergoing metamorphoses."

[11] Mary Ellen Lamb, "The Red Crosse Knight, St. George, and the Appropriation of Popular Culture," *Spenser Studies* 18 (2003): 185–208; also Lamb's *Popular Culture of Shakespeare, Spenser, and Jonson* (London: Routledge, 2006), 163–93.

[12] Andrew Hadfield suggests that Redcrosse is first seen as "an old-fashioned hero from a romance," and Una as "a medieval religious figure": *Edmund Spenser: A Life* (Oxford: Oxford University Press, 2012), 259.

[13] *Faerie Queene*, I.vi.9, II.i.13; cf. III. viii.32 (Florimell).

[14] In the 1596 *Faerie Queene*, "blubbred" also describes the eyes of the abject "Squire in squallid weed" beside a headless lady and bereft of his own lady (V.i.13–14). He bursts "forth teares, like springs out of a banke" (15). In *Daphnaïda*, 551, the pathetic Alcyon's face is said to be "blubbred": *The Yale Edition of the Shorter Poems of Edmund Spenser*, ed. William A. Oram, Einar Bjorvand, and Ronald Bond (New Haven, CT: Yale University Press, 1989).

[15] *Faerie Queene*, II. i.40, ii.3, 7–9.

[16] *Online OED* (accessed October 24, 2015), s.v. *blubbered*, 1; s.v. *dignity*, 1.a–b, 2.a–b, 3.a; cf. s.v. *condign*, esp. 3.a–b. *Blubbered* derives from the verb *blubber*, "to bubble, bubble up; to give forth a bubbling sound, as a spring, boiling water" (s.v. *blubber, v.*, 1). The origin of the verb is likely onomatopoeic. It was applied to the foaming, billowing sea or to bubbles on other bodies of water, such as a brook or waterfall. It described tears (usually of women or children) in the Middle Ages and came also to mean "swollen and disfigured with weeping." Compare s.v. *blubber, n.¹*, 4: *OED* recognizes use of *blubber* for whale fat first in 1665, but the use of whale oil for lamps goes back to the sixteenth century. *Dignity*, as worth, honor, desert, merit (*OED*, 1.a–b) or as *condignity* in the Latin tradition of interpreting Romans 8 and in secular law, too, meshes with concepts of merit, worth, justification, and punishment.

[17] Where King James has "goodliness," Geneva has "grace." The Vulgate has *gloria*, "glory," and some modern translations, "beauty." All versions checked have "flesh," "grass," and "flower." In Spenser's phrase, "verdant gras," the adjective suggests the greenness of spring, fertility, and the like, and its burning suggests something harmful, destructive.

[18] On Spenser's use of Ariosto in figuring Florimell, see Paul J. Alpers, *The Poetry of The Faerie Queene* (Princeton, NJ: Princeton University Press, 1967), 194–96. Alpers describes Spenser's debt as imitation, which, I would add, need not be parodic but readily becomes so.

[19] Cheney was the first to suggest that Arthur and Guyon, with precedent in Ariosto, share a single horse, because Guyon lost his to Braggadocchio (10).

[20] Harry Berger, Jr., "'Kidnapped Romance': Discourse in *The Faerie Queene*," in *Unfolded Tales: Essays on Renaissance Romance*, ed. George M. Logan and Gordon Teskey (Ithaca, NY: Cornell University Press, 1989), 208–56 at 226.

[21] Berger, "'Kidnapped Romance,'" 213–14. Like Alpers (395), Berger (214–16) interprets Florimell's flight to find Marinell as "sexual fearfulness" in general, rather than as justified fear of violent rape by the forester. Such readings reduce all female resistance, not to mention choice and preference, to unreasonable fear. Textual specifics indicate a different reading.

[22] For the animal comparisons, see III.iv.46, 49; for the mythic ones, III.vii.26.

[23] See my *Reading the Allegorical Intertext: Chaucer, Spenser, Shakespeare, Milton* (New York: Fordham University Press, 2008), 95; cf. 94–96.

[24] *Online OED*, s.v. *soil, n.³*, III.5 (accessed October 25, 2015). Other meanings listed are also relevant. For a provocative contrast, now or then, see Cynthia E. Garrett, "Sexual Consent and the Art of Love in the Early Modern English Lyric," *Studies in English Literature* 44.1 (2004): 37–58, esp. 38–41, 54.

[25] *Faerie Queene*, I.ii.7, vi, 5, 19, 31.

[26] On Renaissance hyperbole and catachresis, see my *Translating Investments: Metaphor and the Dynamic of Cultural Change in Tudor-Stuart England* (New York: Fordham University Press, 2005), 157, 159.

[27] Harry Berger, Jr., "Spenser's *Faerie Queene*: Prelude to Interpretation," *Southern Review: An Australian Journal of Literary Studies* 2 (1966): 18–49 at 24–25. Alpers finds Spenser's "extravagance" in this passage successful and not at all ironic (26–29). These contrasting views are broadly representative.

[28] The word "superficially" is tempting but misleading to describe the emotional effect of the dwarf's news on Una: see James W. Broaddus, "Spenser's Redcrosse Knight and the Order of Salvation," *Studies in Philology* 108.4 (2011): 572–604, for evidence of its physical effect on her heart, proof that her love and her very life are a unity (602–3).

[29] Claire McEachern, *The Poetics of English Nationhood, 1590–1612* (Cambridge: Cambridge University Press, 1996), 78. One wonders which other, comparable Renaissance poems McEachern has in mind in calling Spenser's "least inward."

[30] Kathryn Walls, *God's Only Daughter: Spenser's Una as the Invisible Church* (Manchester, UK: Manchester University Press, 2013), e.g., 178; cf. 10. Walls opposes emblematic to mimetic, thus the opposition of symbol to narrative and loosely of timelessness to time. She suggests that Una is paradigmatic for *The Faerie Queene* as a whole. On the meaning of *emblem* and *emblematic*, see Tamara A. Goeglein, "The Emblematics of Edmund Spenser's House of Holiness," *Spenser Studies* 25 (2010): 21–51, esp. 21–24: Goeglein speaks of an emblem as being embedded within a narrative, comparable to the embedding of an ekphrasis (33); also Goeglein's essay "Death is in the 'I' of the Beholder: Early Modern English Emblems of Death," in *Emblems of Death in the Early Modern Period*, ed. Peter Daly and Monica Calebritto (Geneva: Librairie Droz, 2014), 59–95 at 65–66. Thus embedded, an emblem, mutating or developing in narrative, becomes more and other than merely a self-consistent image per se. Walls conceives of Una as unchanging, wholly self-consistent, after her off-stage (off-page) transformation at Archimago's hermitage (17–18, 17–18n51, 38).

[31] See my discussion of Redcrosse's hell in Book I: *The Growth of a Personal Voice: "Piers Plowman" and "The Faerie Queene"* (New Haven, CT: Yale University Press, 1976), 37–40; or, more extensively, "Redcrosse and the Descent into Hell," *ELH* 36.3 (1969): 470–92 at 485–89.

[32] On Archimago as Judas, see Walls, 101. On the lion, see Richard Halpern, "Una's Evil," *The Spenser Review* 40.3 (2010): 1–7 at 2 (article numbered 40.25); pagination starts after p. 6: www.english.cam.ac.uk/spenseronline/static/pdfs/2010_Volume_40_Number_3.pdf (accessed September 20, 2017).

[33] "As if he were the snake in the Garden" is the meaning I evoke here, although the phrase could also mean "as if she were the snake"—a perverse role reversal in what is becoming an upside-down world. (Upside-down and inside out are not necessarily identical.)

[34] Momentarily, Satan is an autonomous figure in the narrative of Book I.iv.36 when he appears on the wagon beam of Lucifera's coach. If he is a historical aspect or an expression of another figure here, Lucifera would be the leading candidate, but, on Lucifera, see my *Light and Death: Figuration in Spenser, Kepler,*

Donne, Milton (New York: Fordham, 2017), 56–57; also my "Redcrosse and the Descent into Hell," 478–79.

[35] "Animated" might have been represented as "anima-ted" for emphasis here. The only soul (or souls) to be found in all members of the genus animal is not the intellectual soul, which only the rational animal, or human being, possesses. Not necessarily limited to animal species, love and hate, attraction and repulsion, make the world go round, as we learn in the Temple of Venus in Spenser's Book IV. A Neoplatonizing World Soul would extend animation of a rudimentary kind beyond the animal genus.

[36] *Faerie Queene*, I.xii.8, vi.4, 9–10.

[37] For significant development of McEachern's argument about Una, see Jennifer Rust, "'Image of Idolatryes': Iconotropy and the Theo-Political Body in *The Faerie Queene*," *Religion and Literature* 38.3 (2006): 137–55, e.g., 137, 151; also Claire Falk on Una as an "invisible image," a visible marker pointing to the invisible: "'Heavenly Lineaments' and the Invisible Church in Foxe and Spenser," *Studies in English Literature* 53.1 (2013): 1–28, esp. 15–25.

[38] Harry Berger, Jr., treats Una in three relatively recent articles: "Displacing Autophobia in *Faerie Queene* I: Ethics, Gender, and Oppositional Reading in the Spenserian Text," *English Literary Renaissance* 28 (1998): 163–82; "Archimago: Between Text and Countertext," *Studies in English Literature* 43.1 (2003): 19–64; and "Sexual and Religious Politics in Book I of Spenser's *Faerie Queene*," *English Literary Renaissance* 34.2 (2004): 201–42 at 210. These essays will be cited by the year in which they were published, i.e., 1998, 2003, 2004. In Joseph Campana's sensitive argument, "Duessa bears the burden of female matter," and Berger's readings want "a sense of the materiality that grounds poetry": *The Pain of Reformation: Spenser, Vulnerability, and the Ethics of Modernity* (New York: Fordham University Press, 2012), 69, 102–3, and all of chapter 2.

[39] Syrithe Pugh, *Spenser and Ovid* (Aldershot, UK: Ashgate, 2005), 50–57, 66–68. Rust, 143–51, treats Una among the satyrs extensively, reading the episode as a parody of the Queen's iconotropic body.

[40] *Paradise Lost*, V.117–19: the lines are spoken by unfallen Adam after intuiting that Eve's dream is evil (96–98). Milton told Dryden that Spenser was "his Original": Barbara K. Lewalski, *The Life of John Milton* (Oxford: Blackwell, 2000), 508.

[41] Logically, this would make Una an accident. See Judith H. Anderson, *Words That Matter: Linguistic Perception in Renaissance English* (Stanford, CA: Stanford University Press, 1996), 88.

[42] For example, my "July Eclogue and the House of Holiness: Perspective in Spenser," *Studies in English Literature* 10.1 (1970): 17–32, and, in compressed form, my *Growth of a Personal Voice*, 44–49, esp. 46 (unity and continuity).

[43] On this maxim in Book V, see my "'Nor man it is': The Knight of Justice in Book V of Spenser's *Faerie Queene*," *PMLA* 85 (1970): 65–77 at 66–67; cf. *Reading the Allegorical Intertext*, 50–51.

156   NOTES

⁴⁴ Lancelot Andrewes, *Works*, 11 vols. (Oxford, UK: John Henry Parker, 1841–54; repr. 1967), 5:265. Andrewes refers to Augustine's *De Civitate Dei* (*City of God*) and to Paul's Epistle to the Romans. Andrewes's words are later than Spenser's Book I but consistent with the bishop's earlier views. The subject is complicated; see, for example, Susan E. Schreiner, *Are You Alone Wise?: The Search for Certainty in the Early Modern Era* (Oxford: Oxford University Press, 2011), chap. 4, also 108: Calvin was "Suspicious of all appeals to the Spirit alone, to the Spirit-guided church or an invisible church."

⁴⁵ As mentioned, these articles have some overlap with McEachern, whose book comes earlier, and with Halpern, whose article comes later. Halpern cites two of Berger's articles, one treating Una in canto xii and the other treating the lion, and the trio of Abessa, Corceca, and Kirkrapine. Walls cites Halpern for support, as well as Berger 2003, and so it goes.

⁴⁶ In Berger's view, Redcrosse "responds to her recrimination like a little boy who has been scolded and told to be good. . . . She has become his savior, governess, and guide, and she shares these offices with the strong women who dominate the House of Holiness. Should this be expected to close up the secret breach of the self-loathing sinner who wants the punishment he knows he deserves? Who has just defied or flinched from the power of the terrible gift of divine forgiveness? That this power of donation is vested in Una, the almighty humble loving virgin, engenders the threatening effects of the secret breach: the threat of infantilization; the threat of emasculation; the threat, one hesitates to say, of castration" (1998:176).

⁴⁷ I take it that Berger's Una is being scapegoated here, though I'm not sure by whom. Berger ventriloquizes the reigning view of Spenser's religious culture when he refers in greatly heightened rhetoric (1998:176) to Una's intervention as emasculating Redcrosse. He wants to expose this culture's ideological exploitation of woman, together with its manipulation of its own believers, to wit, Redcrosse. What bothers me are discrepancies between the narrative and this reading of it. The narrative seems to get in the way, as does the figural being of Una.

⁴⁸ Metaphor differs from metonymy, or substitution—that is, from coding or recoding. Simultaneously, metaphor respects both similarity and difference: my love is a rose, but my love is not (really) a rose.

⁴⁹ On non-residency or absenteeism, see Mary Robert Falls, "Spenser's Kirkrapine and the Elizabethans," *Studies in Philology* 50 (1953): 457–75.

⁵⁰ Berger's Kirkrapine is more complicated. His meaning transmigrates to Archimago, "whose investment in and as St. George illustrates Kirkrapine's theft," and comments on Redcrosse's effectual theft of Christian armor when he abandons Una (Berger, 2004:226). This perceptive insight makes way for the claim that Redcrosse becomes or embodies Archimago by acquiescing in the tempter's imagination and bad agency. Again, I wonder whether psychic displacement is warping the text. Archimago penetrates, manipulates, and poisons Redcrosse's imagination during the knight's time in the hermitage, but he does so without

replacing or simply becoming it. Redcrosse, who has been given the armor of the Christian and still possesses some of its potency after leaving Archimago's hermitage, next defeats the pagan Sans Foy. If this victory turns out to be Pyrrhic, it is still a victory, not a defeat. The meaning of Redcrosse's betrayal of Una fans out to the Abessa, Corceca, Kirkrapine trio, rather than their meaning funneling back into his; it extends out, not narrows in, with significant historical and philosophical ramifications.

[51] Examples include Abessa's pot as an allusion to the Old Testament's Hagar; Una's animals, the trio of lamb, ass, and lion, as (associatively) Trinitarian; identification of her dwarf with the notion of religious *adiaphora*, although the consistency of this meaning throughout Book I is questionable for me. Another is Walls's suggestion of the relevance of the "palmesel" to the satyrs' worship of Una's ass. The palmesel, part of the celebration of Palm Sunday in Germany, was a "life-sized wooden carving of Christ on a donkey, which ran on wheels," Eamon Duffy, *The Stripping of the Altars: Traditional Religion in England. 1400–1580* (New Haven, CT: Yale University Press, 1992), 26; Walls, 119n38. Reference to this custom was available in an anti-papist tract translated in 1570 by Barnaby Googe, briefly Spenser's contemporary in Ireland twelve years later (Walls, 119–22). On Googe in Ireland, see *The Spenser Encyclopedia*, ed. A. C. Hamilton, Donald Cheney, W. F. Blissett, David A. Richardson, and William W. Barker (Toronto: University of Toronto Press, 1990) s.v., *Googe Barnabe* (*sic*); also Hadfield, 124–25, 229.

[52] Hamilton, ed. (2007), 36n19, suggests that Una's outcry "breaks the encoiling rhythm" of Error. He also glosses Redcrosse's "griefe" (19) as "anger." That "gall" in stanza 19 is the source of anger is not the only conclusion the *Online OED* suggests, s.v. *gall n.*[1]: see not only 3.a. "Bitterness of spirit . . . rancour," whence Hamilton's anger; but also 3.b. "Spirit to resent injury or insult" (accessed January 10, 2016). Be that as it may, the reason for Redcrosse's "griefe" at this point is not unambiguous: shame, frustration, disappointment, and anger with himself at his vulnerability are possibilities. The object of his "high disdaine," which, Hamilton implies, is elevated or ennobling, is ambiguous as well: is this object himself or the serpent strangling him—or both? Una's intervention seems the right moment to redouble his force in God's fight, not to stop fighting and start praying.

[53] *Online OED*, s.v., *add*, v., 1.b (accessed March 15, 2014).

[54] Another pressure point comes with Walls's identification of the Lion as Christ—historically and visibly with Christ's Incarnation (1)—and the lion's dismembering of Kirkrapine as Christ's expulsion of the money lenders from the Temple (101). The far more open, insistent association of Arthur with Christ in canto viii and of the Crucifixion, not with Sans Loy's slaying the lion, but with Arthur's battling and defeating Orgoglio, the sinful flesh, is unacknowledged or explained away by Walls: e.g., Arthur's breaking open the iron door of Orgoglio's hellish dungeon, which Walls admits is "reminiscent of Christ's Descent into Hell," indicates that the Prince wants to preach to him (186–89).

[55] Even Redcrosse's hell is not exclusively inner, but is strikingly related to cultural history, which, as history, has external, objective existence, for example, as the cult of Aescupalius, Greek drama, ancient myth, *The Aeneid*, and so on; it is not a question of inner *or* outer, but of inner *and* outer. Hell, moreover, is usually considered a real place in Tudor religion. Spenser's hell in Book I parodically mirrors unity and wholeness, distorting them.

[56] Hamilton, ed. (2007), 155n40.9; *Faerie Queene*, I.i.47, ll.4–6.

[57] *Online OED*, s.v. *melancholy* (accessed December 7, 2015).

[58] For more on the initial description of Arthur, see Anderson, *Reading the Allegorical Intertext*, 130–34, and 54–60 on Spenser's use of Sir Thopas in characterizing Redcrosse and Arthur.

[59] To find such parody merely corrosive or destructive is to succumb to the attitude of Jonathan Swift's satiric poem about Celia, whose idealizing admirer, Strephon (a pastoral name), realizes with disillusioned horror that she experiences the basic functions of the human body and even that, "Oh! Celia, Celia, Celia shits": "The Lady's Dressing Room," www.poetryfoundation.org/poem/180934 (accessed September 11, 2017). Swift's poem suggests that the opposite of naïve idealization is naïve disgust or world-weary cynicism.

[60] The phrase "in the middest" comes precisely at the middle of Book III: Hamilton, ed. (2007), 348n43. Other examples of Spenser's regard for space and time are numerous: for example, their meaningful disjunction in the opening picture of Redcrosse, Una, and the dwarf (I.i.1–6) and their observance throughout *Epithalamion* (e.g., the falling of night and the truncated stanza at the end).

[61] At the wedding of Peleus and Thetis, Ate throws in the golden apple that eventually led to the Trojan War: see Hamilton, ed. (2007), 222n55.4–9; cf. 671n22.

[62] On Archimago's name and epithet "old man," see Hamilton, ed. (2007), 41n43.6; Anderson, *Reading the Allegorical Intertext*, 58, 66, 284–85.

[63] *Online OED*, s.v. *writ*, 2.c, 3.a, b. (accessed December 7, 2015).

[64] See Andrew Zurcher, *Spenser's Legal Language: Law and Poetry in Early Modern England* (Woodbridge, UK: D. S. Brewer, 2007), 65: Zurcher finds Duessa's accusation of prior contract loaded with legal diction. On Spenser as deputy clerk, see Hadfield, 187, 192, and on Spenser as litigant, 202–6, 291–92. See also see Anderson, *Reading the Allegorical Intertext*, 168–79, esp. 176–77.

[65] Eamon Duffy's sympathetic treatment of Roman Catholic ceremonies in Tudor England refers to its "cult of the dead" (466); on the popular celebration of *Corpus Christi* in England, see Duffy, 43–44, 566, 580. For fuller treatment, see Rubin's *Corpus Christi*. Broaddus makes a similar observation about Duessa's seeking the "corse" of her lord, but he finds Una Roman Catholic as well, the Truth that lingered in Catholicism: "Spenser's Redcrosse Knight," 575, 577–78. Compare James Kearney, "Enshrining Idolatry in *The Faerie Queene*," *English Literary Renaissance* 32.1 (2002): 3–30: Kearney considers the presence of Catholic objects and practices in Spenser's first book a futile effort to appropriate or redeem them.

[66] Another parallel occurs in *Paradise Lost*, where Milton's God, in discussion with his Son, voices much the same justification for saving fallen humanity and paying Adam's debt: III.129–31, 285–301. Milton, too, was acquainted with *Piers Plowman*.

[67] William Langland, *Will's Visions of Piers Plowman, Do-Well, Do-Better and Do-Best*, ed. George Kane and E. Talbot Donaldson (London: Athlone, 1975). I have silently changed thorns to *th* and removed editorial brackets in the text; those remaining are glosses borrowed from Donaldson's translation: *Piers Plowman: An Alliterative Verse Translation by E. Talbot Donaldson*, ed. Elizabeth D. Kirk and Judith H. Anderson (New York: W. W. Norton, 1990). The apparatus of the Kane–Donaldson edition includes variants from Robert Crowley's two editions and subsequent reprint of 1550, which I have checked and found insignificant for my purposes in the lines that I cite. Crowley's last edition was reprinted by Owen Rogers in 1561.

[68] Briefly, see my "Artegall" in *The Spenser Encyclopedia*, 62–64, esp. 63 bot. to 64 top; my *Growth of a Personal Voice*, 164–70, further develops the redemptive role of love in Book V.

[69] I would not identify Una as directly and immediately with Christ, the invisible Church, and additional equivalents at the end as do Walls's medievalizing methods of biblical exegesis, e.g., 176–205. For Berger's interpretation of the final canto of Book I, see 2003:49–55; it extends his earlier, psychoanalytical remarks about Una and Redcrosse. Broaddus, "Spenser's Redcrosse Knight," 601, follows Berger in thinking Redcrosse's response to Archimago/Duessa's writ "dishonest," but he also considers Una "the embodiment of Christian Charity," who shadows forth "'glorifying righteousness'" (602, 604, but cf. 601).

[70] *Epithalamion*, 119, in *The Yale Edition of the Shorter Poems of Edmund Spenser*. Hamilton does not note the use of "sunshyny face" in *Epithalamion*, likely because, although the two phrases make a connection, the contexts otherwise indicate a difference. Falk (18) rightly emphasizes the invisibility of the biblical woman in the (blinding) sun, but underemphasizes Una's human dimension at the end. The difference between what prophetic vision actually sees and ordinary physical sight is pertinent.

[71] On Spenserian eros, including *Epithalamion* and the rest of Spenser's poetry (but not Book I), see William A. Oram, "Spenser's Crowd of Cupids and the Language of Pleasure," in *Rhetorics of Bodily Disease and Health in Medieval and Early Modern England*, ed. Jennifer C. Vaught (Farnham, UK: Ashgate, 2010), 87–104. On the "discourses of joy" in *Epithalamion*, including "psalmic praises, hymnody, spiritual comfort, heavenly foretaste, matrimony, and finally sex," see James S. Lambert, "Spenser's *Epithalamion* and the Protestant Expression of Joy," *Studies in English Literature* 54.1 (2014): 81–103 at 83.

[72] *Faerie Queene*, I.ii.1, vii.6–7, xi.31. On Redcrosse's wet dream, see Anderson, "Redcrosse and the Descent into Hell," 473–76, and *Growth of a Personal Voice*, 29–32. On his looseness, see James W. Broaddus, "A Galenic Reading of the

Redcrosse Knight's 'goodly court' of Fidessa/Duessa," *Studies in Philology* 109.3 (2012): 192–98.

[73] *Measure for Measure*, in *The Riverside Shakespeare*, ed. G. Blakemore Evans et al., second ed. (Boston, MA: Houghton Mifflin, 1997), I.ii.147 (and note); also Anne Barton's introduction, 582. Compare Debra Kuller Shuger, *Political Theologies in Shakespeare's England: The Sacred and the State in "Measure for Measure"* (Houndmills, UK: Palgrave, 2001), 25–29, 98, 146n37. Zurcher, 90–94, summarizes the forms of "legal" marriage in sixteenth to seventeenth-century England; cf. 94 regarding "the legally valid custom of the spousal."

[74] On Augustine's threefold present, see Paul Ricoeur, *Time and Narrative*, trans. Kathleen McLaughlin and David Pellauer, 3 vols. (Chicago: University of Chicago Press, 1984), 1:5–30.

2 Belphoebe's "mirrours more then one": History's Interlude

[1] Reference is to *Edmund Spenser: The Faerie Queene*, ed. A. C. Hamilton, text edited by Hiroshi Yamashita, Toshiyuki Suzuki, and Shohachi Fukuda, rev. second ed. (Harlow, UK: Pearson, 2007), II.iii.21–31, and 183n21–31: notes cited as Hamilton, ed. (2007). Hamilton calls these stanzas a blazon, as they are in part, but they are also, inclusively, a portrait that draws heavily on a variety of imagistic and pictorial modes.

[2] For Diana of Ephesus in the Bible, see Acts 19:28. (Google affords abundant images of Ephesian Diana.).

[3] Here I reflect my article on Belphoebe in *The Spenser Encyclopedia*, ed. A. C. Hamilton, Donald Cheney, W. F. Blissett, David A. Richardson, and William W. Barker (Toronto: University of Toronto Press, 1990), 85–87 at 85. I remain indebted to Harry Berger Jr.'s ground-breaking chapters on the portrait of Belphoebe in *The Allegorical Temper: Vision and Reality in Book 2 of Spenser's "Faerie Queene"* (New Haven, CT: Yale University Press, 1957), 120–49.

[4] See esp. Berger, 125–28.

[5] *Edmund Spenser: The Faerie Queene*, 716.

[6] On the Queen's two bodies, see David Lee Miller's study of *The Poem's Two Bodies: The Poetics of the 1590 "Faerie Queene"* (Princeton, NJ: Princeton University Press, 1988).

[7] See *Essays by Rosemond Tuve: Spenser, Herbert, Milton*, ed. Thomas P. Roche, Jr. (Princeton, NJ: Princeton University Press, 1970), 124–27.

[8] Hamilton, ed. (2007), 185n28.1–2, offers the biblical references. Guillaume de Lorris and Jean de Meun, *The Romance of the Rose*, trans. Harry W. Robbins, ed. Charles W. Dunn (New York: Dutton, 1962), 440–41 (20785–20816); cf. 451–52 (21225–27); see Hamilton, ed. (2007), 184nn26.9–27.1. Anxious critical efforts to distance the pillars and temple from Belphoebe's legs and torso ironically attest to its suggestiveness: e.g., Anne Ferry, *The Art of Naming* (Chicago:

University of Chicago Press, 1988), 161–62. See the comparison of Serena's thighs to a "triumphal Arch" in the cannibal episode of Book VI.viii.42—with a difference, too, of course.

⁹ Hamilton, ed. (2007), 185n30.7–9. Quotation from Edgar Wind, *Pagan Mysteries in the Renaissance*, rev. ed. (Harmondsworth, UK: Penguin, 1967), 115. Spenser probably never saw Botticelli's painting, but the painting participates in a widespread cultural context.

¹⁰ Lyly's *Endymion*, including characters named Cynthia and Sir Thopas, was played before the Queen's court in 1588: *Oxford Dictionary of National Biography* (*DNB*; accessed online January 5, 2016). Marlowe's *Doctor Faustus* belongs to the late 1580s, too (exact date uncertain): *Oxford DNB* (accessed online January 5, 2016).

¹¹ *1 Henry IV*, I.iii.201–2, V.1.131–32 (dated 1596–97), in *The Riverside Shakespeare*, ed. G. Blakemore Evans et al., second ed. (Boston, MA: Houghton Mifflin, 1997).

¹² See Frances A. Yates, *Astraea: The Imperial Theme in the Sixteenth Century* (London: Routledge & Kegan Paul, 1975), 29–74, esp. 65–66, 72–73.

¹³ On the sixth proem, see my *Reading the Allegorical Intertext: Chaucer, Spenser, Shakespeare, Milton* (New York: Fordham University Press, 2008), 42–53; the following paragraph extends 335n6.

¹⁴ For Aristotle, color constitutes the subject of vision and the cause of the visible. For a Neoplatonizing scientist such as Johannes Kepler, light, rather than color, is the cause of the visible, but color is still material, "light entombed in a pellucid material": Judith H. Anderson, *Light and Death: Figuration in Spenser, Kepler, Donne, Milton* (New York: Fordham University Press, 2017), 123–25.

¹⁵ *Online OED*, s.v. covet, 1.b, c; 2.a, 3.a–c (accessed January 2, 2016). The relevant commandment is the tenth, although one might also think of a jealous God in the first. (The queen is a far cry from Spenser's God, however.)

¹⁶ "The 11th: and last booke of the Ocean to Scinthia," ll. 69, 497 ff., cf. ll. 29–30, in *The Poems of Sir Water Ralegh*, ed. Agnes M. C. Latham (London: Routledge & Kegan Paul, 1951); reference is to this edition. On the dating of *Cynthia*, see Latham's introduction, xxxvi–xl; and Stephen J. Greenblatt, *Sir Walter Ralegh: The Renaissance Man and His Roles* (New Haven, CT: Yale University Press, 1973), 12–13.

¹⁷ Spenser calls Ralegh "shepheard of the Ocean" in *Colin Clouts Come Home Againe*, *The Yale Edition of the Shorter Poems of Edmund Spenser*, ed. William A. Oram, Einar Bjorvand, Ronald Bond, Thomas H. Cain, Alexander Dunlop, and Richard Schell (New Haven, CT: Yale University Press, 1989), l. 66, cf. ll. 164–67, 173–75. On possible earlier versions of Ralegh's *Cynthia*, see Agnes M. C. Latham, ed., *Sir Walter Raleigh: Selected Prose and Poetry* (London: Athlone, 1965), 25; on the style of *Cynthia*, 210–11. Also Greenblatt, 77–98, esp. on pastoral, 80, 84–85.

[18] Hamilton, ed. (2007), 337n35.5–6. These allusions are widely recognized. In Book III, Belphoebe's posture, her bending over Timias, also recalls the tapestry of Malecasta and looks ahead to such figures as Venus in the Garden of Adonis and Britomart with the prostrate Scudamour in canto xi.

[19] Mary Villeponteaux, "*Semper Eadem*: Belphoebe's Denial of Desire," in *Renaissance Discourses of Desire*, ed. Claude J. Summers and Ted-Larry Pebworth (Columbia: University of Missouri Press, 1993), 29–45, takes "enuy" as greed—jealousy or covetousness (42–43); but see *Online OED*, s.v. *envy*, $v.^1$: 3.a: "to refuse to give (a thing) *to* (a person)," which is the meaning that best fits both context and syntax here (accessed April 15, 2016). On the difference between envy and jealousy, see Anderson, *Light and Death*, 54–58.

[20] Donald Cheney, *Spenser's Image of Nature: Wild Man and Shepherd in "The Faerie Queene"* (New Haven, CT: Yale University Press, 1966), 102.

[21] The reference is to Ralph Church's edition, 1758: Spenser's *Works: A Variorum Edition*, ed. Edwin Greenlaw, Charles Osgood, and Frederick Morgan Padelford, 11 vols. (Baltimore, MD: Johns Hopkins Press, 1932–57), 3:248 (lii).

[22] Jessica C. Murphy, "'Of the sicke virgin': Britomart, Greensickness, and the Man in the Mirror," *Spenser Studies* 25 (2010): 109–27 at 114.

[23] On the Spenser–Ralegh connection, see James P. Bednarz, "Ralegh in Spenser's Historical Allegory," *Spenser Studies* IV (1984): 49–70; also Andrew Hadfield, *Edmund Spenser: A Life* (Oxford: Oxford University Press, 2012), 231–35.

[24] *Edmund Spenser: The Faerie Queene*, 735 (DS 17).

[25] *Online OED*, s.v. *stair*, 1.a: "An ascending series . . . of steps"; 2.a: "One of a succession of steps"; 2.d. *fig*.: "A step of degree in a (metaphorical) ascent or in a scale of dignity"; 2.e: "A high position" (accessed January 2, 2016).

[26] Suggestive in this regard is the enumeration of chastity's possibilities as "a weapon, a tool, a mystification, an evasion, a sovereign prerogative, or a communal covenant": Kathryn Schwarz, "Whose Body?" in *Rethinking Feminism in Early Modern Studies: Gender, Race, and Sexuality*, ed. Ania Loomba and Melissa E. Sanchez (London: Taylor & Francis, 2016), 213–28 at 215–16.

[27] Paul Ricoeur, "The Metaphorical Process as Cognition, Imagination, and Feeling," in *On Metaphor*, ed. Sheldon Sacks (Chicago: University of Chicago Press, 1978, 1979), 141–57 at 146. Hate, standing on one side of Spenser's Concord, ineffectually and unavailingly bites his lip, gnashes his teeth, and threatens with his club. But he remains where he is and gets nowhere. On stationary or immobile figures, see also my fourth chapter.

[28] For example, A. C. Hamilton, ed., *The Faerie Queene* (London: Longman, 1977), 354n54.9. As of Hamilton's 2001 and 2007 editions, his note cites my argument as a gloss. His original edition was unusual in recognizing that the alexandrine needed glossing.

[29] Compare Louis Adrian Montrose's analysis of Petrarchan sublimation in "'The perfecte paterne of a Poete': The Poetics of Courtship in *The Shepheardes*

Calender," *Texas Studies in Literature & Language* 21 (1979): 34–67, esp. 54 (November Eclogue).

[30] *Edmund Spenser: The Faerie Queene,* 721 (CV1).

[31] In *Mirror and Veil: The Historical Dimension of Spenser's "Faerie Queene"* (Chapel Hill: University of North Carolina Press, 1977), 113–14, Michael O'Connell rightly locates a "sense of paradox" in the final stanzas of Book III.v, the result especially of the word "Nathlesse." This sense also follows from my own reading of the penultimate stanza ("ensample dead") and fittingly concludes the canto. For a harsher take on Belphoebe's response to Timias, see Villeponteaux, "*Semper Eadem,*" 42–43.

[32] See my *Reading the Allegorical Intertext,* 126–34, esp. 126–29. My earlier argument, which offers further evidence, is greatly curtailed in the present paragraph, which, conversely, also adds and expands some details.

[33] "Layamon's *Brut,*" in *Arthurian Chronicles Represented by Wace and Layamon,* intro. Lucy Allen Paton (London: J. M. Dent, 1912), 264; Laȝamon, *Brut,* ed. G. L. Brook and R. F. Leslie, EETS 227 (London: Oxford University Press, 1963–78), II:750.

[34] Gerald Prince, "The Disnarrated," *Style* 22.1 (1988): 1–8.

[35] See Patricia Fumerton, "'Secret' Arts: Elizabethan Miniatures and Sonnets," in *Representing the English Renaissance,* ed. Stephen Greenblatt (Berkeley: University of California Press, 1988), 93–133, esp. 93–106. Specifically on Timias's ruby heart, see Allan H. Gilbert, "Belphoebe's Misdeeming of Timias," *PMLA* 62 (1947): 622–43.

[36] For Melissa E. Sanchez, Timias and Amoret are versions of the same self-destructive excess of devotion: *Erotic Subjects: The Sexuality of Politics in Early Modern English Literature* (Oxford: Oxford University Press, 2011), 70–71.

[37] O'Connell, 116; and A. L. Rowse, *Ralegh and the Throckmortons* (London: Macmillan, 1962), 164, 204–6. Also Ralegh, Sir Walter, in the *Oxford DNB* (accessed online January 7, 2016).

[38] For a more positive reading of the jewel and dove episode, see Patrick Cheney's construction of an elaborate *roman à clef: Spenser's Famous Flight: A Renaissance Idea of a Literary Career* (Toronto: University of Toronto Press, 1993), 142–48. Cheney's reading and mine could co-exist, appropriately testifying to yet another doubleness in the poem. Spenser's episode does not overlook the plight of Amoret to concentrate only on Ralegh, however.

[39] Compare *Faerie Queene,* V.xii.36, VI.vi.1.

[40] *Online OED,* s.v. *quean,* 1; s.v. *queen* (etymology): these words have an ablaut relationship (accessed January 3, 2016). Thomas P. Roche, Jr., ed., *The Faerie Queene* (Harmondsworth, UK: Penguin, 1978), 1176, glosses *quean* as *hag,* as does Hamilton, ed. (2007). This meaning seems obvious from several examples in the *OED* and is the most appropriate one for Spenser's context.

[41] Helge Kökeritz, *Shakespeare's Pronunciation* (New Haven, CT: Yale University Press, 1960), 88; E. J. Dobson, *English Pronunciation 1500–1700,* second ed., 2 vols. (Oxford, UK: Clarendon, 1968), 2:640, 612n2.

[42] *The Vision of William concerning Piers the Plowman in Three Parallel Texts*, ed. Walter W. Skeat (London: Oxford University Press, 1886), C.IX.45–46 (my punctuation). For a concise discussion of Langland's punning on *quean/queen* and its basis in Old English, see Mary Carruthers, *The Search for St. Truth: A Study of Meaning in "Piers Plowman"* (Evanston, IL: Northwestern University Press, 1973), 60–61n19. Carruthers discusses wordplay in Langland's line "here nis no quen queyn*tere that* quyk is o lyue" (A.II.14: George Kane, ed.: I have replaced a thorn with *th*).

[43] Geoffrey Chaucer, *Works 1532*, supplemented by material from the editions of 1542, 1561, 1568, and 1602 (London: Scolar, 1969), f. 104 v., Manciple's Prologue, l. 34; f. 165 v., *The Romaunt of the Rose*, column a, l. 19.

[44] Quotation from Middleton is from Charles Barber's edition (Berkeley: University of California Press, 1968); Barber considers the play on *king's evil* "doubtless." For the same view, see James T. Henke, *Renaissance Dramatic Bawdry (Exclusive of Shakespeare): An Annotated Glossary and Critical Essays*, Jacobean Drama Studies, 39 (Salzburg: Institut für Englische und Literatur, Universität Salzburg, 1974), 2:249.

[45] On the presence of Aemylia and other dimensions of meaning in IV.viii, see my essay "Whatever Happened to Amoret? The Poet's Role in Book IV of *The Faerie Queene*," *Criticism* 13 (1971): 180–200, esp. 181–85; also chapter 4 in the present volume.

[46] Near the end of the poet's praise of antiquity and denunciation of the present in canto viii, he only appears to compliment the queen. Instead, he speaks with an evasive, disnarrative ambiguity that is to become increasingly characteristic of his compliments to her and, apparently, of his disillusionment with her. In viii.32.8, "her glorious flowre" is beauty's (l. 1). In viii.33.5, the word "her," although ambiguous, logically refers to beauty's glorious flower in l. 6 (chastity, to judge from Book III); from this flower proceed the "drops" or dew or nectar of virtue. The near but failed reference of pronouns in these stanzas to the living queen is further testimony of the distance between her and the ideal image.

[47] On the bisexuality of the cave beneath the mount in the Garden of Adonis, see my *Reading the Allegorical Intertext*, 221–23; and Lauren Silberman, *Transforming Desire: Erotic Knowledge in Books III and IV of "The Faerie Queene"* (Berkeley: University of California Press, 1995), 47–48. On Lust's bisexuality, see chapter 3 in the present volume, including note 80.

[48] Compare James E. Berg's contrast between the modern term *character* and a Theophrastan character, explained in note 6 of my introduction to this volume.

[49] Compare Marvin Hunt's suggestive analogy of the placement of Sidneian characters within a plot to Saussure's linguistic chessmen operating according to rules of play: "Characteronymic Structures in Sidney's *Arcadias*," *Studies in English Literature* 33.1 (1993): 1–19.

[50] For a constructive reading of Amoret, see Dorothy Stephens, *The Limits of Eroticism in Post-Petrarchan Narrative: Conditional Pleasure from Spenser to*

Marvell (Cambridge: Cambridge University Press, 1998), 25–46. See also my discussion of Serena in chapter 4, including notes.

[51] On the adulterous temptation to Amoret of her "Venereal disposition," see Anne Paolucci, *The Women in Dante's "Divine Comedy" and Spenser's "Faerie Queene"* (Dover, DE: Griffon House, 2005), 122–23.

[52] On Scudamour's seizure of Amoret in the Temple of Venus and its cultural origins, see my *Reading the Allegorical Intertext*, 149–53, esp. 144 (present quotation), 148, 152–53. Sanchez, reading the Temple for its erotic politics, suggests that it shows "a masochistic enjoyment of powerlessness" (*Erotic Subjects*, 64, 71–75). See also Cynthia E. Garrett, "Sexual Consent and the Art of Love in the Early Modern English Lyric," *Studies in English Literature* 44.1 (2004): 37–58, for further light on Scudamour's *raptus* of Amoret, including reference to Ralegh (43).

[53] See Alan Sinfield's discussion of Shakespeare's characters in *Faultlines: Cultural Materialism and the Politics of Dissident Reading* (Berkeley: University of California Press, 1992), 52–79; but also Elisa Oh's exploration of female strategy in "The Silences of Elizabeth I and Shakespeare's Isabella," *English Literary Renaissance* 45.3 (2015): 351–76.

3 Britomart: Inside and Outside the Armor

[1] For a sketch of these dimensions, see my "Britomart" in *The Spenser Encyclopedia*, ed. A. C. Hamilton, Donald Cheney, W. F. Blissett, David, A. Richardson, and William W. Barker (Toronto: University of Toronto Press, 1990), 113–15 at 113. I now put greater emphasis on Britomart as a combination of Mars and Venus.

[2] On the origin and range of the term *figure*, see the editors' introduction to Judith H. Anderson and Joan Pong Linton, ed., *Go Figure: Energies, Forms, and Institutions in the Early Modern World* (New York: Fordham University Press, 2011), 1–18.

[3] On the anagram, see Arthur F. Kinney, "Lear," *Massachusetts Review* 17 (1976): 677–712 at 684.

[4] *Hamlet*, I.ii.85, *The Riverside Shakespeare*, ed. G. Blakemore Evans et al., second ed. (Boston, MA: Houghton Mifflin, 1997); reference is to this edition. See Katharine Eisaman Maus, *Inwardness and Theater in the English Renaissance* (Chicago: Chicago University Press, 1995), 1–34 (including, 1–3, a critique of other arguments, and, on the line I cite from *Hamlet*, 1–2). For a strong denial in Hamlet's instance, see Francis Barker, *The Tremulous Private Body: Essays on Subjection* (London: Methuen, 1984), 35–38: Barker is likely right that Hamlet's interiority remains a mystery but mistaken that it is therefore nonexistent.

[5] Quotations are from *Edmund Spenser: The Faerie Queene*, ed. A. C. Hamilton, text edited by Hiroshi Yamashita, Toshiyuki Suzuki, and Shohachi Fukuda, rev. second ed. (Harlow, UK: Pearson, 2007), here III.i.9 (my emphasis); Hamilton, ed. (2007) refers to his glosses.

[6] Helen Cooper, *Shakespeare and the Medieval World* (London: Bloomsbury, 2010), 180–83. Cooper also traces Ariosto's Bradamante, another of Britomart's models, to a medieval source.

[7] Una is first named in *Faerie Queene*, I.i.45, as Truth in I.ii.arg., as actor in I.ii.9. Belphoebe's name first appears in II.iii.arg., then in III.Pro.5, and, within a canto, in III.v.27. Britomart, named in III.i.arg., acts in III.i.8.

[8] Alan Sinfield, *Faultlines: Cultural Materialism and the Politics of Dissident Reading* (Berkeley: University of California Press, 1992), 61, 65. See also Yu Jin Ko's introduction to Yu Jin Ko and Michael W. Shurgot, ed., *Shakespeare's Sense of Character: On the Page and From the Stage*, (Farnham, UK: Ashgate, 2012), 1–16: "at the heart of Shakespearean character" is a "web of relationship" with others (9). Compare the ethical dimension of "intersubjectivity" in Bruce W. Young, "Shakespearean Character and Early Modern Subjectivity: The Case of King Lear," in *Shakespeare's Sense of Character*, 35–51, e.g., 36–37, 50–51; and William Flesch, "What Makes Someone a Character in Shakespeare?" to which he answers, "interaction": ibid., 53–64 at 60. Compare Paul Yachnin's and Jessica Slights's introduction to their *Shakespeare and Character: Theory, History, and Theatrical Persons* (Houndmills, UK: Palgrave Macmillan, 2009), 1–18; also Sharon O'Dair's, "On the Value of Being a Cartoon, in Literature and in Life," in *Harold Bloom's Shakespeare*, ed. Christy Desmet and Robert Sawyer (Houndmills, UK: Palgrave, 2001), 81–96: O'Dair chides "essentialist humanism" and modern critical practice for "insufficient appreciation of the extent to which self and structure are interrelated" (89–90, cf. 95). R. A. Foakes argues that Sinfield's "continuous or developing interiority of consciousness" (*Faultlines*, 62) is "an act of interpretation," rather than "in the text or action of the play": "Reviving Shakespearean Character Criticism," *In the Footsteps of William Shakespeare*, ed. Christa Jansohn (Münster: LIT, 2005), 191–204 at 203–4. See also note 9 below in this chapter.

[9] Elisa Oh, "The Silences of Elizabeth I and Shakespeare's Isabella," *English Literary Renaissance* 45.3 (2015): 351–76, interprets womanly silence as a strategic, open-ended eluding of patriarchal power and thereby an alternative to Sinfield's reading. Oh's alternative does not disqualify Sinfield's positive criteria of consciousness, as distinguished from its eventual lack.

[10] I extend and modify Sinfield, *Faultlines*, 59. For another take on "character effects," see William Dodd, "Character as Dynamic Identity: From Fictional Interaction Script to Performance," 62–79, in *Shakespeare and Character*: we should take "character as an *effect* and not as an *origin* of speech"; such a "discourse biography" results in a social, moral, cultural identity (62–63). Such biography may be compatible with Dodd's "mimesis," but dubiously with agency. In a written forum on character in *Shakespeare Studies* 34 (2006), Alan Sinfield ("From Bradley to Cultural Materialism," 25–34) aligns the opposition of "old historicism" to formalist imagism with the newer opposition of historicism to "postmodern principles and deconstructive mechanisms" (25, 27–28), and then

reaffirms his own Althusserian (and implicitly Jamesonian) cultural materialism (30, 33). In the same forum, Jonathan Crewe ("Reclaiming Character?" 35–40) refers suggestively to "virtual persons" in drama (35); Tom Bishop ("Personal Fowl: 'The Phoenix and the Turtle' and the Question of Character," 65–74) relates the term "person" in religious discourse to the mix of secular and religious in Shakespeare. In "Character Criticism, the Cognitive Turn, and the Problem of Shakespeare Studies," *Shakespeare Studies* 42 (2014): 196–228, Edward Pechter offers a useful history of character, from Samuel Johnson to current neo-cognitivists. See also Lorna Hutson, *The Invention of Suspicion: Law and Mimesis in Shakespeare and Renaissance Drama* (Oxford: Oxford University Press, 2007), 6, 116–20, 128: Hutson locates Hamlet's interiority in his reflexive, spoken resistance to the "forensic habit of inference . . . associated with the mimesis of dramatic inference" (145).

[11] In "'Of the sicke virgin': Britomart, Greensickness, and the Man in the Mirror," *Spenser Studies* 25 (2010): 109–27, Jessica C. Murphy analyzes Britomart's malady in physical terms, refusing the *specificity* of Britomart's love insofar as Artegall, seen in the magic globe and described for two stanzas, is not an immediate bodily presence (109–10, 112). She relates Glauce's herbal remedies to greensickness without factoring in their failure—i.e., Glauce is mistaken—(117) and reads Britomart's arming simply as her "becoming a man" (119). On Britomart's volcanic response to Artegall's image, which recalls Orgoglio and the dragon of Book I, see also Rebecca Totaro, "Britomart's Meteorological Wound," *Archiv für Studium der Neueren Sprachen und Literaturen* 165 (1[250]) (2013): 42–65: 56–57, 59 (wound); 60–62 (Busiranic imagery); cf. Marion A. Wells, *The Secret Wound: Love-Melancholy and Early Modern Romance* (Stanford, CA: Stanford University Press, 2007), 225. On Britomart's response to Artegall's image and its transformation by Merlin to ethical agency, see Genevieve Guenther, "Spenser's Magic, or Instrumental Aesthetics in the 1590 *Faerie Queene*," *English Literary Renaissance* 36.2 (2006): 194–226.

[12] Lynn Enterline, *The Rhetoric of the Body from Ovid to Shakespeare* (Cambridge: Cambridge University Press, 2000), 19, 25–26; also Enterline's *Shakespeare's Schoolroom: Rhetoric, Discipline, Emotion* (Philadelphia: University of Pennsylvania Press, 2012), 85–88.

[13] For other influences on Britomart's performance by the seaside, including her virtual sonnet, see my *Reading the Allegorical Intertext: Chaucer, Spenser, Shakespeare, Milton* (New York: Fordham University Press, 2008), 70–74.

[14] See *Online OED*, s.v. *consciousness*, 1. "Internal knowledge or conviction; the state of being mentally conscious or aware of something." *OED* examples date from 1605 and 1614, but the first persuasive example of *consciousness* comes in 1642, from Massinger's *Maid of Honour*, I.ii.sig. C4: "The consciousness of mine owne wants." The two earlier examples offered are not persuasively different from *conscience,* a word to which the *OED*'s entry directs additional reference. See *OED*, s.v. *conscience*, II. "Senses without a moral dimension" and II.7 "Inward

knowledge or consciousness of something within or relating to oneself; internal conviction, personal awareness." Almost all the sixteenth-century examples of this definition are religious, which makes the *OED*'s general heading ("without a moral dimension") puzzling and likely too modern for most of them, a recurrent problem in the updated *OED*. Finally, see *OED*, s.v., *aware*, 1. "Watchful, vigilant, cautious, on one's guard"; 2. "Informed, cognizant, conscious" (entries accessed January 8, 2016).

[15] On the implications of being "Venus mayd," cf. Anne Paolucci, *The Women in Dante's "Divine Comedy" and Spenser's "Faerie Queene"* (Dover, DE: Griffon House, 2005), 122–23: Amoret is "constantly having to fight . . . temptation from within," namely, "a Venereal disposition"; regarding her transfiguration, cf. also 69–70: "not Amoret at all," the figure in Busirane's masque is its "central symbol" or "central emblem."

[16] *Faerie Queene*, III. iv.6, 8–9, 12, ix.40.

[17] On Malecasta's tapestry, see William A. Oram, "Spenser's Crowd of Cupids and the Language of Pleasure," in *Rhetorics of Bodily Disease and Health in Medieval and Early Modern England*, ed. Jennifer C. Vaught (Farnham, UK: Ashgate, 2010), 87–104 at 97–98.

[18] *Faerie Queene*, III.x.60, xi.1, 26 (Gealosy); xi.22, 26 (Mulciber). Busirane, like Mammon, is a hoarder, as his second chamber, a golden one, and his imprisonment of Amoret, at once virgin wife and love-principle, show. Malbecco, another hoarder, is jealous of his wife and of his money; his story introduces the cantos of Busirane (III.xi.1). With respect to Scudamour, who is also a jealous possessor, Busirane tries to exercise adverse possession, a legal concept effectually holding that if you successfully encroach on another's land long enough, you have a valid claim to it.

[19] See Leonard Barkan, *The Gods Made Flesh: Metamorphosis and the Pursuit of Paganism* (New Haven, CT: Yale University Press, 1986), 2–5; Ann Rosalind Jones and Peter Stallybrass, *Renaissance Clothing and the Materials of Memory* (Cambridge: Cambridge University Press, 2000), chap. 4, esp. 89–97; Heather James, "Ovid and the Question of Politics in Early Modern England," *ELH* 70 (2003): 343–73 at 358–63; Syrithe Pugh, *Spenser and Ovid* (Aldershot, UK: Ashgate, 2005), 146, 240.

[20] Susanne Wofford, remarking puns on *read* ("rede") in *Faerie Queene*, III. xi–xii, focuses attention on Britomart's gazing: "Gendering Allegory: Spenser's Bold Reader and the Emergence of Character in *The Faerie Queene* III," *Criticism* 30 (1988), 1–21. William Oram's succinct remarks on the House of Busirane are to the point: "Spenserian Paralysis," *Studies in English Literature* 41 (2001): 49–70 at 60. On "rede," in *The Faerie Queene*, see A. Leigh DeNeef, *Spenser and the Motives of Metaphor* (Durham, NC: Duke University Press, 1982), 142–56. Rachel Eisendrath differentiates Britomart's responses to the tapestries from her responses to the more objectified decorations in Busirane's second chamber: "Art and Objectivity in the House of Busirane," *Spenser Studies* 27 (2012): 133–61.

[21] Along with the notion of a chameleon's ability to take on the colors of its surroundings, "negatively capable" alludes here to the critical concept of negative capability, the Keatsian ability to empathize with or blend into a situation not one's own or into what another is experiencing without being judgmental. At times, the Spenserian narrator is didactic or judgmental, at others at variance with his own story, and at still others surprisingly inside it. For a more precisely bounded explanation of Keats's term, see M. H. Abrams, *A Glossary of Literary Terms*, fifth ed. (New York: Holt, Rhinehart & Winston, 1988), 112–13. On the Spenserian narrator, see also my introduction to this volume.

[22] Compare Jones's and Stallybrass's chap. 6 on women's use of mythological sources in their needlework and its utilization for protest, for example, by Mary Stuart. For a witty instance, see *Amoretti* LXXI (the lady's needlework depicting herself as a bee and her Spenserian suitor as a spider).

[23] Katherine Eggert, "Spenser's Ravishment: Rape and Rapture in *The Faerie Queene*," *Representations* 70 (2000): 1–26 at 11–12.

[24] Ovid, *Metamorphoses*, trans. Frank Justus Miller, second ed., 2 vols. (London: Heinemann, 1921), 1:292–93; Bk. VI.51–128 at 68–69.

[25] Hamilton, ed. (2001, 2007), 399n7–25; also Hamilton's 1977 edition of *The Faerie Queene* (New York: Longman), 413n7–25.

[26] Scholarship on the passions of the mind is extensive: for a recent, provocative discussion, rich with reference, see Steven Mullaney, *The Reformation of Emotions in the Age of Shakespeare* (Chicago: University of Chicago Press, 2015), 54–58.

[27] I oppose recent critical efforts to reduce literary allegory to abstraction and then to oppose it to narrative, not recognizing that such allegory is itself a narrative (or dramatic) mode.

[28] Thomas P. Roche, Jr., *The Kindly Flame: A Study of the Third and Fourth Books of Spenser's "Faerie Queene"* (Princeton, NJ: Princeton University Press, 1964), 82.

[29] Compare Graham Allen, *Intertextuality* (London: Routledge, 2000), 44: poetic, like metaphoric, language is double, both X and not X, whereas in traditional logic something is *either* X *or* not X. The virtual identification of poetic with metaphoric language is ancient and widespread.

[30] See Dudley Fenner, *The Artes of Logike and Rhetorike* (Middleburg, Netherlands: R. Schilders, 1584), sig. D1 v., for the translation "maidenly" of Latin "verecunda" in the discussion of metaphor in Cicero's *De Oratore* (ed. G. P. Goold, trans. E. W. Sutton, completed by H. Rackham, 2 vols. [London: Heinemann, 1942], 2:128; Bk. III.xli.165).

[31] Cicero, *De Oratore*, 2:123; Bk. III.xxxviii.156–xxxix.157. For fuller discussion, see my *Translating Investments: Metaphor and the Dynamic of Cultural Change in Tudor-Stuart England* (New York: Fordham University Press, 2005), 129–65 (metaphor and catachresis).

³² *Online OED*, s.v. *derne, adv.; dern, a.* and *n.¹*, 1–2, 5–6 (accessed January 9, 2016); *Middle English Dictionary*, s.v. *derneli(che), adv.*, a-d. The spelling of the adverbial form in Spenser's text suggests familiarity with medieval usage; the contextualized meaning does so more definitely. A current editorial exception is Hamilton, ed. (2007), 404n34: Hamilton still offers "earnestly or dismally," but now prefers "secretly." He rationalizes his preference on the ground that Amoret does not want Busirane to hear her plea. Though moving in the right direction, this gloss oversimplifies the situation. Busirane himself could tell Britomart about his power over Amoret in order to save his neck; at least, he could if he grasped its extent. In any event, Hamilton's explanation would not preclude my less innocent reading. My argument would also lend a more knowing or sinister cast to Lauren Silberman's view of Amoret as "the lady who says yes": *Transforming Desire: Erotic Knowledge in Books III and IV of "The Faerie Queene"* (Berkeley: University of California Press, 1995), 63.

³³ Rhetoric, famously in Plato's *Ion*, is associated with a chain. Alciati's popular emblem book also depicts Hercules, representative of eloquence and rhetoric, "as an old man, trailing after him a crowd of people fastened by the ears with the chains issuing from his mouth." The description is Jean Bodin's in his *Six Books of the Commonwealth*, cited by Jane Aptekar, *Icons of Justice: Iconography and Thematic Imagery in Book V of "The Faerie Queene"* (New York: Columbia University Press, 1969), 229–30n18. Thomas Wilson uses this image of Hercules in the preface to his rhetoric: *Wilson's Arte of Rhetorique 1560*, ed. G. H. Mair (Oxford, UK: Clarendon, 1909).

³⁴ On Petrarchan imagery in *Amoretti*, Theresa M. Krier is enlightening: "Generations of Blazons: Psychoanalysis and the Song of Songs in the *Amoretti*," *Texas Studies in Literature and Language* 40.3 (1998): 293–327; and *Birth Passages: Maternity and Nostalgia, Antiquity to Shakespeare* (Ithaca, NY: Cornell University Press, 2001), 82–105.

³⁵ Paul Ricoeur, "The Metaphorical Process as Cognition, Imagination, and Feeling," in *On Metaphor*, ed. Sheldon Sacks (Chicago: University of Chicago Press, 1978, 1979), 141–57 at 151; also Ricoeur's *Rule of Metaphor: Multi-Disciplinary Studies of the Creation of Meaning in Language*, trans. Robert Czerny (Toronto: University of Toronto Press, 1977), 248, 254–56. I derive "perverse predication" from Ricoeur's "deviant predication." The word *trope* derives from Greek *tropos*, "turn." The rose affords a familiar example of metaphor that is and is not: my love is a rose; my love is not (really) a rose: $A = B$; $A \neq B$.

³⁶ Contrast Susan Frye, *Elizabeth I: The Competition for Representation* (Oxford: Oxford University Press, 1993), 122–24, 129–30; cf. Michael Slater, "Spenser's Poetics of 'Transfixion' in the Allegory of Chastity," *Studies in English Literature* 54.1 (2014): 41–58 at 42–48. Guenther's discussion of Britomart and Amoret emphasizes "irresolvable doubt" and "wonder" (e.g., 219–26).

³⁷ For more on traversal, see pages 103–4 and note 68 in this chapter.

³⁸ *Online OED*, s.v. *bowel, n.*, 3–4, but also 1–2 (accessed January 10, 2016).

[39] *Online OED*, s.v. *as, adv.* and *conj.*, B.I.1.b; V.24 (accessed January 10, 2016).

[40] Ricoeur, "Metaphorical Process," 151; Bourdieu, *Language and Symbolic Power*, ed. John B. Thompson, trans. Gino Raymond and Matthew Adamson (Cambridge, MA: Harvard University Press, 1991), 142–43.

[41] Jean Aitchison, *Words in the Mind*, second ed. (Oxford, UK: Blackwell, 1984), 215, 217, and chaps. 17–18. Aitchison favors an electrical model of selection and comprehension—a kind of electrical circuit board—to an army or "cohort" model. For economy of explanation, I use the cohort model, which Aitchison also recognizes.

[42] Paper delivered July 7, 2001, at the International Spenser Society Conference in Cambridge, UK, to which I refer with Katherine Eggert's permission.

[43] On dead metaphor, see Anderson, *Translating Investments*, 15–22.

[44] *Online OED*, s.v. *stock, n.¹*, A.I.1.a. "A tree trunk deprived of its branches . . . a stump; b. "A log, block of wood"; c. "As the type of what is lifeless, motionless, or void of sensation. Hence, a senseless or stupid person" (accessed January 11, 2016). On the grotesqueness of the hermaphroditic statue and its spectatorial distancing, see Donald Cheney, "Spenser's Hermaphrodite and the 1590 *Faerie Queene*," *PMLA* 87 (1972): 192–200; Eisendrath, 150–51; Catherine Nicholson, "'Against the Brydale Day': Envy and the Meanings of Spenserian Marriage," *ELH* 83.1 (2016): 43–70 at 44–55, 54–55; Nicholson, 54, notes the parodic resonance of Scudamour's embrace of Amoret (III.xii.45.1 [1590]) with the earlier embrace of False Florimell by the witch's son (III.viii.x.1).

[45] On the relation of sex and gender, see Ania Loomba and Melissa E. Sanchez, "Feminism and the Burdens of History," in *Rethinking Feminism in Early Modern Studies: Gender, Race, and Sexuality*, ed. Ania Loomba and Melissa E. Sanchez (London: Taylor & Francis, 2016), 15–41 at 29–32; also note 93 below in this chapter.

[46] For further discussion of Artegall, see the entry on him in *The Spenser Encyclopedia*; my essay on him, "'Nor Man It Is': The Knight of Justice in Book V of Spenser's *Faerie Queene*," in *Essential Articles for the Study of Edmund Spenser*, ed. A. C. Hamilton (Hamden, CT: Archon, 1972), 447–70; or my "Spenser's *Faerie Queene*, Book V: Poetry, Politics, and Justice," in *A Companion to English Renaissance Literature and Culture*, ed. Michael Hattaway, 2 vols. (Oxford, UK: Wiley-Blackwell, 2010), I:263–73. My discussion of Artegall's confrontation with the leveling Giant of Book V is further relevant: *Words That Matter: Linguistic Perception in Renaissance English* (Stanford, CA: Stanford University Press, 1996), 167–89. See also references to Britomart and Artegall in chapter 1 of the present volume and note 85 below in the present chapter.

[47] Edgar Wind, *Pagan Mysteries in the Renaissance*, rev. ed. (Harmondsworth, UK: Penguin, 1976), 91–92 (my emphasis); James Nohrnberg, *The Analogy of "The Faerie Queene"* (Princeton, NJ: Princeton University Press, 1976), 455–57. See also note 56 below in this chapter.

[48] In the *Limits of Eroticism in Post-Petrarchan Narrative: Conditional Pleasure from Spenser to Marvell* (Cambridge: Cambridge University Press, 1998), Dorothy Stephens argues astutely for Britomart as a version of Minerva (e.g. 74, "her Minervan military prowess"; 83, "a masculine goddess born from Zeus's head"; 95, "Minerva, that most masculine of goddesses"). In the Malecasta episode, Stephens assumes that Britomart's helmet is off and her golden hair (coded feminine) cascading (74), whereas, "the braue Mayd would not disarmed bee / But onely vented vp her vmbriere" (III.i.42). Britomart's minimal exposure would actually give a harder edge to Stephens's reading of this episode, and it supports my argument regarding the importance of Venus-Mars to Spenser's *Venus armata*. For physiological background, see Thomas Laqueur, *Making Sex: Body and Gender from the Greeks to Freud* (Cambridge, MA: Harvard University Press, 1990), preface and chaps. 1–2, esp. viii, 8, 11, 30–31; also Valerie Traub's thoughtful introduction in *Desire and Anxiety: Circulation of Sexuality in Shakespearean Drama* (London: Routledge, 1992), 1–22.

[49] See my *Growth of a Personal Voice: "Piers Plowman" and "The Faerie Queene"* (New Haven, CT: Yale University Press, 1976), 4–5.

[50] *Faerie Queene*, III.iii.58–60 (Queen Angela's armor). Malecasta's reading of Britomart, although hardly reliable, is experienced, and it can no more summarily be dismissed than can readings of other figures by vicious interpreters in later books of the poem. Some ambiguity, danger, or confusion is invariably involved.

[51] The dubbing of knights is conventionally their creation (the verb *create* is employed). It coincides with their investment in heraldic arms. In *The Faerie Queene* VI.ii.33, Calidore's dubbing Tristram squire (apprentice to knighthood) coincides with the latter's acquisition of armor by conquest.

[52] Compare Jan Kott's classic essay "Shakespeare's Bitter Arcadia," in *Shakespeare Our Contemporary*, trans. Boleslaw Taborski, second ed., rev. (London: Methuen, 1967), 226–27.

[53] For parody in Arthur's figuration, see my *Reading the Allegorical Intertext*, 55–57, 130–34.

[54] Artegall also wears the armor of the Greek Achilles, which "*Arthegall did win*," presumably an allusion to Hector's killing the disguised Patroclus, which gave the Trojans possession of Achilles's armor (III.ii.25): notable is the implicit fusion of Greek with Trojan, comparable to the joining of Saxon with Briton in Britomart's arming. See also Hamilton, ed. (2007), 306n25.6, 321n60.2. William E. Bolton, "Anglo-Saxons in Faerie Land?: A Note on Some Unlikely Characters in Spenser's *Britain moniments*," *Spenser Studies* 23 (2008): 293–301, aims to discredit Britomart's cross-dressing along with her Saxon armor, overlooking the fact that Redcrosse is Saxon-born (I.x.65). Compare also Kathryn Schwarz, *Tough Love: Amazon Encounters in the English Renaissance* (Durham, NC: Duke University Press, 2000), 16–61: Schwarz perceptively discusses various ways of interpreting Britomart's arming.

[55] On Pubidius, see Harry Berger, Jr., *Revisionary Play: Studies in the Spenserian Dynamics* (Berkeley: University of California Press, 1988), 104. Hamilton, ed. (2007), has further suggestions, 313n13, 630n29.3. Rather than finding comic male/female cooperation in the visit to Merlin, Mary Villeponteaux feminizes the whole visit, considering Merlin's cave vaginal, the site of his emasculation by an enchantress, as well as of his own conception: "Displacing Feminine Authority in *The Faerie Queene*," *Studies in English Literature* 35.1 (1995): 53–67 at 63. (Some figures of men have caves, too, in *The Faerie Queene*.)

[56] Oskar Seyffert, *Dictionary of Classical Antiquities*, rev. ed. by Henry Nettleship and J. E. Sandys (1956; Cleveland, OH: World Publishing, 1963), s.v., *Athēnē*, 80–82 at 80; cf. s.v. *Minerva*, 394. Seyffert notes that Aphrodite (Venus) is also a goddess of storm and lightning (Jovian thunderbolts!) and as such could be depicted in armor; he suggests that these attributes might explain how she came to be associated with Arēs (Mars): s.v. *Aphrodite*, 39.

[57] In *The Faerie Queene*, II.x.25–26, Bladud is portrayed as a beneficial leader possessing wondrous arts, who eventually overreaches. Accordingly, perhaps to shield Britomart from such hubris, her Bladudian spear is rendered ineffectual in her climactic battle with Artegall, and, as part of her more general disfiguration in Book V, it goes missing in her battle with Radigund. Before these battles, it never fails her—whether against Guyon, Marinell, or Paridell. In both the later exceptions, she continues to use a sword. John Lance Griffith locates in Britomart's virtuous purpose the difference between her use of the spear and Bladud's self-indulgent magic: "Britomart's Spear and Merlin's Magic Mirror: Magics Meaningful and Meaningless in *Faerie Queene* Book III," *Medieval and Early Modern Studies* 20 (2012): 73–91 at 81–83.

[58] Hamilton, ed. (2007), 307n30.2.

[59] For example, *The Romaunt of the Rose*, in *Geoffrey Chaucer: The Works 1532, with supplementary material from the Editions of 1542, 1561, 1598 and 1602* (London: Scolar, 1969), f. cxliii v.

[60] On Sidney's speaking picture in Spenser's poetry, cf. Adam McKeown, "Looking at Britomart Looking at Pictures," *Studies in English Literature* 45.1 (2005): 43–63 at 44–49.

[61] See Susanne Wofford, "Britomart's Petrarchan Lament: Allegory and Narrative in *The Faerie Queene*, III, iv," *Comparative Literature* 39 (1987): 28–57 at 39–44.

[62] Although *Sir Gawain and the Green Knight* was never published in Spenser's time and today exists in a single manuscript, the possibility remains of his having seen a manuscript of it or having encountered a source or some other version of the castle trial. Be that as it may, intertextuality, which differs from source study, though it might include sources, can work in both directions for a reader, from former to later, or the reverse: e.g., see Anderson, *Reading the Allegorical Intertext*, 15–16.

[63] James Nohrnberg remarks Britomart's virginal "attraction toward cloistered interiors" but finds it "somewhat paradoxical that Britomart is also the penetrating agent" (532).

[64] On this relation in Book I, see Claire McEachern, *The Poetics of English Nationhood 1590–1612* (Cambridge: Cambridge University Press, 1996), chap. 2, and Harry Berger Jr.'s challenge to her view in "Sexual and Religious Politics in Book I of Spenser's *Faerie Queene*," *English Literary Renaissance* 34 (2004): 201–42. Berger favors an all-encompassing inwardness, McEachern a nearly total outwardness.

[65] Regarding Britomart's faining, cf. Loomba and Sanchez, "Feminism and the Burdens of History," 41: "Desdemona's desire *for* such a man" as Othello "and her desire to *be* such a man, are inextricable."

[66] Quotation from Shakespeare, *Measure for Measure*, II.iv.138.

[67] Judith Butler, *Gender Trouble: Feminism and the Subversion of Identity* (New York: Routledge, 1990), 128–49; and *Bodies That Matter: On the Discursive Limits of "Sex"* (New York: Routledge, 1993), 1–23. On performance, see also Kathryn Schwarz, "Whose Body?" in *Rethinking Feminism in Early Modern Studies: Gender, Race, and Sexuality*, ed. Ania Loomba and Melissa E. Sanchez (London: Taylor & Francis, 2016), 213–28 at 216. On cross-gender identification, see Valerie Traub, *Thinking Sex with the Early Moderns* (Philadelphia: University of Pennsylvania Press, 2016), 24–25.

[68] On transference and traversal, see chaps. 10–19 of Jacques Lacan, *The Four Fundamental Concepts of Psychoanalysis,* book XI of *The Seminar of Jacques Lacan*, ed. Jacques-Alain Miller, trans. Alan Sheridan (New York: W. W. Norton, 1981). Compare Jeffrey Jerome Cohen, "On Saracen Enjoyment: Some Fantasies of Race in Late Medieval France and England," *Journal of Medieval & Early Modern Studies* 31 (2001), 113–46 at 128, 132–33; also Slavoj Žižek, *The Sublime Object of Ideology* (London: Verso, 1989), 30–45; and his "Revisioning 'Lacanian' Social Criticism: The Law and Its Obscene Double," *The Journal for the Psychoanalysis of Culture & Society* 1 (1996): 15–25. Žižek translates cultural ideology to individual fantasy and vice versa in a way that is more suggestive for my view of Busirane's House as a cultural site than is unmediated Lacan. Compare note 70 in this chapter.

[69] Pursuit of the relation of metaphor to metonymy would be distracting here, but my take on it can be found in *Translating Investments*, chaps. 4, 7, and, succinctly, in *Light and Death: Figuration in Spenser, Kepler Donne, Milton* (New York: Fordham University Press, 2016), 160–62.

[70] Žižek's focus on a cultural problem either shifts back to the single character in whom it is internalized and on whom it is based or else it belies its own psycho-basis. This Žižekian-Lacanian basis offers to overlook what specifically and dominantly *differentiates* Britomart from Amoret and Busirane. It also privileges a narrower conception of erotic desire as genital and woman as Busirane's Amoret—whole only when wanting—than is historically justified. Compare Debora Kuller Shuger's argument that in the Renaissance "sexual desire is an inflection of erotic

longing, not its origin or essence": *The Renaissance Bible: Scholarship, Sacrifice, and Subjectivity* (Berkeley: University of California Press, 1994), 178, 180.

[71] Flower and boar are two major, binary forms of symbolism in Book III: see my *Growth of a Personal Voice*, 98–113.

[72] Consider Stephens's argument that Lust's cave is a place where women find a kind of community or intimacy denied them elsewhere (25–26, 41–42).

[73] Although I admire Stephens's work on Spenser's gender-bending, I am sometimes puzzled by her treating a figure such as Amoret—"*Venus* mayd" (and "made") for coupling with "*Cupids* man"—as if she had, and we could grasp, her "consciousness," her "thoughts" and her intentions (e.g., 28, 33, 37); cf. *Faerie Queene*, III.xi.7, IV.x.54. Long before the Temple of Venus, Scudamour's name (Shield of Love), on which Cupid is emblazoned, identifies him as the relatively simple figure "*Cupids* man." See also note 96 below on characterological inference.

[74] On the Venerean veil, see my *Reading the Allegorical Intertext*, 135–53.

[75] Compare this stanza with Britomart's revelation in III.ix.20–24, where she doffs helmet and habergeon alike. In the present passage, the "firie light" suggests heat lightning to Hamilton, ed. (2007); he, too, is reminded of Florimell's comet-like hair (413n13.6–9).

[76] See *The Faerie Queene*, IV.i.47–49: "I saw *him* [i.e., Britomart] haue your *Amoret* at will"; Ate alleges heterosexual sex (49: my emphasis). Compare Slander's comparable reading of Amoret in IV.viii.28–29 ("conuersing"), 35 ("whores"); and Jonathan Goldberg, *Endlesse Worke: Spenser and the Structures of Discourse* (Baltimore, MD: Johns Hopkins University Press, 1981), 59–60. On the reading of "their loues," see Hamilton, ed. (2007), 413n16, who cites Camille Paglia, *Sexual Personae: Art and Decadence from Nefertiti to Emily Dickinson* (New York: Random House, 1991), on the homoeroticism of Britomart and Amoret (182); also Stephens, 38, and Schwarz, *Tough Love*, 168–69. Paglia refers to "homosexual touches" (182); cf. her "Apollonian Androgyne and *The Faerie Queene*," *English Literary Renaissance* 9 (1979): 42–63 at 49–52. Stephens, 76, considers "foolishly anachronistic" the view that Spenser argues "for the virtues of sexual intercourse between women," but she also observes Britomart's "maturation into an intimate—though still highly problematical—friendship with Amoret" in the passages at issue. On *homoerotic* and other "imprecise" or "unintelligible" terms and linguistic uses, see Traub, *Thinking Sex*, 8–17, and on shared beds, 12–13. Textual evidence historically grounds and can refine (not define) such imprecise, catachrestic terminology.

[77] The one lady, Poeana, is lascivious prior to her reform, and the other, Aemylia, was captured by Lust when she tried to elope with her squire of low degree, who was likewise captured by the lust-inducing Corflambo. See chapter 4 for further discussion.

[78] Compare Elizabeth Fowler's point that, in the marriage of Thames and Medway (IV.xi), Medway, the bride, is there by her consent: *Literary Character:*

The Human Figure in Early English Writing (Ithaca, NY: Cornell University Press, 2003), 202, cf. also 203–4. Aside from the retrospective *raptus* of Amoret in IV.x, consent is the dominant ethical emphasis in Book IV. Melissa E. Sanchez gives consent a more sinister, political cast in Book IV: *Erotic Subjects: The Sexuality of Politics in Early Modern English Literature* (Oxford: Oxford University Press, 2011), e.g., 64, 71–75.

[79] For a negative perspective on the encounter between Britomart and Artegall that leads to their accord, see Schwarz, *Tough Love*, 163–70. Schwarz is concerned to expose the contradictions and disabling losses in "the transition from homoerotic violence to heterosexual marriage" (163); cf. Kent R. Lehnhof's reading of Britomart's armor as a bow to the poem's homonormativity, which requires that "her uncomfortable anatomical otherness" be "covered up" as fully as possible: "Incest and Empire in *The Faerie Queene*," *ELH* 73 (2006): 215–43, here 236. I remain interested in the *enabling* possibilities of the encounter, insofar as they can be sustained. They cannot be sustained indefinitely. For an alternative, positive reading of the encounter, see Lisa Celovsky, "Early Modern Masculinities and *The Faerie Queene*," *English Literary Renaissance* 35 (2005): 210–47 at 222.

[80] William Oram observes that Spenser's figure of Lust combines male and female genital imagery, proving a "demonic parallel to the bisexual Venus of canto x": "Elizabethan Fact and Spenserian Fiction," *Spenser Studies* 4 (1983): 33–47 at 42. Stephens considers the figure of Lust "extravagantly male" (42); Goldberg observes that Lust, when first described, is "little more than a gaping mouth dripping blood," the embodiment of desire as a "devouring place" or "devouring mouth" (58). As he describes it, this place is female. With a trunk-like nose and long, wide ears to the waist, however, Lust is also elephantine (and Ollyphantine) and male. On the bisexuality of the cave beneath the mount in the Garden of Adonis, see my *Reading the Allegorical Intertext*, 221–23; also Silberman, 47–48.

[81] Jean-François Lyotard, "The Dream-Work Does Not Think," in his *Discourse, Figure*, trans. Antony Hudek and Mary Lydon (Minneapolis: University of Minnesota Press, 2011), 233–67; and Ricoeur, "Metaphorical Process," 141–57.

[82] Lyotard, "The Dream-Work Does Not Think," 244; cf. Lyotard, *Discourse, Figure*, 15 (phantasm). Lyotard compares the matrix of narrative rhythm to "what Propp called form" (244). On Propp, see *Discourse, Figure*, 145, 406–7n12, 425n26.

[83] *Faerie Queene*, III.ii.25, IV.iv.39, vi.12.

[84] Compare the related confusion/conflation of the roles of hunter and hunted in the imagery of IV.x.55, as Scudamour leads Amoret from the Temple of Venus, a passage I have treated in *Reading the Allegorical Intertext*, 150–51.

[85] Masked Ate's description of Britomart's shield in IV.i.48 is ironically pertinent: telling Scudamour that she does not know the name of the knight who now possesses Amoret, namely armed Britomart, Ate continues, "but in his shield he beares / (That well I wote) the heads of many broken spears." If Britomart's spear and steeple need blunting, the Salvage Knight comparably needs bloodletting, as

earlier suggested: excess, wildness, crudeness (rawness and roughness) are implicit in his disguised figure, whose "mayle" gets "yriv'd" and whose "fingers [go] slacke," his sword thereupon falling (IV.vi.15, 21); sexual allusion is obvious. Like Britomart, Artegall is unmasked before an accord can be reached.

[86] Compare *Amoretti* LXVII, in *The Yale Edition of the Shorter Poems of Edmund Spenser*, ed. William A. Oram, Einar Bjorvand, Ronald Bond, Thomas H. Cain, Alexander Dunlop, and Richard Schell (New Haven, CT: Yale University Press, 1989): "till I . . . with her owne goodwill hir fyrmely tyde; / Strange thing me seemd to see a beast so wyld, / so goodly wonne with her owne will *beguyld*" (my emphasis). Context and genre make a difference, however.

[87] Joseph Anthony Mazzeo's exposition of Machiavelli's *virtù* remains useful: *Renaissance and Revolution: Backgrounds in Seventeenth-Century Literature* (London: Methuen, 1969), 91–94.

[88] On the traditional gendering of wrath, which relates to hate as masculine, see Barbara H. Rosenwein, ed., *Anger's Past: The Social Uses of an Emotion in the Middle Ages* (Ithaca, NY: Cornell University Press, 1998), esp. 1–6, 233–47; Lester K. Little, "Anger in Monastic Curses," ibid., 9–35; Gerd Althoff, "*Ira Regis*: Prolegomena to a History of Royal Anger," ibid., 59–74; and William V. Harris, *Restraining Rage: The Ideology of Anger Control in Classical Antiquity* (Cambridge, MA: Harvard University Press, 2001).

[89] On "fitt," see chapter 2, 53–54.

[90] On the difference between *allegorical* and *allegory*, adjective and noun, see my *Reading the Allegorical Intertext*, 5–7. Mihoko Suzuki observes that, "Britomart, though androgynous, is not self-contained to the point of narcissism" because she seeks Artegall; in other words, she is not subject and object to herself: *Metamorphoses of Helen: Authority, Difference, and the Epic* (Ithaca, NY: Cornell University Press, 1989), 154. In connection with Sidney's *Arcadia*, Schwarz, *Tough Love*, 197, cites Marjorie Garber's illuminating remarks about the use of the term "androgyne" or "hermaphrodite," but, I would add, without an orientation to *figural* or *mythic* thinking, which is not reducible to abstract binaries: Garber denies that a "third term" is properly a *term* or "a sex, certainly not an instantiated 'blurred' sex as signified by a term like 'androgyne' or 'hermaphrodite.' . . . The 'third' is a mode of articulation, a way of describing a space of possibility": *Vested Interests: Cross-Dressing and Cultural Anxiety* (New York: Routledge, 1992), 11. Mythic or figural thinking puts abstraction in question without positing a *space*, which by itself suggests emptiness to me, not a *place* of positive, creative possibility and openness. For yet another alternative, see Celovsky, 211, 214–17, 221.

[91] Quitslund, *Spenser's Supreme Fiction: Platonic Natural Philosophy and "The Faerie Queene"* (Toronto: University of Toronto Press, 2001), 230–35. See also note 92 right below.

[92] See Leone Ebreo [Leo Hebraeus] *Dialoghi d'Amore* [1535] (Heidelberg: Carl. Gebhardt, 1929), Dialogo Terzo, 1–154 at 87 v. to 88 r.; in French, *Dialogues d'Amour*, trans. Pontus de Tyard (1551), ed. T. Anthony Perry (Chapel Hill:

178   NOTES

University of North Carolina Press, 1974) 249, 260; in English, *The Philosophy of Love*, trans. F. Friedeberg-Seeley and Jean H. Barnes (London: Soncino, 1937), 268–69, 302, 354–55, 371–72. Reprints and translations testify to the popularity of Leone's dialogue. Taken whole, his views support Elliot R. Wolfson's explanation of the ultimately androcentric basis of kabbalistic hermaphroditism: *Language, Eros, Being: Kabbalistic Hermeneutics and Poetic Imagination* (New York: Fordham University Press, 2005), chap. 2; cf. chaps. 3–4. Leone's assertion that each male and female includes the other sex/gender illogically gives way to a more conventional allegory of man as intellect and woman as body. Relevant to Leone's assertions is Shuger's contention that, in the later seventeenth century, eros is relocated from the eyes and "brain to regions below the waist" (179). My "Artegall" in *The Spenser Encyclopedia*, 62–64 at 63, already notes that the principle of coupling in Spenser's epic (and in its principal couple) involves four terms, not two.

[93] Compare Laqueur on the so-called one-sex model, which is largely Galen's: "what we call sex and gender were . . . [in this model] explicitly bound up in a circle of meanings from which escape . . . was impossible" (8, 128–29). Laqueur acknowledges the existence of the Aristotelian two-sex model in the period, on which see my *Reading the Allegorical Intertext*, 376–77n10. Traub's view, although not utopian, is somewhat more hopeful: *Desire and Anxiety*, 14–18. See also note 45 above in this chapter and Traub, *Thinking Sex*, e.g., 8, 18.

[94] Earlier, Scudamour has referred to the willingly disarmed Artegall as "a Ladies thrall" (IV.vi.28). Both the facts that Scudamour is the speaker and that he speaks at the anticlimax of the battle of Britomart and Artegall make a big difference. Scudamour, "Cupid's man," is not the most reliable of witnesses, a point his story and Amoret's bring home.

[95] Compare Ricoeur, "Metaphorical Process," 151, on the split reference of metaphor; also Wolfgang Iser, *The Fictive and the Imaginary: Charting Literary Anthropology* (Baltimore, MD: Johns Hopkins University Press, 1993), xiv–xv: Iser's category of the fictive is not tied to "the old fiction/reality dichotomy." Like Ricoeur's metaphor, the fictive "keeps in view what has been overstepped" but is nonetheless "an act of boundary-crossing" that at once "disrupts and doubles the referential world."

[96] William Morse, "'The Play's the Thing: Shakespeare's Critique of Character (and Harold Bloom)," in *Harold Bloom's Shakespeare*, 109–23 at 118, 120. Compare Lorna Hutson, "Law, Probability and Character in Shakespeare," in *Fictions of Knowledge: Fact, Evidence, Doubt*, ed. Yota Baatsaki, Subha Mukherji, and Jan-Melissa Schramm (Houndmills, UK: Palgrave Macmillan, 2012), 61–83. Hutson discusses the "hidden, causal or motivational elements" of speech and action that are "merely inferred" and encourage us to think of fictional persons as having an existence that exceeds the story in which they act (61, 63–64). It hardly requires a boy actor to make a fictive woman speak "from within about the system

of gender": Yanchin and Slights, introduction to *Shakespeare and Character*, 1–18 at 9. Are there limits to inferential reading? What role has evidence, and who is the judge?

[97] *Faerie Queene*, V.vi.34, 37–38, vii.21–23.

[98] *Faerie Queene*, V.vii.8, 16, 19.

[99] For discussion, including Isis Church, see my essay in *Essential Articles for the Study of Edmund Spenser*, at 458–60; and in *A Companion to English Renaissance Literature and Culture*, I:263–73. Also McKeown, 52; and David Lee Miller, "Gender, Justice, and the Gods in *The Faerie Queene*, Book V," in *Reading Renaissance Ethics*, ed. Marshall Grossman (New York: Routledge, 2007), 19–37. Katherine Eggert comments perceptively about sex and gender in the Temple of Isis: *Showing like a Queen: Female Authority and Literary Experiment in Spenser, Shakespeare, and Milton* (Philadelphia: University of Pennsylvania Press, 2000), 40; more recently, Eggert offers an alchemical interpretation of Britomart's vision as a "*coniunctio* of equals" in the Temple: *Disknowledge: Literature, Alchemy, and the End of Humanism in Renaissance England* (Philadelphia: University of Pennsylvania Press, 2015), 187–90 at 188. Compare also Alice Miskimin, "Britomart's Crocodile and the Legends of Chastity," *JEGP* 77 (1978): 17–36; and Kathryn Walls, "Spenser and the 'Medieval Past': A Question of Definition," in *Spenser in the Moment*, ed. Paul J. Hecht and J. B. Lethbridge (Madison, NJ: Fairleigh Dickinson University Press, 2015), 35–66 at 45–47.

[100] Quotation from William Blackstone, *Commentaries on the Laws of England*, as cited in Elizabeth Fowler, 107.

[101] A foreign marriage increases the danger, but a domestic one also incurs it. On Alençon, see *The Spenser Encyclopedia*, 14–15; Andrew Hadfield, *Spenser: A Life* (Oxford: Oxford University Press, 2012), 101, 273.

[102] Hamilton, ed. (2007), 558n30, suggests that the lioness is Britomart and the tiger Radigund, insofar as the lion is a "royal beast." I am less confident of these identifications; cf. the blurring of Redcrosse and Sans Joy in Book I as a griffin with "pray" and "rightfull rauine" and a dragon desirous of these (I.v.8). In the present battle, the lioness is female, and the tiger is not, but the combatants cannot so neatly be distinguished. The lack of a stable distinction between them is another instance of figural undoing and reversing: Mars and Venus wasting each other, an internal and figural matter and not *simply* a dynastic or political one. Compare Eggert, *Showing like a Queen*, 41: "Britomart's task is evidently to subdue herself." While Eggert reads Britomart and Radigund as "scarcely distinguishable," she also reads tiger and lion as female, whereas I think it important that Britomart's Martian and Venerean components *alike* are hemorrhaging in this battle; cf. Paglia, "Appollonian Androgyne," 85; and Suzuki, 177–95. For final complications of gender, cf. V.iv.39 (Lioness), V.vii.30 (Lioness, Lion, she), and V.viii.49 (bitch, Tiger). Raging female at least momentarily morphs into male in the last two passages. See also note 88 in this chapter.

[103] Britomart's progress in Books III–V can variously be translated and theorized: e.g., her assumption of Busirane's abuse of Amoret into theories of transference (10–11, 103–4) or of sadism, masochism, or both; her journey in Book V into a process of sublimation or, again, of transference (see Anderson, "Nor Man It Is," *Essential Articles*, 460); and her fight with Radigund into masochism. In *New Introductory Lectures on Psychoanalysis*, trans. James Strachey (New York: W. W. Norton, 1965), Freud (very) controversially wrote, "The suppression of women's aggressiveness which is prescribed for them constitutionally [i.e., essentially] and imposed on them socially favours the development of powerful masochistic impulses, which succeed, as we know, in binding erotically the destructive trends which have been diverted inwards" (155–16). Because my present concern is with figuration, with metaphorical allegory as a way of thinking, and with significant form and tangible meaning, I want to minimize ahistorical, abstractive translation, even while acknowledging its possibility within a different kind of project.

[104] Quotation from *Colin Clouts Come Home Againe*, l. 802: *Shorter Poems of Edmund Spenser*. On the birth of Venus, see also Hesiod, *Theogony*, in *Hesiod and Theognis*, trans. Dorothea Wender (Harmondsworth, UK: Penguin, 1973), 27–29. For the positive aspects of Britomart's rescue of Artegall, see the parallels to Una observed in my first chapter.

[105] On the Chaucerian persona in the fifth proem, see my *Growth of a Personal Voice*, 184–86, and, for additional contextualization, see my *Words That Matter*, 172–73. Unlike Harry Berger, Jr., I do not find Spenser's narrator consistent even in his masking. Like the figures of *The Faerie Queene*, its narrator evolves and shifts. His own figure is contextualized: see Berger's "Narrative as Rhetoric in *The Faerie Queene*," in *Situated Utterances* (New York: Fordham University Press, 2005), 173–217, and my "Chaucer's and Spenser's Reflexive Narrators," in *Reading the Allegorical Intertext*, 27–41. My discussion of Malfont and Duessa in chapter 4 of the present volume is also relevant.

[106] Artegall's name suggests "art equal," "art of equality," or "equal [to] Arthur." Prince Arthur is identified in the poem as Artegall's maternal half-brother (III. iii.27). In Book III, his name is spelled "Arthogall" or "Arthegall," emphasizing his similarity to Arthur.

[107] Metonymy is "referential, substitutive, coded, ideological," as distinguished from metaphor, which is "deviant, constructive, creative—code-breaking": Anderson, *Translating Investments*, 4.

[108] Shekhar Kapur, *Elizabeth* (1998). Reading Britomart throughout the poem as an allegory of Elizabeth I, Julia M. Walker suggestively sees Mercilla as the icon that replaces Britomart: *Medusa's Mirrors: Spenser, Shakespeare, Milton, and the Metamorphosis of the Female Self* (Newark, NJ: University of Delaware Press, 1998), chap. 3, esp. 112–13. To my mind, replacement comes earlier and for a larger complex of reasons.

4 Phantasies, Pains, and Punishments: A Still-Moving Coda

[1] Quotations from *Edmund Spenser: The Faerie Queene*, ed. A. C. Hamilton, text edited by Hiroshi Yamashita, Toshiyuki Suzuki, and Shohachi Fukuda, rev. second ed. (Harlow, UK: Pearson, 2007), here III.xii.26. Notes are cited as Hamilton, ed. (2007), unless otherwise indicated.

[2] Paolucci, *The Women in Dante's "Divine Comedy" and Spenser's "Faerie Queene"* (Dover, DE: Griffon House, 2005).

[3] In order, see Kathryn Schwarz, *Tough Love: Amazon Encounters in the English Renaissance* (Durham, NC: Duke University Press, 2000); Melissa E. Sanchez, *Erotic Subjects: The Sexuality of Politics in Early Modern English Literature* (Oxford: Oxford University Press, 2011); Theresa M. Krier, *Gazing on Secret Sights* (Ithaca, NY: Cornell University Press, 1990), 67–82 (portrait of Belphoebe); Elizabeth Fowler, *Literary Character: The Human Figure in Early English Writing* (Ithaca, NY: Cornell University Press, 2003), 193–214 (Medway and Florimell).

[4] For example, William Shakespeare, *The Winter's Tale*, ed. Stephen Orgel (Oxford: Oxford University Press, 1996), IV.4.140–43; Ben Jonson, *The Forrest*, in *Works*, ed. C. H. Herford and Percy and Evelyn Simpson, 11 vols. (Oxford: Clarendon, 1925–52), 8; also my discussion of still movement in Jonson: *Words That Matter: Linguistic Perception in Renaissance English* (Stanford, CA: Stanford University Press, 1996), 116–21.

[5] For various approaches to Mutability and Nature (mine included), see *Celebrating Mutabilitie: Essays on Edmund Spenser's Mutabilitie Cantos*, ed. Jane Grogan (Manchester, UK: Manchester University Press, 2010). See also note 15 below in this chapter.

[6] The argument that the rule of a woman is unnatural was familiar in Spenser's time and particularly associated with Protestant Reformers: e.g., see Patricia Parker, *Literary Fat Ladies: Rhetoric, Gender, Property* (London: Methuen, 1987), 54–66. Parker also argues that Acrasia refers to Queen Elizabeth. On issues of sex and gender the figure of Acrasia raises, consider Harry Berger, Jr., "Wring out the Old: Squeezing the Text, 1951–2001," *Spenser Studies* 18 (2003), 81–121, and Judith H. Anderson, *Reading the Allegorical Intertext: Chaucer, Spenser, Shakespeare, Milton* (New York: Fordham University Press, 2008), chap. 15.

[7] See my *Reading the Allegorical Intertext*, chaps. 9, 15, and "Acrasia" in the index; the version offered here derives from pages 234–37. The chapters cited abound in critical annotation.

[8] On the words "crime" and "sin," see Stephen Greenblatt, *Renaissance Self-Fashioning: From More to Shakespeare* (Chicago: University of Chicago Press, 1980), 172. See also the debate between Richard Danson Brown and J. B. Lethbridge regarding the significance (or its lack) of Spenser's rhyming in their *Concordance to the Rhymes of "The Faerie Queene"* (Manchester, UK: Manchester University Press, 2013), 1–180.

[9] William Shakespeare, *Antony and Cleopatra*, ed. John Wilders (London: Routledge, 1995), II.ii.245–47.

[10] Jean-Luc Nancy, *The Ground of the Image*, trans. Jeff Fort (New York: Fordham University Press, 2005), 9, 20. On "exhilaration," see "jouissance" (Nancy, 9), plus Valerie Traub's explanation of *jouissance* as a "complex, self-contradictory concept," not simply equivalent to "pleasure": *Thinking Sex with the Early Moderns* (Philadelphia: University of Pennsylvania Press, 2016), 29.

[11] On the Palmer as an artist, a spinner of myth, see my "Knight and the Palmer in *The Faerie Queene*, Book II," *Modern Language Quarterly* 31 (1970): 160–78, esp. 162–65. The Palmer is a rational, sometimes rationalizing spinner; even his "subtile" net is "formally," or regularly, rationally, logically "frame[d]" (II.xii.81).

[12] See Leonard Barkan, *The Gods Made Flesh: Metamorphosis and the Pursuit of Paganism* (New Haven, CT: Yale University Press, 1986), 2–5; Ann Rosalind Jones and Peter Stallybrass, *Renaissance Clothing and the Materials of Memory* (Cambridge: Cambridge University Press, 2000), chap. 4, esp. 89–97; Heather James, "Ovid and the Question of Politics in Early Modern England," *ELH* 70 (2003): 343–73 at 358–63; Syrithe Pugh, *Spenser and Ovid* (Aldershot, UK: Ashgate, 2005), 146, 214, 266; Pamela Royston Macfie, "Text and *Textura*: Spenser's Arachnean Art," in *Traditions and Innovations: Essays on British Literature of the Middle Ages and the Renaissance*, ed. David G. Allen and Robert H. White (Newark, NJ: University of Delaware Press, 1990), 88–96.

[13] Variously and at length on Venus and her refractions in *The Faerie Queene*, see my *Reading the Allegorical Intertext*, 14–15 and chaps. 9, 14. These chapters are another reason that I do not treat these figures in detail here.

[14] Amavia has been a traveler, but she is in a single place when we see her and soon immobilized in death. The old hag Occasion in Book II is a boundary case: once fettered, she is certainly situated, but, by nature, she should always be happening, changing, moving on. As a figure, she only enters one scene of Guyon's quest: she is bound in it, then freed. Impatience and Impotence are extensions of Maleger, also in Book II.

[15] For discussion of Lucifera, see my *Light and Death: Figuration in Spenser, Kepler, Donne, Milton* (New York: Fordham University Press, 2017), 57, and 32–37, 46, 49 on the figure of Mutability.

[16] On the descent through the woods/matter in Book I and its sources, see William Nelson, *The Poetry of Edmund Spenser: A Study* (New York: Columbia University Press, 1963), 159; Judith H. Anderson, *The Growth of a Personal Voice: "Piers Plowman" and "The Faerie Queene"* (New Haven, CT: Yale University Press, 1976), 36–37. On *silva* and *hyle*, see also my *Words That Matter*, 104–6. On Milton's Satan in the preceding sentence, see my *Reading the Allegorical Intertext*, 305–7, including 418n103; and *Light and Death*, chap. 3 ("Satanic Ethos: Evil, Death, and Individuality").

[17] *Faerie Queene*, V.ix.36–50, x.1–4.

[18] For a start, see Michael O'Connell, *Mirror and Veil: The Historical Dimension of Spenser's "Faerie Queene"* (Chapel Hill: University of North Carolina Press, 1977), 150–54; also my books *Reading the Allegorical Intertext*, 177–78, and *Words That Matter*, 187–88.

[19] *Faerie Queene*, IV.i.19, V.ix.40–41, 47. A body matching the mind is hardly a feature exclusive to womanly figures, let alone to wicked ones. For examples among the figures of men, consider the goatish Malbecco, who makes the owl-like monster of his mind; Grill, who chooses to remain a pig; and Orgoglio, a "monstrous masse of earthly slyme," who effectually becomes "an emptie blader" (I.vii.ix, viii.24).

[20] Joan Copjec, "The Anxiety of the Influencing Machine," *October* 23 (1982): 43–59 at 44; cf. 52–56. Copjec's observations could be applied to other episodes in Book V.

[21] Over decades, I have repeatedly returned to the depiction of Lady Munera: for examples of the more recent discussions, *Words That Matter*, 169–71, and "Spenser's *Faerie Queene*, Book 5: Poetry, Politics, and Justice," in *A New Companion to English Renaissance Literature and Culture*, ed. Michael Hattaway, 2 vols. (Chichester, UK: Wiley-Blackwell, 2010), I:263–73 at 266–67; cf. also my entry on "Langland, William," in *The Spenser Encyclopedia*, ed. A. C. Hamilton, Donald Cheney, W. F. Blissett, David A. Richardson, and William W. Barker (Toronto: University of Toronto Press, 1990), 425: Lady Munera's "golden hands," for example, recall Lady Meed's ringed "fyngres . . . fretted with gold wyr," and Munera's feet of "trye [precious]" silver suggest network slippers (V.ii.25). Hands held aloft in supplication and crying for mercy at Artegall's feet, Lady Munera is summarily executed and, handless and footless, thrown over the castle wall, "But the streame washt away her guilty blood," equivocally a biblical purgation of guilt or a merely natural cleansing (27). The problem of Lady Munera directly relates to the larger subject of Justice, the social (not personal) virtue that by definition has no respect of person. The first two discussions referenced in this note address this larger context.

[22] For discussion of the Burbon episode, see my chapter in *Essential Articles for the Study of Edmund Spenser*, ed. A. C. Hamilton (Hamden, CT: Archon, 1972), 447–70 at 448–50, or, more recently and summarily, in *A New Companion to English Renaissance Literature and Culture*, 1:271–72. Burbon's and Artegall's identities are double in the episode, as is that of the Knight of Justice, Artegall, in much of Book V.

[23] It is the election year, 2016, in the US as I make this observation.

[24] See *Faerie Queene*, IV.vii.16, viii.50.

[25] The spelling "Paeana" occurs at *Faerie Queene* IV.ix.9, 13. Hamilton, ed. (2007), 475n59.4, derives the name Placydas from Latin *placidus*. I find the Latin origin of *placidus*, namely *placeo*, a slightly fuller and more positive fit.

[26] Jonathan Goldberg, *Endlesse Worke: Spenser and the Structures of Discourse* (Baltimore, MD: Johns Hopkins University Press, 1981).

[27] Poeana's reform is what especially distinguishes her from Lady Munera, whose father, Pollente, and their toll-collector also operate outside their castle, although presumably on their land. Munera's plea for mercy might suggest a capacity to change, but this possibility is not developed in the text beyond the ironic echo of purgation by water (V.ii.27.5). Lady Munera contrasts even more sharply with Briana in Book VI, who not only accepts the opportunity to reform but is also permitted to expose Calidore's violence and call him out for it (VI.i.25, 45).

[28] In *Growth of a Personal Voice*, I have treated Serena and Mirabella in terms of free will (agency), responsibility, and fortune (Machiavelli's *virtù* and *fortuna*).

[29] For Turpine's shaming, see *Faerie Queene*, VI.vi.36, vii.26–27; cf. V.iii.37; for Timias's humiliation, see VI.vii.49, viii.5.

[30] The figures Blandina and Enias might be said to touch Serena's story, too. The connection of stories in romance goes on and on.

[31] Compare Kathryn Schwarz's suggestive critique of institutional priorities that reduce Shakespeare's "women to integers in a cold-blooded calculus": "Whose Body?" in *Rethinking Feminism in Early Modern Studies: Gender, Race, and Sexuality*, ed. Ania Loomba and Melissa E. Sanchez (London: Taylor & Francis, 2016), 213–45 at 214–15.

[32] A touchstone for this view is Gordon Teskey, *Allegory and Violence* (Ithaca, NY: Cornell University Press, 1996).

[33] See Mary Thomas Crane, *Framing Authority: Sayings, Self, and Society in Sixteenth-Century England* (Princeton, NJ: Princeton University Press, 1993), 58. Crane refers specifically to the flowers of rhetoric and to *florilegia*, anthologies of poems.

[34] Pertinently, on intention and will, see Kathy Eden, *Poetic and Legal Fiction in the Aristotelian Tradition* (Princeton, NJ: Princeton University Press, 1986), 98–100, 130–31; also Elliott Visconsi, *Lines of Equity: Literature and the Origins of Law in Later Stuart England* (Ithaca, NY: Cornell University Press, 2008), 5–7. For more on Melibee, see Anderson, *Reading the Allegorical Intertext*, chap. 6.

[35] *Online OED*, s.v. *misfare, n.^{1}*; s.v., *mis, prefix*; s.v. *fare, n.* and *v.* (accessed March 23, 2016).

[36] See *Online OED*, s.v. *hapless*; s.v. *care, n.^{1}*, 1.a. (accessed March 21, 2016).

[37] *Online OED*, s.v. *spoil, v.^{1}*, 10.a.–b., 11.a., c. (accessed March 21, 2016).

[38] Depending on context, horses are traditional symbols of passion, heroic or erotic.

[39.] See the latter portion of note 41 below.

[40] Compare Joseph Campana on Amavia's death: *The Pain of Reformation: Spenser, Vulnerability, and the Ethics of Masculinity* (New York: Fordham University Press, 2012), 121–22.

[41] The word *dame* (< Latin *domina*) can signify a woman of rank or one in charge, as Serena now is, as well as a married woman, the latter a suggestion that could indicate this development during her time with Calepine in the Salvage

man's dwelling: see *Online OED*, s.v. *dame*, I.2.a, II.5, 6.a, 7.a.–b. (accessed March 22, 2016). In canon law, marriage is *essentially* an agreement between two people; cf. Andrew Zurcher, *Spenser's Legal Language: Law and Poetry in Early Modern England* (Woodbridge, UK: D. S. Brewer, 2007), 90–94. (Although Thomas Wilson's dialogic treatise, *A Discourse Upon Usury (1572)*, ed. R. H. Tawney [New York: Harcourt Brace, 1925], treats a different subject, its inclusion of opinions drawing on canon as well as on civil and common law is exemplary and pertinent: e.g., 237, 272–73). The sequence of Calepine's and Serena's dwelling with the Salvage, then Calepine's rescue of a baby is suggestive with respect to the continuation of Amoret's story in Serena's: Ralegh not only had seduced, then married Elizabeth Throckmorton; he had also impregnated her. The Ralegh/Throckmorton affair hovers increasingly over Serena's story, as it did insistently over Amoret's in Book IV.

[42] Citation from the *Online OED*, s.v. *self pron., a.*, and *n.*, C.*sb*. I. From the pronoun: 3, of which the first example given is 1674 (accessed December 14, 2014). But see Goldberg, 91–94n7, and my *Light and Death*, 68–69, including notes 35–38. Examples earlier than 1674 exist in the sixteenth as well as the seventeenth century.

[43] I agree with Hamilton, ed. (2007), 656n31.1–6, that Serena's "former dread" refers to the beginning of her story, but it also includes the triggering sight of Mirabella, Timias, and their captors. See *Online OED*, s.v. *infer, v.*, 3.a-b, 4; s.v. *villainy, n.*, 1.a, 3.a.; s.v. *villainous, adj.*, 1.b., 2.a. (accessed March 22, 2016). In the instance of Serena, inference is loaded with forensic nuance: on inference, see Lorna Hutson, *The Invention of Suspicion: Law and Mimesis in Shakespeare and Renaissance Drama* (Oxford: Oxford University Press, 2007), e.g., 115–16, on the inference of motives and causes.

[44] In the lines cited, as elsewhere, the story of Serena recalls that of Amoret, insistently at times: see Hamilton, ed. (2007), 656n31–51. There are also significant differences between the two.

[45] As clearly instanced in Duessa, a Spenserian figure can have many social, cultural, and historical dimensions, whether intermittently, successively, or all at once. The cannibal episode has been much studied: for a start, see Hamilton, ed. (2007), 657n35; Jonathan Crewe, "Spenser's Saluage Petrarchanism: *Pensées Sauvages* in *The Faerie Queene*," *Bucknell Review* 35 (1992): 89–103, is of particular interest. Compare Rufus Wood, *Metaphor and Belief in "The Faerie Queene"* (Houndmills, UK: Macmillan, 1997), 157–65; Joan Pong Linton, *The Romance of the New World: Gender and the Literary Formations of English Colonialism* (Cambridge: Cambridge University Press, 1998), 109–17. Also Julia Major, "The Arch of Serena as Textual Monument," *Reformation* 9 (2004): 131–71: Serena and the cannibals are a meta-allegory of "the possible fate of Spenser's poem . . . among unfriendly readers" (131). Andrew Hadfield, "Another Look at Serena and Irena," *Irish University Review* 26.2 (1996): 291–302, reads Serena as a type of Elizabeth (293, 299–302).

[46] On the afterimage, in Renaissance optics and psychology a controverted issue, see my *Light and Death*, 127–28, 130, on Kepler, and see my "Working Imagination in the Early Modern Period: Donne's Secular and Religious Lyrics and Shakespeare's Hamlet, Macbeth, and Leontes," in *Shakespeare and Donne: Generic Hybrids and the Cultural Imaginary*, ed. Judith H. Anderson and Jennifer C. Vaught (New York: Fordham University Press, 2013), 185–219 at 186–88, 196–97.

[47] Hamilton, ed. (2007), 658n42.5, on the planned sacrifice of Serena, is puzzling: "In a context that involves the fantasies of a woman in love, the *Altar* suggests the nuptial bed on which the bride awaits the groom 'Like an appointed lambe, when tenderly / The priest comes on his knees t'embowell her' (Donne, 'Epithalamion made at Lincolnes Inne,' 89–90)." This note signals something more salacious for Serena than a fear of further debasement and guilt about her earlier failing. As observed, the priest lowers his knife toward her "brest," not toward her "bowels," a more ambiguous word used of Amoret (but see chapter 3). See also note 48 right below.

[48] See Dorothy Stephens on Serena at this point: *The Limits of Eroticism in Post-Petrarchan Narrative: Conditional Pleasure from Spenser to Marvell* (Cambridge: Cambridge University Press, 1998), 128–34. Stephens particularly examines the description of the naked Serena's mood as "vnwomanly" when morning comes to her and Calepine (132–34). I take her unwomanly mood more simply to reflect her loss of identity, her namelessness as Serena—that is, her loss of herself. Exemplifying an older criticism, Walter F. Staton, Jr. ("Italian Pastorals and the Conclusion of the Serena Story," *Studies in English Literature* 6.1 [1966]: 35–42) finds Spenser's treatment of Serena far subtler than in Italian analogues, yet concludes that she should have thanked Calepine instead of complaining about her embarrassment.

[49] Hamilton, ed. (2007), 659n51.8, remarks that "the sexual meaning [of *knowen*] is suggested" in its second use. It could be, yet this suggestion settles nothing unless we assume Serena merely to be scared of sex, a common default setting for modern critics. Surely there are other possibilities, especially prior to the Victorians. Serena, after all, has spent much time in the forest with Calepine in the Salvage's dwelling, a place with a natural valence (like that of the Salvage himself). See also note 41 above in this chapter.

[50] Meanings of *case* range from fortuitous to physical and mental ones, including conscience and awareness, to legal ones, including equity: e.g., see *Online OED*, s.v., *case, n.¹*: e.g., 2.a. "an event, an occurrence; a chance happening"; 3. "Fortune, chance"; 5.a. "condition, physical or mental state"; 6.a. "A legal action, esp. one to be decided in a court of law"; P7. "case of conscience" (accessed April 18, 2016). For the sexual pun, see *case* (pudendum) in Eric Partridge, *Shakespeare's Bawdy* (New York: E. P. Dutton, 1969), 76–77; also *Online OED*, s.v. *case, n.²*, 1.a, 2.a., 8 (accessed October 21, 2016).

[51] Hannah Arendt, *The Human Condition*, second ed. (Chicago: University of Chicago Press, 1998), 237; cf. 243: I silently changed "himself" to "herself."

[52] Hamilton, ed. (2007), 621n23.2.

[53] See Louis Montrose, *The Subject of Elizabeth: Authority, Gender, and Representation* (Chicago: University of Chicago Press, 2006), 193–200; also, Claire McEachern, *The Poetics of English Nationhood, 1560–1612* (Cambridge: Cambridge University Press, 1996), 34–82.

[54] Neither Hamilton's notes nor the article on Mirabella in *The Spenser Encyclopedia*, 476, remark her connection to the queen, perhaps put off by description of her birth as base and mean (VI.vii.28). But this description could be a subterfuge that masks reference, or, in a book in which gentle is as gentle does, baseness and meanness could be as they do, too, especially since Elizabeth was regarded by some as a bastard: cf. Shakespeare's Edmund on bastardy base in *King Lear*, ed. R. A. Foakes (London: Thomas Nelson, 1997), I.2.9–10. Spenser's Mirabella is also described as "a Ladie of great dignitie . . . lifted vp to honorable place" (vii.28). Sheila Cavanagh offers one of the more detailed commentaries on Mirabella: *Wanton Eyes and Chaste Desires: Female Sexuality in "The Faerie Queene"* (Bloomington: Indiana University Press, 1994), 110–24. Although not connecting Mirabella to the Queen-Ralegh-Serena story, Cavanagh suggests that Mirabella's situation "inverts" the Belphoebe and Timias story, since both involve "a sadomasochistic dyad" (133). Anne Shaver makes the connection to the queen and her treatment of Ralegh explicit: "Rereading Mirabella," *Spenser Studies* 9 (1988 [1991]): 209–29 at 223–24, though without reference to the stanzas I cite and consider definitive. Compare also Zurcher, 173–74.

[55] I include this parallel with Lucifera at the suggestion of an anonymous reader for MIP.

[56] Quoted from the Knight's portrait in Chaucer's General Prologue to *The Canterbury Tales: Works 1532*, supplemented by material from the editions of 1542, 1561, 1568, and 1602 (London: Scolar, 1969), fol. I r.

[57] Harry Berger, Jr., *The Allegorical Temper: Vision and Reality in Book 2 of Spenser's Faerie Queene* (New Haven, CT: Yale University Press, 1957), 66.

[58] See Maurice Evans, *Spenser's Anatomy of Heroism* (Cambridge: Cambridge University Press, 1970), 224; and Anderson, *Growth of a Personal Voice*, 182–83, including notes 48 (Italian *brigante*, "brigand," meaning "devil") and 50 (the Harrowing of Hell in *Piers Plowman*, including the unlocking and breaking open of gates; also the binding of Cerberus by Hercules, customarily seen as an analogy to the Harrowing of Hell).

Index

Abessa, 30–31, 35–36, 157n50
abusio/abuse, 10, 11, 87, 89, 92, 93, 103–4
accord (pun), 108
Acrasia, 3, 11, 19, 59, 123–24, 181n6
"Add faith vnto your force," 37–38
Aemylia, 67, 69, 122, 130, 131–32, 164n45
agency, 133, 134, 139; Britomart, 9, 10, 78, 112, 117; Mirabella, 133; Serena, 133, 142. *See also* choice
Aitchison, Jean, 92, 171n41
Alciati, Andrea, 170n33
allegory/allegorical, 30, 35, 36, 105, 113, 134, 151n14, 177n90
Allen, Graham, 169n29
allusion, 8 (etymology), 15–16
Alma, 11, 123, 126
Alpers, Paul J., 153nn18, 21, 154n27
Althoff, Gerd, 177n88
Amoret, 23, 67, 70–72, 93, 109–10, 147, 165n51; Arthur's rescue of, 8, 66, 108; Belphoebe's twin, 7, 49, 62; Britomart's relationship with, 9–10, 70, 90–91, 105–8, 109; Busirane's capture of, 9, 80–81, 88, 92; identity, 88; Lust's capture of, 66, 108, 109, 132; Serena and, 12, 22–24, 72, 132–35, 137, 141–42, 144–45, 147; Timias and, 8, 63–64

Amoretti (Spenser), 89, 169n22, 170n34, 177n86
Amyas, 130–32
analogy, 2, 16, 28, 45, 72, 107
Anderson, Penelope, 149n1
Andrewes, Lancelot, 34, 156n44
androgyne/androgenous, 113, 177n90
antique image/antiquity, 52–54, 64, 65
Antony and Cleopatra (Shakespeare), 124, 182n9
Aptekar, Jane, 170n33
Arachne, 83–85, 99, 125
Archimago, 27–28, 31–32, 41–45; arrest of, 41; Duessa and, 41–43, 44; parody of Redcrosse, 13, 17–18, 77, 156n50; as Satanic hypocrisy, 27–28.
Arendt, Hannah, 187n51
Argante, 22, 62–64, 81, 82
Ariosto, Ludovico, 14, 152n4, 153n18
Aristophanes, 14, 152n3
Aristotle, 1, 161n14; *Poetics* 15, 152n5
armor: Achilles's, 99, 172n54; Britomart's, 9, 10, 77, 95–114, 115; enabling, 99, 101, 105
Artegall, 14, 18, 46, 119, 171n46; armor of, 99, 172n54; battle with Britomart, 10, 96–97, 108, 109, 110, 111–12, 114; Britomart's relationship with, 10, 21, 45, 79; inner Venus of, 96; name, 180n106

INDEX

Arthur, Prince, 41, 67, 69, 153n19; Amoret and, 8, 66, 108; Artegall and, 180n106; as Christ figure, 157n54; Corflambo killed by, 131; Mirabella and, 144, 145; Serena and, 133, 134, 137, 138, 146; Una aided by, 26, 27, 39

As You Like It (Shakespeare), 9, 78, 99

Ate, 41, 106, 107, 127, 128, 158n61, 175n76, 176n85

audacia (boldness), 87

Auerbach, Erich, 150n9

Augustine, Saint, 33–34, 36, 38, 47, 156n44, 160n74

awareness 80–95, 104, 119–20, 148, 168n14. *See also* vnwares (unwares)

Barber, Charles, 164n44

Barkan, Leonard, 168n19, 182n12

Barker, Francis, 165n4

Bednarz, James P., 162n23

Belphoebe, 7–8, 49–73, 133, 147, 166n7; Amoret's twin, 7, 49, 62; as Queen Elizabeth, 7, 50, 64; Braggadocchio and, 51–52, 70; home in woods, 8, 70; portrait of, 7, 49–52, 56, 59, 60; rose of, 56–57, 65, 69, 146; Mirabella and, 12, 72, 133, 145; Timias and, 55–56, 57, 62, 63–64, 65–66

Berg, James E., 150n6, 164n48

Berger, Harry, Jr., 29, 35; *Allegorical Temper*, 145, 160nn3–4, 187n57; "Archimago" (2003), 155n38, 159n69; "Displacing Autophobia" (1998), 34, 155n38, 156nn46–47; "'Kidnapped Romance," 21, 153nn20–21; "Narrative as Rhetoric," 180n105; "Prelude to Interpretation," 24–25, 154n27; *Revisionary Play*, 173n55; "Sexual and Religious Politics" (2004), 155n38, 156n50, 174n64; "Wring out the Old," 181n6

Betrothal, 7, 160n73; of Una, 40–42, 45, 46, 55; of Britomart, 96, 108, 117

binaries, 10, 28, 96, 107, 122, 175n71, 177n90. *See also* opposites

bisexuality/bisexual, 109, 164n47, 176n80

Bishop, Tom, 167n10

Blake, William, 88

Blatant Beast, 22, 68, 118–19, 133–37, 139–40, 147

blubber (verb), 6, 13, 18–19, 22, 25, 152n14, 153n16

Bodin, Jean, 170n33

Bolton, William E., 172n54

Bourassa, André G., 2–3, 150n6

Bourdieu, Pierre, 92, 171n40

bowels (term), 91–92, 170n38

Bower of Bliss, 19, 55, 85. *See also* Acrasia

Braggadocchio, 7, 51–52, 70, 153n19; parody and, 14

Britomart, 9–11, 21, 75–120, 147, 167n11, 180n103; agency of, 9, 10, 78, 112, 117; Amoret's relationship with, 9–10, 70, 90–91, 105–8, 109; armor of, 9, 10, 77, 95–114, 115; Artegall's relationship with, 10, 21, 45, 46, 79; awareness of, 80–95; battle with Artegall, 10, 96–97, 108, 109, 110, 111–12, 114, 172n48; character effects and, 76–80; figuration reversal, 115–20; Guyon's unseating by, 19; Radigund's battle with, 11, 117–18

INDEX

Broaddus, James W., 154n28, 158n65, 159nn69, 72
Brown, Richard Danson, and J. B. Lethbridge, 181n8
Busirane, 9, 22, 80, 88, 103. *See also* House of Busirane
Busiranic art forms, 10, 81–85, 88, 89, 93. *See also* Busirane; House of Busirane
Butler, Judith, 103, 174n67

Calepine, 133, 134, 136–37, 141
Calidore, 14, 18, 133, 134, 136, 146
Campana, Joseph, 184n40
cannibals, 133, 134, 140–41, 185n45
casuistry, 2, 149n5
catachresis, 15, 24, 86, 87, 89
Cavanagh, Sheila, 187n54
Celovsky, Lisa, 176n79, 177n90
Cervantes, Miguel de, 8, 13, 14
chain/enchainment, 90, 108, 170n33
character, 2, 3, 75, 150n6
character effects, 9, 78–80
chastity, 19, 49, 50, 58, 75, 112, 162n26
Chaucer, Geoffrey, 4, 31, 69, 164n43, 187n56. *See also* titles of specific *Canterbury Tales*
Cheney, Donald, 56, 152n4, 153n19, 157n51, 162n20, 171n44
Cheney, Patrick, 163n38
choice, 77, 133, 145. *See also* agency
Cicero, 87–88, 98, 101, 169nn30–31
Coelia, 27, 123, 126
Cohen, Jeffrey Jerome, 174n68
Colin Clouts Come Home Againe (Spenser), 161n17, 180n104
comedy, 13–16, 29, 99
concept, 2–3, 59, 121, 146, 168n18; culturally gendered, 95–96; Una and, 27, 34
Concord (character), 59

consciousness, 9, 11, 78, 104, 167n14. *See also* awareness
continuity, 33, 52, 54, 80, 121
continuous consciousness. *See* consciousness
Cooper, Helen, 77–78, 166n6
Corceca, 30–31, 35, 36, 126
counterfactual, 3, 92
coverture, 117, 161n15
Crane, Mary Thomas, 184n33
Crewe, Jonathan, 185n45
cross-dress, 8, 9, 96, 177n90
Cupid, 81, 86, 95, 96, 142, 175n73
Cynthia (Ralegh), 54–55, 67, 161nn16–17

Daphnaïda (Spenser), 152n14
death, 42, 57, 60, 121; "ensample dead," 57–62, 64, 163n31
DeNeef, A. Leigh, 168n20
dernly/derne (term), 88, 170n32
Despair (character), 34, 36, 39, 130
Diana, 49, 50, 51, 62, 97
dignity (term), 19, 127, 133, 153n16
disnarration, 63, 67, 72, 141, 164n46
Dobson, E. J., 163n41
Dodd, William, 166n10
Dolon, 10, 115–16
Donne, John, 6, 15, 92; 'Epithalamion made at Lincolnes Inne,' 186n47
doubleness, 15–16, 23, 27, 40, 41, 64
dragon, 31, 39, 41
Duessa, 6, 35–36, 41–43, 71, 122, 127–29, 140, 151n14, 184n40; and Eden, 40–46; as Mary Stuart, 127–29, 140; sexual assault on (faked), 6, 18–19; Una and, 18–19, 27, 28–29, 44–45
Duffy, Eamon, 157n51, 158n65

Ebreo, Leone, 113–14, 177n92
Eden, Kathy, 149n4, 184n34

Eden, 7, 28, 31, 65, 147; parody in, 39–47
Eggert, Katherine, 84, 93, 169n23, 179nn99, 102
Eisendrath, Rachel, 168n20, 171n44
elf queen, 41, 77
Elizabeth (Queen), 28, 52–55, 64, 123, 149n1; Acrasia and, 123, 181n6; Belphoebe as, 7, 50, 64; Mary Stuart and, 128; Mercilla as, 56, 123, 128; Mirabella and, 133, 142, 187n54; Ralegh and, 7, 8, 54
emblem, 3, 26, 143, 154n30
enabling armor. *See* armor
"ensample dead," 57–62, 64, 163n31
Enterline, Lynn, 79, 167n12
epic (genre), 2, 14, 26, 146
Epithalamion (Spenser), 45–47, 158n60, 159nn70–71
eros, 20–21, 22, 159n71
erotic coupling, 10, 93–94, 97, 110, 113–14, 175nn73, 76
Error (serpent), 27, 31, 37, 157n52
Escobedo, Andrew, 150n6
Estienne, Henri, 15
ethics, 2, 120, 148
Evans, Maurice, *Spenser's Anatomy of Heroism*, 187n58
Eve (Milton's), 15, 115
experience, 5, 8, 16, 31, 75, 110, 129, 139, 147; Amoret and, 70; Belphoebe and, 8, 7, 11, 71; Britomart and, 11, 80, 103–4, 114, 115–16, 172n50; Redcrosse and, 38; Serena and, 136, 140; Una and, 8, 26, 27, 31, 71

The Faerie Queene, 2, 3; 1590 installment, 6, 10, 13, 17–25, 50, 59, 93; 1596 installment, 4, 10, 11, 12, 14, 53, 89, 93, 94, 120, 131, 152n14

Faerie vision, 66, 67
Faerie/Faerie image, 8, 58, 66–67, 69, 119, 129, 148; Proems and, 52–55; Britomart and, 76, 99, 100–2
fain (verb), 10, 85, 89, 103, 174n65
Falk, Claire, 155n37, 159n70
Falls, Mary Robert, 156n49
False Florimell, 14, 22, 60, 87, 127
fantasy, 9, 10, 89
feign (verb), 3, 10, 85, 89
Fenner, Dudley, 169n30
Ferry, Anne, 160n8
figural being, 7, 25, 81, 106
figural integrity, 11, 27, 112, 116, 129
figural thinking, 98, 177n90
figuration, 2, 3–4, 75, 81, 96, 98, 134, 150n10, 165n2
figure (definition), 3–4
fit/"fitt," 54, 113, 177n89
fixation (psychological sense), 8, 71, 87, 94–95, 121, 126, 129
Flesch, William, 166n8
Florimell, 2, 3, 8, 19–24, 112, 114, 147; chastity of, 58; flight of, 19–22; parody, 14; rescue of, 23–24; sexual assault on, 6, 19
Florio, John, 15
Foakes, R. A., 166n8
forest. *See* wood(s)
form, 3–4, 15–16, 89, 94–95, 104–5, 111–12, 113, 117–18, 124, 134; Britomart and, 95–96, 101–2, 107–9, 111, 115–16; as transformation, 6, 51, 56–57, 61, 108, 111–12, 114–16, 145. *See also* Busiranic art forms; performance
fortune, 133, 134, 142, 145
Fowler, Alastair, 152n10
Fowler, Elizabeth, 175n78, 179n100, 181n3
Freud, Sigmund, 32–33, 180n103

friendship, 14, 49, 75, 109, 131
Fumerton, Patricia, 163n35

Garber, Marjorie, 177n90
Garden of Adonis, 9, 11, 22, 62, 70, 109, 113
Garrett, Cynthia E., 153n24, 165n52
gender, 3, 34, 96, 113–14, 171n45, 179n102
George, Saint, 17, 18, 40
Glauce, 79, 80, 82, 93, 94, 98, 101, 114, 167n11
Gloriana, 31, 52, 54, 64
Goeglein, Tamara A., 154n30
Goldberg, Jonathan, 132, 175n76, 176n80, 183n26, 185n42
Googe, Barnaby, 157n51
grace (heavenly), 25, 27, 35, 44–45, 52, 55
Greenblatt, Stephen J., 161nn16–17, 181n8
Griffith, John Lance, 173n57
Guenther, Genevieve, 167n11, 170n36
Guyon, 14, 18, 19, 21, 153n19

Hadfield, Andrew, 152n12, 158n64, 162n23, 179n101, 185n45
Hamilton, A. C., 40, 45, 49, 86, 93, 101, 112, 131,136, 143; ed., *Edmund Spenser: The Faerie Queene*, 151n1; ed., *The Spenser Encyclopedia*, 157n51
Hamlet (Shakespeare), 76, 79, 115, 165n4
Harris, William V., 177n88
Harvey, Gabriel, 14
hate, 111, 162n27, 177n88
Hellenore, 7, 22, 122, 129–30
Henke, James T., 164n44
Henry IV, Part I (Shakespeare), 52, 161n11
Henry plays (Shakespeare), 5, 52

hermaphrodite, 10, 93–94, 96, 107, 177n90
hermit, 133, 134, 138–39
Hesiod, 180n104
history, 1–2, 8, 27–28, 30, 66, 137, 142, 147; Belphoebe and, 49–51, 54, 60–61, 64, 66, 70, 71–72; Britomart and, 9, 78, 80; Duessa and, 127–29; form and, 13–16, 105
hoarder, 83, 86, 87, 168n18
House of Busirane, 9, 80–95. *See also* Busirane; Busiranic art forms
House of Pride, 40. *See also* Lucifera
House(s), 8, 30–31, 122–23. *See also* specific houses, *topos/topoi*
Hunt, Marvin, 164n49
Hutson, Lorna, 149n4, 167n10, 178n96 185n43
hypocrisy, 27–28. *See also* Archimago

idealization, 2, 7, 27, 41, 52, 94, 158n59; Amoret and, 66, 69; as antique image, 55, 64, 69, 164n46; Belphoebe and, 7, 49–50, 57–65. *See also* antique image/antiquity
identity, 3, 10, 88, 96, 103–4, 122, 133
ideology, 28, 89, 115, 119, 134, 180n107
Impatience (character), 69, 182n14
(im)possible puns, 68, 92–3
Impotence (character), 69, 182n14
inly, 17, 26, 77
inner, 39–40, 69, 87, 96, 102, 107, 146, 158n55; and Serena, 138, 140
integrity (as a figure), 11, 112, 116, 129. *See also* figural being
intention, 2, 9, 79, 184n34
interiority, 8, 9, 76, 78, 104, 165n4, 167n10. *See also* inner

intertextuality, 2, 8, 16, 102, 125, 173n62
Invisible Church, 26, 28, 30, 33, 36, 38, 159n69
irony, 14, 27, 35, 94, 103, 115–16, 130, 134, 144
Iser, Wolfgang, 178n95
Isis, 11, 115–16, 123

James, Heather, 168n19, 182n12
jealousy/Gelosy (character), 83, 86–87, 89, 95, 116, 130, 168n18
Jones, Ann Rosalind, and Peter Stallybrass, 168n19, 169n22, 182n12
Jonson, Ben, 15, 122, 181n4
Justice. *See* law

Kahn, Coppélia, 149n2
Kapur, Shekhar, *Elizabeth*, 119, 180n108
Keats, John, 169n21
kind/-ness, 7, 28, 29, 129, 143
King Lear (Shakespeare), 5, 79, 105, 187n54
Kinney, Arthur F., 165n3
Kirkrapine, 28, 31, 156n50, 157n54
Ko, Yu Jin, 166n8
Kökeritz, Helge, 68, 163n41
Kott, Jan, 172n52
Krier, Theresa M., 170n34, 181n3
Lacan, Jacques, 36, 103, 110, 128, 174n68
Lady Munera, 126, 129, 183nn21–22, 184n27. *See also* law
Lamb, Mary Ellen, 152n11
Lambert, James A., 159n71
Langland, William. *See Piers Plowman*
Laqueur, Thomas, 172n48, 178n93
law, 2, 42, 43, 44, 100, 149n5; as justice, 14–19, 56, 68, 97, 99, 117–18, 120, 126–28; and Malfont, Munera, 129

Layamon's *Brut*, 62, 163n33
Lehnhof, Kent R., 176n79
lens(es), 2, 6, 9, 75, 109, 130
Lethbridge, J. B. See Brown, Richard Danson
Letter to Ralegh, 50, 54. *See also* Ralegh, Sir Walter
Lewalski, Barbara, 150n13, 152n7, 155n40
Linton, Joan Pong, 150n9, 165n2, 185n45
lion, 27, 28, 30, 31, 39, 154n32, 157n54
Little, Lester K., 177n88
liuing (living), 42, 57, 58–59, 60–61
Loomba, Ania, 1, 149nn2–3, 162n26, 174n67
Lucifera, 11, 40, 63, 123, 126, 144, 154n34, 182n15, 187n55
Lucrece (Shakespeare), 79
Lust (character), 8, 65, 66, 70, 108, 132, 151n14, 175n72, 176n80
Lyly, John, *Endymion*, 52, 161n10
Lyotard, Jean-François, 3, 110–11, 176nn81–82
lyric, 7, 11, 50, 52, 62–63, 65, 110, 121, 146

Macbeth (Shakespeare), 72, 78
Macfie, Pamela Royston, 182n12
Machiavelli, Niccolò, 112, 177n87
Major, Julia, 185n45
Malbecco, 22, 83, 86–87, 95, 101, 129–30, 183n19
Malecasta, 123; Britomart's relationship with, 21, 80, 82, 86, 94; parody, 14, 19
Maleger, 182n14
Mammon, 43–44, 86
The Manciple's Prologue (Chaucer), 164n43
Marlowe, Christopher, 52, 161n10
Mars, 10, 95, 97, 100, 113

mask/masque, 10, 86–87, 90, 103, 112, 114, 119, 180n105
Masque of Cupid, 64
Maus, Katharine Eisaman, 165n4
mayle (pun: mail/male), 111, 113
Mazzeo, Joseph Anthony, 177n87
McCabe, Richard A., 152n4
McEachern, Claire, 26, 28, 29, 54, 154n29, 156n45, 174n64, 187n53
McKeown, Adam, 173n60, 179n99
Measure for Measure (Shakespeare), 46, 78, 103, 160n73, 174n66. *See also* betrothal
Melibee, 14, 65, 133, 135, 146
Mercilla, 56, 123, 127–28, 180n108
Merlin, 60, 79, 87, 89, 91–92, 98, 103, 110, 113–14, 156n48, 169n29, 180n107
metaphor, 2, 35–36, 92, 93, 110, 156n48
methexis, 124
metonymy, 103, 115, 119, 156n48, 180n107. *See also* substitution
Middleton, Thomas, 69
Miller, David Lee, 160n6, 179n99,
Milton, John, 40, 150n13, 155n40, 182n16. *See also Paradise Lost*
mind, 9, 21, 77
Minerva/Athena, 10, 97, 99, 101, 118
Mirabella, 122, 142–46, 147; as Queen Elizabeth, 133, 142, 187n54; Serena and, 132–33, 134, 139, 145–46
mirror, 16, 21, 124, 144
"mirrours more then one," 14, 52, 53
Miskimin, Alice, 179n99
Montrose, Louis Adrian, 162n29, 187n53
moon (etymology), 50
Morse, William, 115, 178n96
Mother Hubberd's Tale (Spenser), 117

movement. *See* still moving
Murphy, Jessica C., 56, 162n22, 167n11
Mutabilitie Cantos, 14, 122, 147, 151n19
Mutability (character), 5, 14, 123, 181n5, 182n15
myth, 7, 9–10, 12, 21–22, 96, 98, 113; and Belphoebe, 49–50, 54, 56–57, 59–61; and Britomart, 75, 79, 81–83

namelessness, 17, 105, 133, 186n48
names (subject), 76, 133
Nancy, Jean-Luc, 124, 182n10
narrative, 1–5, 7–8, 12, 14, 27–28, 32, 39, 63, 105, 120, 122; Amoret and, 60, 70; Belphoebe and, 50, 52, 71; Britomart and, 98, 105, 107–8, 115, 119; Copjec and, 128–29; Lyotard and, 110–11; Serena and, 135; Una and, 27–28, 32, 37, 46. *See also* allegory/allegorical, disnarration, story/storytelling
narrative figuration, 4, 5, 11. *See also* figural being; figural integrity; figuration; narrative
narrator, 4–5, 17–24, 116, 118, 124, 130, 148, 169n21, 180n105; and Britomart, 76–77, 106, 116–19, 120; in Eden, 41, 44; in House of Busirane, 81, 83–84, 92; and Serena, 135–36, 138
nature, 87, 97, 106, 123, 141n1; Belphoebe and, 49–51, 54; Book I and, 23, 27, 28, 29–30, 38; Hellenore/ Una and, 129; Mirabella and, 143; Proem III, 54; Serena and, 135. *See also* kind/-ness
Neoplatonism, 20, 155n35
Nicholson, Catherine, 171n44
nothing (pun), 93

Occasion (character), 69, 182n14
Ocean to Scinthia (Ralegh), 54–55, 67
O'Connell, Michael, 163nn31, 37, 183n18
O'Dair, Sharon, 166n8
Oh, Elisa, 165n53, 166n9
old fisherman, 21, 22, 94–95
old man, 72, 158n62
old woman, 8, 67–68, 72, 132
Ollyphant, 22, 81
opposites, 7, 10, 20, 21, 28, 56, 59, 97, 116, 128. *See also* binaries
Oram, William A., 159n71, 168n17, 168n20; ed.,*The Yale Edition of the Shorter Poems of Edmund Spenser*, 152n14
Orgoglio, 41, 143, 157n54, 183n19
Othello (Shakespeare), 72, 78, 174n65
outer, 39–40, 76, 158n55, 174n64
Ovid, 7, 9, 19, 21, 29–30, 79, 81–85, 125, 169n24

Paglia, Camille, 175n76, 179n102;
Paolucci, Anne, 121, 122, 151n17, 165n51, 168n15, 181n2
Paradise Lost, 5, 31, 56, 115, 127, 152n7, 155n40, 159n66. *See also* Milton, John
Paridell, 22, 95, 101
Parker, Patricia, 181n6
parody, 7, 8, 13–17, 99; comic, 13–16, 29; content and expression, 15; definition of, 14–16; in Eden, 39–47; erotic, 22; etymology, 15; *Faerie Queene* (1590), 17–25, 45; role of, 6; sacred, 6, 15, 45, 130
pastoral, 14, 55, 135, 146–47
Pastorella, 133, 146–47, 148
Paxson, James J., 149n6
Pechter, Edward, 167n10
Penthesilea, 49, 50, 51
performance/per-*form*, 10, 103–4, 140
persona, 2, 3, 4, 119

Petrarch, Francesco (also Petrarchan, Petrarchism), 9, 15, 51, 60, 61, 79, 80, 81, 140, 162n29
Philotime, 63
Phoebe, 50, 62. *See also* Diana
Piers Plowman, 4, 43, 44–45, 68–69, 159nn66, 69, 164n42, 187n58.
place, 82, 122–23. *See also topos/topoi*
Placydas, 131–32, 183n25
Plato, 1, 170n33
Poeana, 122, 126, 130, 131–32, 175n77, 184n27
poet, 4–5, 57, 94, 128. *See also* poet-narrator; narrator
Poetics (Aristotle). *See* Aristotle
poet-narrator, 7, 119, 120. *See also* narrator; poet
portrait (Belphoebe's), 7, 49–52, 56, 59, 60
precedents, 6
Prescott, Anne Lake, 151n3
Prince, Gerald, 63, 163n34
probability, 2
Proem III (*Faerie Queene*), 7, 52–55, 57–58, 63
prosopopeia, 3
psychoanalysis, 3, 34–35, 90. *See also* Freud; Lacan
Pugh, Syrithe, 29–30, 36, 155n39, 168n19, 182n12
Puttenham, George, 3, 16, 150n7, 152n9

quean(e)/queanly (term), 68–69, 163n40, 164n42
Quintilian, 15, 152n6
Quitslund, Jon, 113–14, 177n91

Rabelais, François, 8, 13, 14
Radigund, 11, 117–18, 123, 126, 179n102
Ralegh, Sir Walter, 57, 61–62, 67, 163n37; *Cynthia*, 54–5,

161nn16–17; Queen Elizabeth relationship with, 7, 8; Elizabeth Throckmorton and, 8, 66–67, 69, 142, 185n41; *Ocean to Scinthia*, 54–55, 67
rape, 9, 23, 89, 91, 93; *raptus*, 70, 109
Redcrosse, 17, 31, 32, 36, 37, 38, 79, 152n12; Archimago and, 13, 17–18, 77, 156n50; attempted suicide, 34; betrothal of, 40; Duessa and, 28, 42, 44, 127, 159n69; Una's relationship with, 7, 14, 26–27, 29, 35, 45, 46, 156nn46–47
refiguration, 73, 122. *See also* transfiguration; transformation
religion, 2, 25, 36, 37–38
rhetoric, 2, 3, 87–88, 170n33
Rhu, Lawrence F., 152n4
Ricoeur, Paul, 3, 59, 89, 92, 110, 160n74, 162n27, 170n35, 171n40, 176n81, 178n95
Roche, Thomas P., Jr., 87, 163n40, 169n28
romance (genre), 14, 126, 146
Romance of the Rose, 51, 114
Rose, Margaret A., 16, 151nn3, 15, 152n5
rose (Belphoebe's), 8, 56–57, 61–63, 65, 89; cf. 124, 146
Ross, Charles, 152n4
Rowse, A. L., 163n37
Rubin, Miri, 15, 152n8, 158n65
Rust, Jennifer, 155nn37, 39

Salvage Man, 133, 134, 136–37, 138
Sanchez, Melissa E., 1, 149nn2–3; 162n26, 163n36, 165n52, 171n45, 174nn65; 176n78, 181n3
Sans Joy, 37, 40, 179n102
Sans Loy, 18, 22, 24, 28
satyrs, 7, 22, 23–24, 27, 29–30, 129

Schwarz, Kathryn, 149n2, 162n26, 172n54, 174n67, 175n76, 176n79, 177n90, 181n3, 184n31
Scudamour, 70, 72, 81–82, 94, 114, 165n52, 175n73, 178n94
The Second Shepherd's Play, 15
self, 138–39, 185n42
self-betrayal, 116
self-cancellation, 133
self-citation, 6, 16, 17, 18, 46
self-reflective, 15, 84, 99
senseless stocks, 93
Serena, 22, 23, 72–73, 122, 133–42, 147; Mirabella and, 132–33, 134, 139, 145–46; Timias and, 133, 134, 137–39, 144, 145. *See also* Amoret
serio ludere, 8, 25
sex, 6, 34, 113–14, 171n45
Seyffert, Oskar, 173n56
Shakespeare, William, 5, 13, 46, 52, 75–76, 92, 99, 122, 124; character and, 2–3, 9, 78–80, 150n6, 165n4; Hamlet, 76, 79, 115, 167n10; Shakespeare's women, 5, 9, 11, 72, 103, 120, 124. *See also* titles of plays
Shaver, Anne, 187n54
The Shepheardes Calender (Spenser), 117
Shuger, Debra Kuller, 160n73, 174n70
Sidney, Sir Philip, 101, 173n60
Silberman, Lauren, 164n47, 170n32
silhouette(s), 10, 17, 96, 107
Sinfield, Alan, 9, 11, 75, 78–79, 104, 150n6 151n16, 165n53, 166nn8–10;
situate/situation, 11, 71, 122–23, 125–26
Slander (character), 8, 66, 68, 69, 126; Amoret and, 65, 66, 70, 175n76
Slater, Michael, 170n36
Slights, Jessica, 150n6, 166n8, 179n96

sociocultural (context, shaping), 94, 114, 145
Spenser, Edmund. *See* poet-narrator
Stallybrass, Peter. *See* Jones, Ann Rosalind
Staton, Walter F., Jr., 186n48
statue, 94, 96, 119, 125
Stephens, Dorothy, 164n50, 172n48, 175nn72–73, 175nn72–73, 76, 176n80, 186n48
still movement, 11–12, 24, 121–22, 127, 130, 133, 148
stillness. *See* still movement
story/storytelling, 5. *See also* narrative
structure(s), 2, 11, 95, 119
sublation, 46, 92, 93, 110, 134; in lyric, 11, 63, 121, 146
substitution, 11, 103, 115, 119, 132, 156n48
Suzuki, Mihoko, 177n90, 179n102
symbol, 45, 54, 61, 64, 75–76, 95, 104–5, 107, 121

The Tale of Melibee (Chaucer), 15. *See also* Chaucer, Geoffrey
The Tale of Sir Thopas (Chaucer), 15, 41. *See also* Chaucer, Geoffrey
Temple of Venus, 10–11, 59, 72–73, 82, 110–12, 114, 165n52, 176n84; and Amoret, 11, 70, 89, 94, 110
terminology (subject), 2–4, 177n90. *See also* specific terms
Teskey, Gordon, 153n20
text, 1–2, 36, 38, 110
theory, 1, 3, 5, 110, 180n103
Throckmorton, Elizabeth, 8, 66–67, 69, 185n41
time, 41, 49, 121, 129
Timias, 21; Amoret and, 8, 63–64; Belphoebe and, 55–56, 57, 62, 65–66; Serena and, 133, 134, 137–39, 144, 145

topos/topoi, 8, 30, 39, 70, 82. *See also* place
Totaro, Rebecca, 167n11
transference, 11, 174n68, 180n103
transfiguration, 9, 11. *See also* refiguration; tropic conversion
translation, 35, 87, 103, 140
Traub, Valerie, 149nn1–3; 172n48, 174n67, 175n76, 178n93, 182n10
traversal of fantasies, 10, 103, 170n37, 174n68
Troilus and Cressida (Shakespeare), 78
tropic conversion, 134, 140
trouthe/troth, 33, 35, 44, 45, 147
Truth/truth, 28; Una as, 7, 27, 30–31, 33–34, 44, 77, 166n7. *See also* trouthe/troth
Twelfth Night (Shakespeare), 9, 78
twins, 12, 22, 49, 62, 122, 146

Una, 6–7, 8, 17, 25–39, 129, 147, 152n12, 154n30; assault on, 6, 18–19, 24–25; betrothal of, 40–41, 45–47; Duessa and, 18–19, 28–29, 44–45; Florimell and, 2, 19, 21–24; as Invisible Church, 26, 28, 30, 38, 159n69; Redcrosse and, 7, 14, 26–27, 29, 35, 44–46, 156nn46–47; as Truth, 7, 27, 30–31, 33–34, 44, 77, 166n7

Venus armata, 10, 97, 103, 172n48
"Venus mayd" (pun), 81, 88, 106, 168n15, 175n73
Venus, 62, 118, 125; Belphoebe as, 51; Mars and, 10, 95, 97, 100, 113. *See also* Temple of Venus
Venus-Virgo, 10, 49, 95, 97
Vergil, 29, 55, 128

Villeponteaux, Mary, 162n19, 163n31, 173n55
virginity: Belphoebe and, 7, 8, 49, 58; Britomart and, 58, 95
Virgo. *See* Venus-Virgo
Visconsi, Elliott, 184n34
vnwares (unwares), 66, 80, 86, 108, 135, 136

Walker, Julia M., 180n108
Walkington, Thomas, 15, 152n5
Walls, Kathryn, 17, 26, 29, 31, 33, 36–39, 154nn30, 32; 157nn51, 54; 179n99
Wells, Marion A., 167n11
wholeness, 27, 49, 56, 65, 92, 115, 136, 141, 158n55
whore, 28, 54, 68, 151n14, 175n76
Wilson, Thomas, 170n33, 185n41
Wind, Edgar, 97–98, 104, 161n9, 171n47

The Winter's Tale (Shakespeare), 181n4
witch (Book III), 22, 60, 69, 126
Wofford, Susanne, 83–84, 168n20, 173n61
Wolfson, Elliot R., 178n92
woman (term), 1
woman-figure, 49, 126, 134, 146. *See also* woman; women
women (term), 1
Wood, Rufus, 185n45
wood(s), 7, 8, 17, 19, 29–30, 31–32, 37, 70

Yanchin, Paul, 150n6, 166n8, 179n96
Yates, Francis A., 161n12
Young, Bruce W., 166n8

Žižek, Slavoj, 174nn68, 70
Zurcher, Andrew, 149n4, 158n64, 160n73, 185n41, 187n54